THE QUACK CORPS

A Marine's War — Pearl Harbor to Okinawa

by

Arthur W. Wells

DolArt Published

1629 Sunset Avenue, Chico, California 95926

Copyright: © 1992-2001 Arthur W. Wells.
All rights reserved.

Second Edition

Library of Congress Library Card No. 92-96867
ISBN 0-9633631-2-3

SOURCES:
Naval Historical Center, Washington, D.C.
U.S.S. Pennsylvania Action Report for 7 December, 1941.
War Diaries: *U.S.S. LST-23; U.S.S. LST-272;* U.S.S. *LST-340; U.S.S. LST-354.*
U.S. Marine Corps Historical Center, Washington, D.C.
Muster Rolls: Marine Detachment, *U.S.S. Pennsylvania;* "C" Company, First Battalion, Second Marine Brigade; Five Inch Artillery Group, First Defense Battalion Fleet Marine Force; Second Marine Amphibian Truck Company, Second and Fourth Marine Divisions, Fleet Marine Force, Pacific.
Arthur W. Wells 1943, 1944 and 1945 letters to Dolores Alden.
Former members of the Second Marine Amphibian Truck Company, World War II

To *Dolores:*

A mental picture of her smiling face gave me the will to survive

and

To the men of the Second Marine Amphibian Truck (DUKW) Company

Who others called

THE QUACK CORPS

PREFACE

Their numbers were small, those Marines on navy ships and Pacific island stations when war began with the Japanese, 7 December, 1941. Many of them didn't live to see its end, almost four years later.

Among the survivors of the surprise attack on Pearl Harbor was a Missouri farm boy, a member of the Marine Detachment, *U.S.S. Pennsylvania*. He enlisted in July 1940 and attended boot camp in San Diego, California. Upon completion of boot camp, he was sent to "C" Company, 1st Battalion, 6th Marine Regiment, Second Marine Brigade, an infantry regiment. A company senior noncommissioned officer encouraged him to make the attempt to attend the U.S. Naval Academy, Annapolis, Maryland.

Corp. Arthur W. Wells
San Francisco, early 1942

To attend the academy, an enlisted Marine was required to serve nine months of sea duty in a capital ship of the U.S. Navy. Capital ships were battleships, aircraft carriers and cruisers.

Before duty in a ship, enlisted Marines were required to attend Sea School, located on the U.S. Marine Base, in San Diego. Upon graduation, he boarded the battleship *U.S.S. Pennsylvania*, Flagship of the U.S. Pacific Fleet, in April 1941. The ship's home port was Pearl Harbor, Oahu, Territory of Hawaii

Wounded during the Japanese attack, he returned to the *Pennsylvania* before she sailed for San Francisco, in late December 1941, for bomb damage repairs and installation of new anti-aircraft weaponry. She returned to Pearl Harbor in August 1942 and he transferred in September to the *U.S.S. New Mexico*, also a battleship, as the senior non-commissioned officer with Vice-Admiral William Pye's Marine Flag Detachment.

After a tour of the South Pacific in *New Mexico*, his next unit was the Marine Barracks, Navy Yard, Pearl Harbor. It was followed by the First Defense Battalion, on one-square-mile-of-land Palmyra Island. It lay 1100-miles southwest of the Hawaiian Islands and was used by the U.S. to aid in their defense, along with Johnston, Midway and Wake Islands..

Following a furlough in the U.S., and short months of duty at Camp Elliott, near San Diego,, the Marine Corps formed the First and Second Marine Amphibian Truck (DUKW) Companies in December 1943, and he became a member of the Second.

Second DUKW, as it was called by its personnel, was the first Marine company to land on Japanese soil, Saipan, June 15, 1944, followed by the invasion of Tinian, July 24, 1944, and Okinawa, April 1, 1945.

He left the company to return to the United States for discharge, September 9, 1945, before it sailed from Saipan to aid in the occupation of Japan..

Contents

Pearl Harbor Bombed! 9
U.S. Navy Hospital 22
The City by the Bay 32
Return to Pearl Harbor 42
USS New Mexico 51
Palmyra Island 61
Furlough and Camp Elliott 70
A Quack Marine 79
Hitting Hawaiian Surf 89
Fire Storm in West Loch! 100
Saipan! 113
Moving forward on Saipan 140
Rest and Tinian 163
In the Marianas 176
Okinawa! 198
A Second Invasion of Okinawa 225
War's End! 245
Going Home! 258
A Warrior Returns! 272
Grey? Bald? Paunchy? 277

Chapter 1
Pearl Harbor Bombed!

The huge red ball blossoming under the plane's wing filled the porthole on *U.S.S. Pennsylvania,* as the fighter banked and climbed for altitude. The plane had just completed a strafing run on Ford Island, located in the middle of Pearl Harbor. I didn't need for anyone to remind me that it was an unfriendly because I recognized it as a Jap Zero.

As the striker for Corp. Thomas N. Barron, Marine Detachment Clerk, I usually caught Sunday morning duty for turning in the detachment's daily report to the ship's office prior to 0800. I had just dropped it off and stopped for a bull session with a deck division friend when the sound of explosions reverberated through the ship. We laughed at a nearby sailor's remark, "That's just like the Army to wait until Sunday to hold gunnery practice." But we rushed to a porthole when another sailor yelled, "The Japs are attacking!"

The pace had been leisurely on the ships in Pearl Harbor, the 7th of December 1941, because Sunday was the day for rest and relaxation after the usual weekly few days at sea where the crews practiced day and night for war. Some men were still ashore; some of those aboard were still feeling the effects of a night out in Honolulu. Others were writing letters, pressing uniforms, shining shoes, straightening wall-locker gear, or rapping in bull sessions. With the surprise and suddenness of the Japanese attack, some of them would die with a shoe still in hand, or with thoughts of how to word the next sentence in a letter, or with mouths open as they began the next sea story—their war had ended before it had officially begun!

I turned from the porthole and raced aft, heading for my battlestation high on the mainmast—I was the pointer on the

The Quack Corps

U.S. Navy photo
U.S.S Pennsylvania—Destroyers *Cassin* and *Downes* forward.

director controlling the port 5-inch .51-caliber broadside guns.

As I dodged others racing to their stations, the expressions on faces registered, shocked disbelief, anger and determination, and some had fear stamped indelibly into their paled and drawn features. The mouths of others spewed curses as they damned the Japs, in almost a scream.

Pearl Harbor Bombed!

U.S. Navy photo

U.S.S Pennsylvania at sea prior to World War II.

Though Marines usually didn't take their rifles to shipboard battlestations, I instinctively thought of my "best friend." As I sped through the Marine Compartment, I noticed Sgt. Bud Tinker standing near the weapons locker and I slowed to ask whether I could get my rifle. He didn't have a key so I resumed my sprint aft.

To get to my battlestation, I had to climb a ladder up the outside of the most starboard leg of the mainmast's tripod. Countless times up and down it in practice had given me the agility and confidence of a monkey. As I sped upward, I rammed my head against the ass of a sailor climbing above me, just below the searchlight platform. I fumed while the clumsy overweight man dragged his bulky body, at what seemed like a snail's pace, the rest of the way to the platform. He spun to face me, "What the hell's the idea of running into me?" he demanded.

"Get your fat ass out of my way!" I retorted.

11

The Quack Corps

He didn't make a comeback but stepped aside, and I resumed my trip. After reaching my station, I helped the men already there lower the storm windows into recesses. I uncovered the gun director, donned a soundpower phone headset, and made checks with the captains of the port side Marine-manned broadside guns, Number-8 and -10. The 5-inch .51-caliber guns were not designed for use against aircraft and the director and gun crews could do nothing but watch harbor activities. The Marine officer commanding the director station, 2dLt. Leyton M. Rogers, ordered all phones secured except for the one connecting with the ship's gunnery control.

As a 19 year old, I didn't want to miss anything and my eyes darted about the harbor trying to keep tabs on every Jap plane, every bomb and torpedo, and every ship. My attention switched back and forth from Ford Island to Battleship Row, and to *Helena* and *Oglala* berthed in the *Pennsylvania*'s regular 10-10 Dock berth, with *Oglala* outboard of *Helena*. *Pennsy*, as Flagship of the Pacific Fleet, usually enjoyed the choice berth because Admiral Husband E. Kimmel wasn't about to ride his barge across channel whenever he wanted to board or debark from his flagship. But now *Pennsylvania* was in Number-1 Drydock with screws off, just forward of her usual 10-10 berth.

Battleship Row was across the channel and I had an unobstructed and relatively closeup view of it by looking across *Pennsylvania's* starboard quarter.

I didn't think of the dangers caused by strafing Jap planes, or of low-level American small-caliber fire, or of a 5-inch AA gun's projectile hitting the mast when it was fired at low-flying planes. I was so engrossed in watching events across the channel that I didn't notice when three Jap planes strafed *Pennsylvania*'s port side at about 0805.

The gun director crews were supposed to huddle between the tripod's legs running up through the station during strafing attacks but I leaned out a window for a better view of

Pearl Harbor Bombed!

low-flying planes or flights passing over at higher altitude. Twice, Lieutenant Rogers grasped my trouser belt and pulled me inboard. Even though he reminded me to stay between the legs, I would become engrossed in following the action and ease back to an opening.

With the ship shuddering from the constant concussions caused by the firing of her 5-inch and 3-inch guns, and the explosions of bombs and torpedoes in the harbor, I didn't consciously feel, hear, or see the gigantic explosion that demolished *Arizona*. Only minutes after the attack had begun, the dreadnought turned into a mass of twisted, torn and fire-scorched steel.

I didn't pay much attention to activities around *California*, or the tanker *Neosho* directly across the harbor, or Ford Island. My concentration focused on *Oklahoma* and *West Virginia* as torpedoes ripped again and again into their bowels.

Oklahoma's masts appeared to be moving closer and I realized she was listing heavily to port. I watched in awe as she continued turning, so fast her masts splashed the water, until her keel was exposed to the dimmed light of a smoke-shielded sun. When she rolled, I could see men spilling off her decks into the water to port and others frantically scrambling over her hull to starboard.

I was in a quandary as I debated with myself whether I should salute. To me, the ship was dying in shame and I didn't feel she rated a salute, but I wanted to pay respects to the many men who were dying with her. By the time I'd firmed my decision, she had capsized so I snapped a quick, reverent, salute.

As *Oklahoma* rolled, a float-equipped scout plane slid off the aft-turret catapult and floated into the burning oil at the channel side of the ship. My attention switched to *West Virginia* and other activities and I didn't watch the plane's final fate but it must have burned and sank.

I watched while torpedo planes continued attacking *West Virginia*. In what seemed only a matter of seconds after a plane

The Quack Corps

dropped a torpedo, a plume of water spouted at the outboard side of the ship ... she appeared to rise, shudder, and then settle back even lower in the water than she had been before as the explosions tore out her bowels.

How could anything possibly penetrate a battleship's thick armor I had wondered ... that it could be done was being demonstrated to me in a most dramatic and definite way!

The planes were below my height when they dropped low to lay their deadly cargoes into the water, as they made torpedo runs on *Helena* and *Oglala*. I could see the cockpit instruments and the expressions on the pilots' faces. The white of their teeth flashed as they grimaced with concentration or grinned in exultation at the success of their missions. Then, as the planes banked and climbed for altitude, I was almost eyeball-to-eyeball with the rear gunners as they looked down their gun sights and sprayed deadly bullets over the topsides of the ships. How I wished for my rifle!

My eyes focused on a plane struggling to gain altitude after attacking Ford Island. Flames and smoke streamed out behind it. It slipped off to the left and glided to a crash on or near the U.S. Navy Hospital grounds. It was the only plane I saw shot down during the attack!

A flight of five planes flew over *Pennsylvania* at high altitude and the ship's AA guns concentrated on them. I fumed with frustration as I saw the shells bursting below the planes or, judging from the volume of fire, not even exploding. The planes continued serenely on their way and disappeared unscathed over the billowing smoke hovering above the harbor. The sight of them added to the frustration of watching torpedo and bomber planes dropping their instruments of destruction, then escaping apparently undamaged into the billowing smoke.

Approximately 30-minutes after the attack began, orders were passed for the director crew to clear the mainmast and go below. I dropped down the tripod leg ladder, grasping the

Pearl Harbor Bombed!

handrails loosely and tightening my grip occasionally to control my speedy descent ... my feet were catching every third or fourth rung! I ran to the boat deck and joined a line of sailors and Marines passing ammunition to a 5-inch .25-caliber AA gun--I felt better now that I was helping to fight Japs.

As I cradled each projectile against my chest, I prayed that it would knock an enemy plane from the air. Odd thoughts can enter one's mind at unexpected moments: grease from the ammo was smearing my white skivvy shirt and I directed extra curses at the Japs for that!

So many men were lending a hand on the boat deck that they were getting in each other's way. It also exposed more than necessary to strafing planes so all Marines were ordered below. I didn't want to sit in the Marine Compartment with nothing to do, unable to keep tabs on harbor activity, so I went to Number-7 Casemate. It and -9 were starboard side and the 5-inch broadside guns in them were manned by Marines, as were Number-8 and -10 on the port side. Again, I had nothing to do but observe . . . and talk.

Sgt. R. L. Taylor and I were standing in the center of the casemate talking when a Marine sitting in the gun's pointer seat yelled, exultantly, "A battleship is going out!"

I rushed to the casemate opening and saw *Nevada* emerging almost like a ghost from the thick smoke ... slowing making her way by Battleship Row and heading toward the harbor's entrance.

A swarm of Japanese planes darted through the air above her and bombs were exploding in the water alongside and on her decks. When one exploded in the water just off her starboard bow and near a sailor coiling rope on the fo'c'sle, he dropped the rope and streaked aft. It appeared that his upper body was lagging behind his churning legs, because he ran leaning back and the back of his head appeared to be almost between his shoulder blades. I sensed his desperation and em-

The Quack Corps

pathized with him but in other circumstances it would have been hilarious!

His timing was poor, however, because when he reached about amidships on the port side, a bomb hit *Nevada* in that area. Debris spurted high into the air, including a cotton bunk mattress. I envisioned a genie sitting on a Persian rug as the mattress soared high above the ship and then fluttered and yawed as it dropped to the water. I've always wondered whether the sailor was wounded or killed by that bomb.

I felt pride as I watched the gallant old battlewagon slowly, determinedly, and *majestically* fighting her way through rising geysers of water, shrugging off multiple bomb hits, with her guns defiantly spitting flames and projectiles at the darting planes swarming like bees above her while striving desperately to stop her. The old ship fighting her way down harbor was the most inspiring sight I saw during the entire war!

I wouldn't learn of *Nevada*'s fate until later, because *Pennsylvania*'s PA system blared: "A strafing attack is coming. Take cover!"

Sergeant Taylor yelled, "Get inboard!" And I ducked into the passageway connecting the two casemates. He joined me by the guns' ammunition hoist and we resumed our conversation.

Next, I was fighting for consciousness and it was like trying to climb out of an inky-black abyss. During those moments that I was aware of my surroundings, the pile of men on the deck of Number-7 Casemate felt like a nest of squirming worms as they struggled to untangle. As I'd gain consciousness for a moment, I could feel the crushing weight from above and the warmth and softness of wriggling bodies beneath me. Suddenly, the weight was gone and I felt someone tugging the back of my skivvy shirt, pulling me off the pile. He helped me to stand.

Pearl Harbor Bombed!

At 0906, a bomb had penetrated the deck of the boat deck and had apparently hit the base of the broadside gun in Number-9 Casemate before rolling over on the deck and exploding. The blast had funneled through the connecting passageway hurling men like projectiles against the wall-lockers attached to the forward bulkhead of Number-7.

I glanced toward the casemate opening and saw Sergeant Taylor standing nearby. His face was blackened but he acted uninjured, even though he had been between me and the exploding bomb. "Sickbay! Main deck forward!" he yelled. Feeling woozy and rudderless, I grasped the back of a Marine's skivvy shirt and followed him down the ladder to the Marine Compartment located below the casemates.

After stumbling over a stretcher in the compartment and learning that the man in it, PFC Nelson R. Holman, had a broken leg, my next awareness was of standing just inside the sickbay. My eyes roved over it ... taking in the sparkling white bulkheads, the white bunk coverings and the compartment's clean-as-a-new-pin look. Even the terra-cotta color battleship linoleum covering the deck looked immaculate to me ... except for a huge pool of blood on the deck by the bunk nearest the entrance. But there wasn't any blood on the bunk! Later, someone informed me that a close buddy of mine had lain there and his life had flowed out with that pool of red. Shrapnel had taken a huge chunk out of his back and nothing could be done to save him.

I didn't see a single man ... dead or alive. The sickbay was completely empty! It was quiet, peaceful, and a haven from the carnage I had witnessed topside. But I felt deserted because those who could tend to my needs had disappeared. In doubt as to what to do and unable to make a rational decision, I ambled aft to a compartment where mess tables had been setup for morning chow. Dishes, food, tables, and silverware were helter-skelter on the deck. A sailor was standing in the compartment and I asked him if he knew where sickbay had been moved. He didn't know. Another sailor entered the compartment and the sailor with me asked him. He informed us that it had been moved to second deck and forward by Number-1Turret's barbette.

I made my way to it and saw many wounded men laying in bunks lining the passageways and sitting or laying on the deck. I felt very weak and eased myself to the deck and leaned back against the barbette. I didn't see any doctors but several corpsmen were busily attending to wounded men.

After leaning against the barbette for several minutes with my eyes closed, I sensed the approach of a corpsman and opened them. He squatted beside me and inquired about my injuries, then asked, "Can you stand up?"

I didn't realize that my khaki pants were blood soaked. After I pushed myself to my feet, he didn't wait for me to drop my pants but began slitting up the left trouser leg with a scalpel. The higher he slit while searching for the source of the blood, the more worried I became that the worst had happened and mentally vowed: "If they got my nuts, I'll kill everyone of the little bastards!" Fortunately, the shrapnel wound was in my upper thigh, just below the buttock. He hastily bandaged it and moved on to another man.

Remembering a few empty bunks, tiered three high, when I entered the temporary sickbay, I headed for a clean-looking center bunk. A young sailor manning a soundpower phone nearby remarked in a reproving tone of voice, "I put clean coverings on just this morning. You'll get them bloody." I stared at him with a "Tough! You just try to keep me out of it" look. As I eased into the bunk, he didn't make any more remarks.

A doctor dressed in civilian clothes entered the sickbay, quite some time later, and began checking wounded men. He worked his way around the barbette and upon reaching my bunk, questioned, "Marine, what happened to you?"

"Shrapnel in the leg and a knock on the head, Sir," I replied.

Pearl Harbor Bombed!

He checked the corpsman's bandaging job. Then, without checking my head or asking how I felt, he said, "You can return to your station."

I crawled out of the bunk and started around the barbette. But, after a few steps, I felt vomit beginning to rise and dashed for a tin mop bucket setting nearby on the deck. After I had finished, the doctor ordered me back into the bunk. As I didn't feel up to going any place under my own power, I crawled back into it.

A short time later, sailors dashed into the compartment and grabbed all of the fire extinguishers. Their actions caused PFC Tommie J. Dale, in a bunk across the passageway, and I to worry that *Pennsylvania* was afire. We began discussing the best and fastest way to abandon ship.

Two destroyers, *Cassin* and *Downes,* were in the dry dock with *Pennsylvania.* They were beam-to-beam forward of the battleship. Private First Class Dale and I didn't know that the destroyers had been hit by bombs and were burning. The heat from their fires was bubbling the paint inside *Pennsylvania*'s bow.

Some time later, the ship's crew began transferring men from the sickbay to the nearby naval hospital. A bullet had torn off part of Dale's heel and he was suffering severely. When men started to take me out first, I requested that they take him because of his pain. At that time, my head and the shrapnel wound were not hurting.

Later, two very-young sailors brought a stretcher to my bunk. They stood by it discussing how they could manage to get me out of the bunk and onto the stretcher. I'd remember it with amusement later because I solved their problem. I suggested they wait a minute and crawled out of the bunk to lay down on the stretcher.

They carried me aft but stopped when they reached the first ladder going up to the main deck. They set the stretcher on the deck and for several minutes discussed how to get me up the ladder. Again, I suggested they wait a minute and got off the stretcher, climbed the ladder, and they folded the stretcher and brought it up. I laid back down on it and they carried me to the quarterdeck.

As we neared the head of the gangway to 10-10 Dock, the ship's PA system blared: "A stretcher is needed for a severely wounded man!" and gave the location.

"Leave me here and go get him," I suggested to the sailors. "I'll be okay." They stopped. I got off the stretcher and sat on a nearby bit.

While I sat in the warm sun waiting for the sailors to return, I wasn't conscious of any guns firing. Number-3 and -4 Turrets blocked my view of Battleship Row, but I noticed that *Helena* was still afloat at 10-10 Dock. I also noticed a Navy officer, a sailor, and Marine were standing at the head of the gangway.

Though my head felt like it was detached and floating several feet above the deck watching what went on below, I still was mentally alert enough to know that the Japs had made a shambles of Pearl Harbor. I wondered how much damage had been done to *Pennsylvania*. But I was too dazed to give much thought to future happenings. Feeling very tired, I considered laying on the teakwood deck but resisted the urge.

Floating in and out of awareness, I didn't know whether the severely wounded man was carried off via way of the quarterdeck gangway. Curious about him, I wondered if another gangway had been put in place forward. After awhile, I began to worry that the sailors had forgotten me. But, eventually, they returned and carried me to the dock.

They placed me on a cotton mattress in the bed of a civilian pickup truck. The driver headed for the U.S. Navy Hospital at breakneck speed. When the truck hit a bump in the road it bounced me into the air above the mattress. The pickup had a 2 x 6 board bolted across the top of its bed. Mesmerized, I stared fixedly at the board and began worrying that a large

Pearl Harbor Bombed!

bump would throw me into it. The driver apparently didn't realize that the rough ride could do more damage than lack of speed in getting me to the hospital. Even though I was still woozy from the bomb blast, it was an unforgettable ride.

When we arrived at the hospital, the attendants moved me to another mattress, laying on the deck just inside the entrance. Private First Class Dale was on one of the nearby mattresses. Once more, the stretcher bearers started to give me priority and I again suggested that they take him first. He thanked me and they took him away. It was the last time I'd ever see him.

Eventually I was taken into a ward and put to bed. After a quick check by ward medical personnel and a morphine shot, I drifted into an untroubled sleep.

I awakened after dark to the sound of guns firing in the harbor area. Later, I learned that a flight of six *Enterprise* planes had been coming in for a landing on Ford Island and four were shot down by friendly forces.

After the guns quit firing, the only sounds to be heard in the darkness were the muted voices of medical personnel and the moans of the wounded.

Chapter 2
U.S. Navy Hospital

It unnerved me when bodies were removed from the adjacent bunks the first two mornings of my stay, even though still in a stupor from the bomb and morphine. I wondered if it was an omen that my condition might be worse than suspected—I didn't realize the frequent vomiting was probably a result of my head injury.

On Tuesday, 9 December, the doctor checked the shrapnel wound and ordered ward personnel to let me shower and return to my ship. I crawled out of the bunk to head for the shower. After reaching the aisle at the foot of the bunk, I vomited on the deck. He ordered me back into the sack. He also ordered the corpsman accompanying him to have my head X-rayed.

The X-rays didn't show any skull fracture. Nevertheless, my head, from top center to just below my left ear, ballooned to such an extent that only the tip of my ear could be seen in a mirror. Later, when I applied for glider pilot training, the physical examination revealed that my left eye was weakened by the injury.

Besides the head and shrapnel injuries, the areas of my skin not protected by clothing were covered with small red spots. It appeared hordes of mosquitoes had feasted on me. Small pieces of bomb materials caused some of them but paint chips probably the others. As an example, H.M.S. *Warspite,* a British battleship heading to the States for repairs had entered Pearl Harbor sometime prior to the 7th. Her Royal Marines invited *Pennsylvania*'s Marines aboard for a visit. German bombs had damaged her off Crete and the areas subjected to the explosives' blast had every square inch of paint scoured

U.S. Navy Hospital

from the bulkheads. The U.S. Navy hadn't taken heed of the fires and other dangers caused by thick coats of paint, because most ships with any age, like the *Pennsylvania,* still had multiple layers of paint on interior bulkheads.

When I began feeling better, I checked through the wards for other Marines off *Pennsylvania.* I spotted the name of a Marine who had reported aboard only days before the attack. The upper portion of his body was horribly burned. He was unrecognizable because his eyes were swollen shut and he no longer had eyebrows or eyelashes. His hands were useless. With the severity of his burns, I felt it best to check with a corpsman to see whether it was all right to talk with him. "Go ahead. With burns that bad, he'll probably be dead in 10-days or so anyway," he responded.

I walked to the head of the bunk and spoke softly to him. He responded. I informed him that I was also in *Pennsy*'s detachment, but my wounds were not serious. After we talked for a few minutes, he asked, "Will you write to my parents and let them know that I'm all right"? I assured him that I'd take care of it.

While writing later, I struggled while trying to find the right words to reassure his parents without letting awareness of the corpsman's words seep through. I decided to write only that his hand had been hurt, without giving details and didn't mention why he wasn't dictating the letter. I wasn't very steady on my own feet and trying to write with the corpsman's words ringing in my ears, didn't make for a very steady hand ... my usually hard-to-read scrawl was even worse in that letter.

The Navy was apparently being deluged with requests from parents, other relatives, and girlfriends for information about the well-being of their loved ones; it made extra efforts to get mail quickly to the island.

The Marine received several letters and I read them aloud to him. Tears oozed from his swollen eyes as I read those from

The Quack Corps

his parents and girlfriend. While trying to console him, and to help raise his spirits, I asked about his dog that his father had mentioned in a letter.

Talking about dogs seemed to be safe ground so after exhausting the subject of his, I talked about the dogs back on our farm in Missouri. I related amusing tales about Ol' Liver, a half-shorthair pointer. He meant death to groundhogs but was worthless for hunting squirrels, rabbits and other Missouri game. Ol' Liver was very fond of biscuits so we referred to him as a "biscuit hound". He chuckled at the tales and appeared in better spirits when I left the ward. Surprisingly, he lived and returned to limited duty in the Marine Corps. Later, his stepsister wrote to thank me and we corresponded for the duration of the war. His parents also wrote expressing gratitude and invited me to visit them whenever possible.

Private First Class Raymond "J" Laughlin was in my ward. We had made several liberties together, but he ignored me when I attempted conversation with him. Laughlin had received burns but was ambulatory, because they were not extensive. He acted in a daze and seemed to be giving me the cold shoulder. I thought it a little strange that he'd treat a liberty buddy that way, even under those circumstances. I understood the reason for the treatment when a corpsman informed me that both of his eardrums had burst. After that, I made certain that he was looking at me whenever trying to make conversation.

In one of the wards, I noted women, out of uniform, hovering over nude and horribly burned men. Some were cleaning or picking something off the men's' skin, while others were trying to ease their discomfort by fanning. Curious that nurses would be working out of uniform, I asked a corpsman, "Why aren't those nurses in uniform"?

"They're not nurses. They're civilian volunteers. Many of them are Honolulu prostitutes."

U.S. Navy Hospital

"Prostitutes! I didn't know the Navy allowed them in a Navy installation."

"Usually not. Scuttlebutt had the Navy refusing to allow them on base but the women raised so much hell and told the Navy: 'Those sailors have been supporting us for a long time. Now, we're going to help them.' I suppose the Navy decided to pretend it doesn't know they're prostitutes."

The warm sun and gentle Hawaiian breezes had a healing and soothing effect, so I spent most of the daylight hours sitting on a bench at Hospital Point, watching harbor activities and thinking.

I could see men clamoring over the exposed bottom of *Oklahoma,* knifing through the steel with cutting torches to rescue men trapped in compartments ... compartments that before the attack were below decks. It was a dangerous job because fumes might explode, but rescue work continued and many men were saved.

Later, a sailor with the rescue crew from *Maryland* told me: "We had to let the metal cool before removing the cutout sections. The men would have burned themselves severely in their desperate scramble to escape. In some instances, we threw blankets, food, and containers of water to them ... some were acting crazy and it wasn't safe to bring them out until they calmed a bit. But others told us: 'Take my buddy first ... he's in a bad way.'"

Ships passing my bench diverted attention from other harbor activities. Most were destroyers. My curiosity was piqued with wonder as to where those entering the harbor had been and where those leaving were going. The newer destroyers entering, riding high in the water with fuel and stores depleted, reminded me of fleet greyhounds as they glided silently and gracefully through the harbor channel. Had any of them engaged the Japanese at sea? I wondered.

The aircraft carrier *Saratoga* hadn't made an appearance for some time. I also wondered about the whereabouts of the carriers *Lexington* and *Enterprise*. They had entered and left the harbor recently. They must be somewhere in Hawaiian waters, I speculated, unless they too were in a watery grave.

How could the Jap planes manage to get in without being detected by a patrol plane or ship? Patrolling had been done because I had watched Navy PBYs take off and land in the water by Ford Island at set times. Also, single destroyers had entered and left the harbor on apparently set schedules.

The devastating defeat was shameful and humiliating to me and, based on what I had observed, so few enemy planes had been shot down.

The months of practice, practice, and more practice hadn't been enough but *Pennsylvania*'s and other ships' crews fought gallantly and courageously with the available weapons.

The anti-aircraft guns on most of the ships had been ineffective in repelling the low-flying Japanese planes. Most of the AA guns were outdated and were the wrong type for repelling planes during an attack of that nature. Others had mentioned new AA guns which reputedly were very effective against low-flying planes. Apparently, most were being sent to England. Though England's fight was also ours, I still felt bitter that we had been left out on a limb with outdated and too few guns.

My anger at the Japs was predominantly because they had killed buddies-in-arms. Of course, anger also boiled because they had attacked my country. My concept of war was not to inform the enemy of your attack plans, so I was looking for an American to blame for the surprise of the attack and for the lack of sufficient weaponry. When the word was passed that Secretary of the Navy Frank Knox planned to visit the wards, my bitterness focused on him. He was a likely candidate, in particular for the weaponry shortage on the ships.

Afraid of an angry reaction if he stopped to talk to me, I thought it best to be out of the ward. Even under the circumstances, I knew it wasn't likely that an enlisted Marine, even a

U.S. Navy Hospital

bandaged one, would get away with blowing his stack at that high-ranking official. I resented his visit because I felt that he was only trying to placate the wounded men.

I was sitting on a bench adjacent to a road cutting through the hospital grounds when the secretary and his entourage drove by. Uncovered, a salute wasn't in order because Marines don't salute while bareheaded. Normally, I would have stood at attention while they passed, but I kept my seat and pretended to be staring into the distance. In a way, I was hoping the officers in a following jeep would stop to reprimand me for not standing at attention. Blowing my stack at one of them would probably have had more far-reaching effects. All of us Marines had felt so frustrated during the attack, because we had been trained to fight but could do little during the battle. Our .30-caliber rifles would have been more effective than most of *Pennsylvania's* AA guns. The machine guns, high on the masts, were the exception but they could provide only so much firepower.

A couple of days after the attack, Marine Detachment 1stSgt. William Smith visited the detachment's hospitalized men. He informed me that four of my best buddies had been among the six Marines killed by the bomb and sixteen Marines had been wounded. One of the men killed had been standing behind the open hatch cover in the deck of Number-9 Casemate ... he died from the bomb's concussion, without a mark left on his body.

Later, I learned that rumors led my father to believe that I was killed in the attack. He lived on a farm. A Western Union Messenger made six attempts to find him then delivered a telegram on the seventh attempt that read:

Washington, D.C., 11:42 p.m. 12/11/41. Thomas H. Wells (father) R.R. No. 2, Crocker, Missouri. Deeply regret to inform you that your son, Private First Class Arthur W. Wells, U.S. Marine Corps, has been

> wounded in action in the performance of his duty and in the service of his country X The Major General Commandant appreciates your great anxiety and will furnish you further information promptly when received X To prevent possible aid to our enemies please do not divulge the name of his ship or station. T. Holcomb The Major General Commandant.

The Marine Corps didn't pass the word that he had been notified, so I wondered whether my family even knew what had happened to me.

My head was still extremely painful and swollen but I was anxious to return to *Pennsylvania*. I thought of her as home. I had a score to settle and I wanted to be with the men I knew and trusted while settling it. And I began badgering the doctor to release me from the hospital. At first, he refused and I threatened to go AWOL and return to the ship anyway. He recognized my determination, and also probably knew that only time would heal my wounds. He released me on 13 December, with orders to report to the ship's doctor. He didn't give me any papers. I guessed that he would be too busy to be concerned with checking on me so I conveniently forgot about his order. I wasn't taking any chances that I'd be sent off the ship.

During 1stSgt. Wm. Smith's first visit to the hospital, I had requested a change of clothes. He brought them on his next visit. The moment the doctor left my bunk, I dressed, stuck my blood-stained khaki pants under my arm, and headed for the ship. I didn't want to wait for transportation but after walking only a short distance, a passing jeep stopped and gave me a ride. The driver dropped me off at the foot of *Pennsy's* gangway and I reported aboard for duty.

During my absence, the Marines in the detachment had wielded chipping hammers with a vengeance in the Marine Compartment; it had a fresh coat of sparkling white paint. Also word had been passed to ships throughout the Navy to

U.S. Navy Hospital

remove excess layers of paint, greatly reducing bomb-hit fire hazards.

In addition, to help reduce bomb-flash burns, high command required all men in the combat zone to wear long-sleeve shirts and long pants—amazing the protection that had been provided by a thin cotton skivvy shirt.

Late in the afternoon of my first day back aboard, a Marine came off watch and entered the Marine Compartment without unloading his rifle. While securing it, he accidentally pressed the trigger and the bullet ricocheted off the compartment bulkheads. Fortunately, it didn't hit anyone. In peacetime, he would have been court-martialled but this time he just received a good reaming-out by one of the sergeants.

I wanted to see what damage the bomb had caused, so the day after returning aboard I climbed the ladder to Number-7 Casemate. The only visible damage were dents in the wall-lockers mounted on the forward bulkhead—one dent looked to be about the shape and size of my head! Next, I went through the passageway where I had been standing during the attack to inspect -9. Repairs had been made to its deck and overhead, but the base of the broadside gun had a gouge in it that appeared to have been made by the nose of the bomb. During my eyeballing of the casemate, a sailor informed me that eighteen sailors had joined the six detachment Marines in death.

After leaving the casemates, I walked to the quarterdeck for a look at my mainmast battlestation. While there during the attack, I was never conscious of strafing but I could see pockmarks all over the mast—some were undoubtedly caused by low-level, small-caliber American fire.

Pennsylvania's battle report for 7 December shows three planes strafed the ship at about 0805 with other attacks later. *Pennsylvania* and *Downes* were hit at 0906 with one bomb hitting each of the ships. Other bombs dropped during that attack either hit the dock abreast of the ship or the water outside the

The Quack Corps

dry dock. The report also reveals that *Pennsylvania* left dry dock on 12 December.

The roster attached to the Marine Detachment office filing cabinet revealed the following casualties:

KILLED 12/7/41

LNAME	FNAME	RATE
Barron	Thomas N.	Corp.
Nations	Morris E.	Corp.
Stewart	Floyd "D"	PFC
Tobin	Patrick P.	PFC
Vincent	Jesse C. Jr.	Corp.
Wade	George H. Jr.	PFC

WOUNDED 12/7/41

LNAME	FNAME	RATE
Board*	Woodrow W.	Pvt.
Bozek	Walter J.	Pvt.
Crawford*	Claude C., Jr.	Corp.
Dale*	Tommie J.	PFC
Dillon*	George J. Jr.	PFC
Draben*	Warren C.	Pvt.
Eue*	Gordon A.	PFC
Francis*	Hollis B.	PFC
Gordon*	Roger A.	Pvt.
Holman*	Nelson R.	PFC
Jones*	Ervin B.	Pvt.
Kuehl*	Russell K.	Pvt.
Laughlin*	Raymond "J"	PFC
Mabey*	Kember D.	Pvt.
McFall	John H.	Pvt.
Rodland*	Bert W.	Pvt.
Wells	Arthur W.	PFC

*Transferred off the ship.

U.S. Navy Hospital

At first, Marine Detachment Clerk, Corp. Thomas N. Barron was reported as missing in action. Later, First Sergeant Smith commented that his body had been found in the dry dock when it was drained. With his death, I inherited his title and duties. The added responsibilities saved me from doing guard duty and mustering for formations, except when the entire ship's crew, to the man, was required to do so.

Chapter 3
The City by the Bay

When I reported back aboard *Pennsylvania*, on 13 December, First Sergeant Smith ordered that I wasn't to man my battlestation until cleared by the ship's doctor to do so. I didn't know that I had already made my last climb up the mainmast ladder.

No longer would the wild ride thrill me during the mainmast's soaring arc as the ship rolled and pitched in heavy seas, nor would I be able to watch the crew members as they went about their duties on the deck far below. Never again would I be able to stretch my arm out a gun-director-station opening and almost touch the close-at-hand rainbows in the sun's rays. I wouldn't feel the shiver of the mast as the dreadnought's bow plunged into huge waves in an angry sea, nor the thrill of the upward thrust as she was lifted atop the waves as they passed along her keel. The 5-inch .51-caliber gun crews wouldn't have me to tell them about what lay over the horizon. Though I'd miss the thrills given by my perch high above the main deck, there was one compensation ... I wouldn't have to choke and gag in the smokestack gases when the ship headed upwind or blew tubes.

I missed my perch, 20 December, 1941, when *Pennsylvania*'s screws began spinning and she moved away from 10-10 Dock to put to sea. Usually tugs moved the ship from the dock, but, this time, Captain C. M. Cooke, Jr. ordered the screws reversed and he maneuvered the ship smoothly, under her own power, away from the dock and into the channel.

As the ship moved down channel toward the harbor entrance, crews of other ships lined the rails and exploded with big cheers. I could feel *Pennsy*'s deck quivering under my feet

The City by the Bay

and watched her massive wake crashing against the channel banks as Captain Cooke ordered flank speed to make a running start for the open sea. Spray flew as the ship's bow plunged into the offshore rolling ground swells. The ship maintained flank speed until clearing the most dangerous areas for laying-in-wait submarines. Nothing untoward happened until the ship was at sea for a couple days, then scuttlebutt had a torpedo crossing her stern but I have never talked to anyone who could verify it.

Pennsylvania had left Pearl Harbor amid a multitude of rumors about her destination and probable activities. Some of the scuttlebutt was unrealistic and really far out. After the ship had sailed an easterly zigzag course for a few days, the rumor that the ship was heading for San Francisco proved to be correct. As the Golden Gate Bridge appeared over the horizon, the elation I normally would have felt was tempered by shame for the crushing defeat at Pearl Harbor.

The ship approached the entrance to San Francisco Bay and thousands of people were massed on vantage points and watching from the hills of the city. Apparently, the word began to circulate the moment the ship and her escorts loomed on the horizon. I guessed this wasn't the only day San Francisco residents had looked seaward, with nervousness and fear that any masts visible far out to sea rose above Japanese hulls.

As *Pennsylvania* moved slowly and silently through San Francisco Bay, and later to the Hunter's Point Naval Shipyard, the PA system blared: "You are not to divulge any information about what happened at Pearl Harbor! You are not to reveal damage to ships and installations to anyone, including members of your family!"

When *Pennsy* neared the dry dock at Hunter's Point, it appeared that everyone in the shipyard dropped tools to stare at the silently approaching ship. They were getting their first look at a battleship survivor of Pearl Harbor. I didn't hear a

The Quack Corps

single cheer … from ship or shore…because we were not returning as winners.

Shortly after the ship entered dry dock, the Marines moved into nearby barracks. Billeting on board would interfere with modernizing, re-gunning, and other work on the top decks and masts.

Pennsylvania had arrived on 29 December and Captain Cooke didn't let any grass grow before granting liberty, with the first one on New Year's Eve. Taking liberty wasn't appealing to me because the shame and humiliation of our shattering defeat kept me from feeling up to facing the civilians. They might accuse us of turning tail and running from the Japs because the ship had returned Stateside. I knew if people made remarks of that type I'd be fighting more than the Japanese because I wouldn't tolerate accusations towards me and my shipmates of cowardice. My non-liberty plans changed when a buddy was unexpectedly assigned guard duty. He had made plans for a date and couldn't reach the girl by phone to let her know that he couldn't show. Corporal Marvin Weatherly knew that I didn't plan to take liberty so he asked me to go ashore to deliver a message for him. He pointed out that it was a long way to 46th Street so to make my trip worthwhile, why didn't I just take his place on the date. I didn't know how the girl would feel about that, so I informed him I'd deliver his message but was returning to the ship afterward. In any case, I didn't want to make any promises until I had met the girl.

Three of us from the detachment shared a taxi to downtown San Francisco where I caught a city bus to the girl's home. It turned out that my buddy was just a friend of the family. The girl, petite and overly passionate Inez, became the first on a list that made San Francisco a memorable stay. The trauma caused by war's beginning, and the fear of an uncertain future, made the women of the city enthusiastic about helping a Missouri farm boy, in Marine dress blues, overcome shyness and build a storehouse of pleasant memories.

The City by the Bay

Following Inez was Irene, with flashing black eyes and equally black hair, a temper to match, and whose golden voice pleased patrons of area nightclubs and radio listeners. Then, Peggy, a vivacious and fun-loving San Francisco area newspaper society editor and senator's daughter. Next was Margaret, a private secretary and my favorite, with the clear and unblemished skin like so many of the girls raised in the moisture-laden air of Oregon. Added to the list were Marie, whose voluptuous body had graced a swimsuit in Billy Rose's Aquacades at Treasure Island during the 1939 World's Fair, and Collette, a dancer at Bimbo's 365 Club on Market Street. Others, almost faceless and nameless.

I enjoyed the pleasures of San Francisco only as duty allowed, for modification and regunning of the ship proceeded at a fast pace.

Even before the crew had moved off *Pennsylvania*, shipyard workmen swarmed over the ship. Height was cut off the mainmast. The 5-inch .51-caliber broadside guns were removed. The openings through which the guns had projected and the portholes were covered with steel. Removed also were the old 5-inch .25-caliber and 3-inch .50-caliber anti-aircraft guns, some with barrels twisted and drooping from the heat generated by firing so rapidly and long at Pearl Harbor. The five-inch'ers were replaced with 5-inch .38-caliber guns, vastly improving the ship's long-range AA protection. Also, sprouting on her top decks and superstructure like spines on a cactus were dozens of 20mm and mid-range guns.

With the broadside guns no longer aboard and the mainmast lowered, my gun-director battlestation had ceased to exist. I lost the $5.00 extra pay per month for being a Gun Director Pointer, First Class, though I could still wear the insignia on the sleeve of my blue uniform blouse.

Scuttlebutt floated that the new guns had been en route to the ship but hadn't yet left the States when the Japs attacked at Pearl Harbor. What the crew would have given to have had them that day!

Lowering of the mainmast, and other changes, gave the ship's topside and superstructure a more rakish look. Her 1916 bow style looked out of place but, in time, I knew I'd become accustomed to her lines.

The ship moved out of dry dock at the end of March 1942 and sailed to a berth at a pier at the foot of Market Street, near downtown San Francisco. Now, we could catch a streetcar on Market after only a short walk. The time saved in getting to our liberty destinations, and the money saved to get there, enabled us to spend more time enjoying the pleasures offered in San Francisco.

In Pearl Harbor, topside activities on *Pennsylvania* were observed only by service personnel, a few visiting wives, and shipyard workers. Berthed so near downtown with activities visible from the windows of high buildings and the hills, the ship became a showcase for the civilians of San Francisco. Though *Pennsy* Marines were accustomed to spit-and-polish, it became even more pronounced in detachment formations, standing watches, close-order drill practice on the piers, and in Color Guards.

Though still feeling the shame of Pearl Harbor, we were proud of being Marines and the chance to renew that pride was helpful to morale. The popping as hands slapped rifles while in formation and the unconscious renewal of, "Eyes straight ahead! Chin up! Chest out! Suck in that gut!" strained the buttons on shirts or blue blouses even more. NCOs and officers barked commands with more snap and the men in formation marched with renewed pride. Though the shame of the defeat would always be with us, we were recovering from feeling like beaten puppies. We were also spoiling for the chance to use those new guns on the Japs!

With the broadside gun battlestations no longer in existence, the Marines were assigned to 20mm AA guns located on the boat deck. The spit-and-polish routine was interrupted by hours of learning all we could about them before the ship left port. Characteristic of Marines, and just as we had with our rifles in boot camp, we disassembled and assembled them so many times that we could do it in the darkness of night. I taught and directed the activities of four Marine crews manning 20mm guns located to starboard and aft on the boat deck. I spent hours away from my detachment clerking duties to try and stay ahead of the men in learning about the 20's.

As with the other weapons manned in the past, we were anxious to fire the new guns to see what they could do. Our anticipation rose when *Pennsylvania* moved from the pier on 14 April and pointed her bow west to sail out of San Francisco Bay. Many of her Navy crew were replacements for more experienced men sent to man newly commissioned ships. The new men needed training in at-sea duties and, with the rest of the crew assigned to AA gun stations, learning how to hit an enemy plane with the new guns.

The ship's crew wasn't told of the scheduled date and time of sailing. But, again, the grapevine had been busy and thousands of people crowded the hills of San Francisco watching as *Pennsylvania*, accompanied by other ships, sailed under the Golden Gate.

I didn't expect that the ship would head into the war zone with so many inexperienced crew members. But I had learned that I didn't always guess the Navy's intent correctly, and I may be taking my last look at San Francisco as it disappeared over the stern.

Other ships in the fleet also had many new men in their crews so we remained near the West Coast. The gunners manning the AA guns practiced by firing at a target sleeve towed by an airplane.

Marine training had focused on the use of a variety of weapons since day one of service and many in the detachment had fired at towed sleeves with machine guns. It wasn't a real

The Quack Corps

feat of marksmanship to hit a sleeve, because it was towed on a course parallel with the ship at an unchanging speed and altitude and the planes and ship didn't perform evasive maneuvers. The major test was the pitch and roll of the ship but we quickly learned the feel of that and made the necessary adjustments. After only a few days of practice, most of the Marines became proficient at hitting the sleeve. But many of the Navy gunners hadn't had occasion to fire automatic weapons and needed more practice.

Loss of a target sleeve often meant securing from practice. For the Marines, hitting the sleeve had lost its challenge and one day a Marine on a 20mm commented that we could secure from practice if we could clip the towline. So competition began among the gun crews to see who could be the first to clip it. After only a short time, the target fluttered into the ocean. In subsequent gunnery practice, the towline was frequently cut with a 20mm shell whenever the Marine crews felt practice had gone on long enough. It wasn't long until *Pennsy's* captain guessed what we were doing. So he cramped our style by ordering the Marine crews to take the last firing runs, with the remark, "Those damn Marines shoot down too many sleeves!"—his Marine Orderly passed the word to us about that comment. So, we manned the guns but sat in boredom as each sailor manning a 20mm fired his full allotment of rounds.

After a few days at sea, the flotilla returned to port. A few days later, the in-and-out-of-port routine resumed as destroyers led the parade of ships leaving San Francisco Bay. As I recall, the other battleships accompanying *Pennsylvania* were *Maryland*, *Tennessee* and *Colorado*. The cruises gave the new men additional training in their shipboard duties and continued gunnery practice. I also thought the in-and-out-of-port routine served as a good front so the civilians wouldn't feel the ships were hiding in port but, instead, were going out to make sure the Japanese didn't get close to the States.

The City by the Bay

I learned that a boyhood friend was a sailor aboard *Colorado*. She was berthed at a nearby pier so I decided to visit him. I didn't realize the ordeal I'd go through just to visit another serviceman. When I requested permission from the young ensign on duty as Officer of the Deck to come aboard, he put me through the wringer. I guess the ink hadn't yet dried on his commission, because he apparently was enamored of his rank or over-zealous in his duties. He might have felt that I looked too young to be a Marine corporal. In any event, the grilling went on and on. A Marine was on duty with the O.D. He was standing behind the officer grinning, which I thought odd.

Eventually, the O.D. gave permission for me to board and had word passed for Roy Hargis to report to him. Usually, a man with a visitor took responsibility for his guest. This time, the O.D. called for a Marine guard, ordered him to keep us by Number-3 turret, and allowed only 10 minutes for visiting. Then, he ordered the guard, "Take this man back to *Pennsylvania* and be certain that you see him on board!" I began the walk back to my ship with the guard trailing behind. When we were out of the O.D.'s sight, he called, "Wait up, corporal." He caught up with me and continued, "I'll walk with you. I'm not going to embarrass you by making it appear that you're a prisoner. You're not the only one that son-of-a-bitch has treated this way."

"I've been taken for a lot of things but it's the first time I knew that I looked like a spy."

"I think he must see spies in his dreams," he commented, with a laugh. We talked about duty on our respective ships during the rest of the walk to *Pennsy*.

Just before we reached the foot of the gangway, he said, "I'm not about to walk up that gangway with you. I'm sorry about your embarrassment."

"It wasn't your fault. Maybe we'll see each other again on liberty," I answered. He turned and headed back to his ship,

The Quack Corps

without a backward glance. The men in *Pennsy's* detachment had a laugh about my spy experience.

Though it had been irritating, and added to the detest I was beginning to feel for new ensigns, it couldn't have been nearly as unnerving as the experience undergone by the task force's scout plane pilots. The force was cruising off the Northern California Coast when fog formed so quickly that the pilots couldn't make it back to the ships. They made emergency landings on the water and the task force began the hunt for them. Lookouts posted on the bows and on other parts of the ships cocked their ears for the planes' motors. Complete silence was ordered so the lookouts could have a better chance of hearing the motors when the pilots sporadically revved them.

After a plane was located, a battleship maneuvered to pick it up. I watched as *Pennsylvania* made a turn to port so a plane could taxi into the calmer waters created by the turn and alongside the ship's stern. A davit hoisted the plane aboard and placed it on the aft-turret launching catapult. Every plane was recovered except one that crashed into a battleship's superstructure, *Colorado* as I recall, while flying in the dense fog.

Pennsy was threading her way through the minefields as she approached the Golden Gate. Below decks, I heard the sounds of explosions. The decks vibrated as she picked up speed, and I rushed topside. She was heeling over as she twisted and turned through the minefield course. I rushed out onto the quarterdeck. A PBY plane was circling in the distance, and periodically dropping depth charges. An old four-stacker destroyer, *U.S.S. Crosby* I believe, was laying-to near where the PBY was circling. Of course, I thought they had a Jap sub cornered.

In a few minutes, a submarine shot up through the water's surface at what appeared to be about a 45-degree angle. That sub popping out of the water looked like a big fat cigar! She was already making headway when her bow dropped back to

The City by the Bay

the water. She was an American submarine making a practice dive. Apparently, the PBY crew hadn't received the word, nor did they pay heed to the signal flown by the destroyer. The sub followed *Pennsylvania* into San Francisco Bay, then veered toward the Mare Island sub base. She was low in the stern, apparently as a result of the depth charging. Later that day, scuttlebutt floated on *Pennsy* that the sub had lost nine men.

In the few months since *Pennsylvania's* arrival, the threat of attack on the west coast by Jap ships had lessened. The people in San Francisco felt safer. And, the new men who had joined the ships' crews only short months before had gained their sea legs. They also had acquired a good working knowledge of the ships and new guns. I felt each trip out of San Francisco might be the last because the time was undoubtedly drawing near that the ships would join the other naval forces in the Pacific War Zone.

Chapter 4
Return to Pearl Harbor

The U.S. coastline disappeared over the stern of *Pennsy* 1 August, 1942, and the flotilla commander set a zigzag course heading west. It wasn't by choice that I hit the deck to man my battlestation and watched the sun rise in the east every morning. Then, to man the station again that evening and watch it fade below the western horizon—the danger of enemy attack was greatest at dawn and at dusk.

The raucous PA announcement: "General Quarters! General Quarters! All hands man your battlestations! All hands man your battlestations!" happened frequently as the huge screws pushed the ship westward. In addition to dawn and dusk GQ's, battlestations were manned every time a bogey (unidentified plane or ship) showed on radar, visually, or when screening destroyers had an underwater sound contact. Each time one of those GQ's sounded, a chill coursed up my spine.

On 14 August, Diamond Head loomed on the horizon. When *Pennsylvania* neared the entrance channel to Pearl Harbor, the anti-sub nets were pulled back and she entered much more sedately than when leaving it eight months before.

Just after passing the sub nets, the crew secured from General Quarters. I took up stance amidships by myself at the starboard rail. Tension welled up and I wasn't in any mood for conversation. The ship sailed silently by Hospital Point and the bench where I had spent many hours while hospitalized. Then, *Pennsy* swung to port to begin the familiar circling of Ford Island. As the island drew near, I noted the destroyed aircraft hangars and other evidence of the attack still on it.

Pennsylvania passed the capsized hulk of *Utah*. I felt some satisfaction that the Japs had made at least one mistake, because the torpedoes wasted on the old target battleship had been destined for the bowels of an aircraft carrier.

Tension heightened as *Pennsylvania* approached the torn and twisted remains of her sister ship, *Arizona*. It was deathly quiet and the new men in the crew stared in awe. The men who had been there during the attack, with mental visions flashing of diving and banking planes, pyrotechnics and sounds of massive explosions, boiling black smoke, belching of anti-aircraft guns, the horribleness of a buddy's torn and bleeding body or the remembrance of it burned to the blackness of overdone toast. And, too, of massive ships slowly settling until keels buried in the harbor's muddy bottom, or rolling like a child's play boat in a bathtub to expose huge keels to the sun.

And, if as I did, each man reaffirmed his determination that the Japanese nation would pay ... a thousand or more fold ... until it was brought to its knees for what it had done on that Sunday morning. I could already taste the sweetness of vengeance because I knew I might die before complete vengeance was exacted.

The bones of a high school buddy, Wayne Bandy, lay with those of over 1100 men entombed in *Arizona's* bowels. No one would ever know how he had died—whether slowly while gasping for breath in a sealed compartment, or instantly by the force of the dreadnought's explosions, or by searing fire. I hadn't known he was aboard *Arizona* until reading of his death in my home-area newspaper.

As *Pennsylvania* sailed slowly by Battleship Row, it was as if the attack was a rerun and being projected on a gigantic movie screen. Again *Oklahoma's* masts splashed the water when she capsized ... and *West Virginia* settled into the mud as torpedo after torpedo tore into her bowels. While *Pennsylvania* eased into her berth, I visualized the awe-inspiring sight of *Nevada* fighting her way down harbor. I hadn't noticed the hole in the Navy Yard smokestack before, but *Helena's* crew claimed credit for putting it there on 7 December. The remaining evidence of the attack would help stamp it even more indelibly into my memory.

Later, I was in Pearl Harbor and watched *West Virginia* towed in the direction of the sub base. The port side of her hull had been ripped open by torpedoes. The space between decks above her waterline, where they had hit while she was settling deeper and deeper into the water, looked from my vantage point at 10-10 Dock as if there was barely enough room for a man to crawl between. Then even later, I also watched the rusted hulk of *Oklahoma* towed in the same direction—much of her superstructure had been cut away before she was righted.

At her berth, an anti-torpedo net protected the channel side of *Pennsylvania*. The crew settled into an in-port routine, except that liberty was granted during daylight hours only.

Liberty in Honolulu ran a poor second to San Francisco but I decided to go ashore to stretch my legs and get away from the ship's confines. Even though servicemen on liberty were in good numbers prewar, this time I found downtown Honolulu packed with shoulder-to-shoulder uniforms.

Prostitution was permitted in prewar Honolulu and the authorities let it continue. I could hardly believe my eyes when I saw men standing in block-long lines waiting for a turn with a prostitute. Previously, many of the servicemen had acted a little self-conscious while in the area of the hotels featuring prostitutes but now most appeared at ease. Perhaps, many of them wouldn't patronize the cathouses, as Marines called them, in peacetime. Far from home and close contact with women, it gave them the chance to feel the warmth and closeness of a woman and release some of the tensions of war in the best way available, for a nominal fee of three bucks.

In some of the hotels, each prostitute used three rooms, one by a man undressing, another by a man using the services of the prostitute and the other by a man dressing after his turn. Hallway doors were usually open and some of the women didn't even take time to slip on a robe as they rushed from room to room. It was mass production spilling of male sperm and semen. The cycle continued until the servicemen returned to ships or other stations before dark.

Massage parlors had proliferated as had lady barbers. So those men not inclined to patronize the whorehouses could feel the touch of a woman's gentle fingers at the massage parlors or have facials done by a lady barber. Having the facial had a plus because in addition to feeling the touch of a woman's fingers, pores in the facial skin were opened and cleaned.

Spending every night aboard ship gave us a cooped-up feeling, so we looked for ways to relieve the tensions. Kangaroo Courts in the Marine Compartment became the favorite of the Marines aboard. The courts were designed for laughs so trumped-up charges served as rationale for bringing a Marine defendant to trial. The grapevine spread the word about the fun, throughout the ship, and many sailors joined off-duty Marines in the compartment. It was usually so packed that it reminded me of sardines in a can. I laughed so hard during the trials that my stomach ached and my sides got sore.

Platoon Sergeant Stringfellow featured a good sense of humor and the ability to be serious in laughable situations; he served as judge. Another Marine acted as prosecuting attorney, another as defense attorney, one as bailiff and 12 others comprised the jury.

When a new man joined the detachment, it presented another opportunity for a trial, particularly if he was fresh out of Sea School. He was ordered to the ship's bridge to bring us a "sky hook" or to the engine room for a "bucket of steam." Of course, he couldn't get either of them so we tried him for not properly carrying out his orders. At sea, he took up post on the bow to watch for the mail plane wearing a life jacket, his rifle on his shoulder, and a pair of binoculars slung from his neck. The plane never came because the crew didn't get mail deliv-

The Quack Corps

ered to the ship at sea. Then, we put him on trial for not bringing us mail.

Corporal Billy Cooper was on duty as corporal of the guard while a mail watcher was posted. As a different turn of events, he was charged with not advising the mail watcher of which direction the plane would come. I served as his defense attorney, using the argument that the ship had changed course and the captain hadn't informed the corporal of the new heading. Of course, I knew that he didn't stand a chance of acquittal so just waited for the passing of sentence.

This time, the court was really turning things around because I was also pronounced guilty for not presenting a good defense. The sentence that the bailiff pluck hairs from our bare asses with a tweezers was changed when I blurted that I didn't have any hair on mine. Apparently, they *had* noticed that in the showers and promptly changed the sentence to wearing our clothing wrong-side out.

Sailors in one of the deck divisions approached us about holding a trial for a member of their division. He refused to shower and they were tired of his stink. We refused, at first, by pointing out that it could cause trouble between sailors and Marines. We also felt that it'd change the fun purpose of our trials. They continued pressing and we eventually agreed but they would have to furnish all members of the court, except for the judge because he could remain neutral and keep order.

On the night of the trial, the sailors forcefully brought the fiercely resisting defendant into the Marine Compartment. They sat him down and the trial proceeded. The sailor jury sentenced him to taking a bath in the middle of the compartment, using a steel helmet shell for a tub, G.I. saltwater soap, and a G.I. scrub brush for a washcloth.

When ordered to get with it, he refused, at first, but removed his upper garments after the sailors threatened to undress him by force. Then he stopped. Two sailors grabbed his arms, two his legs and two stripped clothing from him while he struggled fanatically.

A bucket of cold water was brought to fill the helmet shell. A sailor handed him the brush and soap and ordered, "Turn to!" but he refused. At his refusal, they grabbed him and began roughly scrubbing with the brush so he decided that he'd better do it himself. Embarrassment and anger got the best of him occasionally and he'd make a rush at one of the sailors or try to escape. A flick on his bare ass with a wet towel reddened it even more and he was forcibly returned to the middle of the compartment.

After they felt he had at least some semblance of a bath, they let him go. Reportedly, he showered regularly after his kangaroo court ordered scrubbing. As feared, his trial seemed to take some of the zing out of the fun we had been having; it was one of the last held while I was aboard *Pennsy*.

The ship's showers didn't have individual stalls. When the water was on for a limited time, men packed the showers and one had to use caution to be sure that he was soaping his own body. Those who were overly modest found that it just wasn't the place for it.

The main deck head was in the bow. Seats were bolted to a long metal trough that had water flowing through it. A vertical piece of metal about the height of a seated man separated each seat from its neighbor.

Shortly after joining the Marine Detachment, I watched a sailor light a large bundle of toilet paper and drop it in the trough. I laughed when heads began popping up above the dividers as each man felt the heat from the burning paper. When a buddy was using a seat the yell would go up, "Fire in the trough!"

On 4 September 4, 1942, Navy Captain T. S. King signed the warrant promoting me to sergeant. The third stripe got me out of the detachment clerk's job and into sergeant's duties

The Quack Corps

with the detachment. Other events would make even further changes in my duties.

Pennsylvania hadn't been the Pacific Fleet Flagship since Admiral Husband Kimmel moved his Flag ashore at war's beginning. So Vice-Admiral William Pye, Commander Task Force ONE, had hoisted his Flag on the ship on 3 April, 1942. The admiral's facial features and stature reminded me of Napoleon in paintings I'd seen.

Admiral Pye transferred his Flag to the battleship *New Mexico* 26 September, 1942. A sergeant and 14 other Marines were to make up his Marine Flag Detachment. Word was passed for volunteers from *Pennsylvania*'s detachment.

As junior sergeant on *Pennsy*, I'd be stuck with the flag job unless one of the other sergeants volunteered. I spent a lot of time trying to sell any one of them on the benefits of being senior NCO with the Flag, using the persuasion, "It'll be easy duty because all you'll have to do is assign men to orderly shifts for the admiral and his staff. You won't have sergeant of the guard duty and will probably have more liberty because you won't have to stay on board in port." The job didn't appeal to any of them and with no choice in the matter, I reluctantly packed my gear for the transfer. With only seven months left of sea duty, I wanted to stay on *Pennsy* because she was a "happy" ship.

As I prepared to leave the ship, "home" for the past 17 months, it was with a multitude of memories, good and bad. I laughed about falling out of my hammock the first night aboard and falling asleep while walking post at the foot of the quarterdeck gangway the second night. I remembered the many hours spent grabassing with the Corp. Robert Barnett and another man in the Marine Compartment. Quite often, they'd hang me out to dry with my web trouser belt draped over an overhead hammock hook. Included, of course, were memories of Honolulu, Long Beach and San Francisco liberties.

Return to Pearl Harbor

While aboard, I had served under three different Marine Detachment commanding officers. First was Major Wilburt S. "Slew Foot" Brown, a tall, lanky, gruff-voiced mustang, who had earned a field commission for his exploits in Nicaragua in the late 1920's or early 30's. He gave me a reaming out my second day of work in the detachment office because I couldn't find the daily report. He apologized later. He left his mark on *Pennsy* and gave us a laugh during an inspection muster under the canvas covering "officers' country" on the quarterdeck—stifled snickers were heard in the enlisted ranks when the Major drew his saber from its scabbard, raised it forward and up in a straight-arm motion, as a part of its manual-of-arms, and cut a long slit in the canvas!

Major Brown was relieved by Captain Robert E. Cushman, Jr., in June 1941. I always considered the Captain to be the most intelligent Marine officer under which I served. After his relief in the spring of 1942 by Captain Robert S. Riddell, I didn't see him again nor did I follow his career. My recognition of his intelligence hadn't been off the mark. Awarded the Navy Cross for actions on Guam during its invasion in 1944, he went on to high command in Korea and in Vietnam, served as Deputy Director of the Central Intelligence Agency during some of President Richard Nixon's years, and became Commandant of the United States Marine Corps. He attended the U.S. Naval Academy at age 16, before graduating from high school. While Commandant of the Corps, his St. Paul, Minnesota, high school decided it was time to present him with a diploma. I left with fond memories of Gunnery Sergeant William B. "Bucky" Harris, a big, curly headed Marine with long years of service in the Marine Corps. He was awarded the Croix de Guerre by the French in World War I. The Gunny treated me like a son. He gave me many pointers about how best to get along in the Corps, such as keep my nose clean and lay off the booze.

The Quack Corps

U.S. Navy photo
U.S.S *Pennsylvania* BB38—U.S.S *New Mexico* BB40, somewhere in the Pacific.

First Sergeant Smith sometimes returned to the ship still under the effects of too much drinking. On Fridays, the ship's captain inspected every area of his ship and it wouldn't do for him to catch the first sergeant sleeping it off. So Gunny Harris delegated me to keep the first sergeant out of the inspection party's way—for some reason, he'd listen to me. Marines took up stations at strategic points. They passed the word when the inspection party headed our way and I'd cajole the first sergeant into going with me to a different area.

The first sergeant was German and had enlisted in the United States Marine Corps prior to World War I. A detachment Marine informed me that Smith was with a unit that captured his hometown in Germany.

Duty on *Pennsy* would be remembered as one of the high marks in my Marine service because her detachment Marines was second to none.

Chapter 5
U.S.S New Mexico

Naval personnel and seagoing Marines usually referred to the *New Mexico* as *New Mex.* Occasionally, I'd hear her called "The Queen of the Seas" but in a derisive or tongue-in-cheek tone of voice. Most of the crew didn't consider her a "happy" ship. The atmosphere aboard differed greatly from what I had experienced on *Pennsylvania.*

The *New Mexico*'s Detachment Marines didn't welcome the Flag Marines aboard with open arms. The addition of 15-more bodies in their quarters caused serious overcrowding. The detachment used compartments on two different decks, which also created some inconvenience. Resentment caused by the overcrowding, and the feeling by some that the Flag Marines "had it made" with easier duties, made the welcome aboard somewhat less than enthusiastic.

The Flag Marines served as orderlies and messengers for Vice-Admiral William Pye and his staff and were not assigned to ship battlestations. They mustered with the ship's detachment for inspections, were subject to its discipline, but were not assigned any duties with it except for helping keep the living quarters ship-shape. I compiled a daily duty roster and provided the detachment office with a copy. In port, the Marine Detachment office crew controlled the liberty cards of the men assigned to duty or not otherwise eligible for liberty.

The lack of ready acceptance of the Flag by Detachment Marines may have been, in part, caused by the first sergeant's attitude. He was at or near middle age, with an arrogant attitude, stubborn and discourteous. He had been a lieutenant in the Chicago Police Department prior to reserve call up.

The Quack Corps

When reporting aboard, I turned the Flag Marine records in to him. After a quick thumb through, he raised his head and, in a threatening and belligerent voice, told me among other things, "You Flag Marines aren't on *Pennsylvania* now! You'll toe the line on this ship!" *Pennsy's* detachment had a fleet-wide reputation for spit-and-polish and it didn't need any defense, so I bit my tongue and kept quiet. With my close daily contact with *Pennsy's* first sergeant, gunnery sergeant and detachment officers in the past, I was beyond the point of feeling awed by *his* stripes.

I warned the men that we would be under close scrutiny for awhile and to keep their noses clean. A couple of days after we boarded the *New Mex*, the Marine Detachment Commanding Officer pulled a surprise inspection and noted improperly stored gear in two lockers. The First Sergeant sent for me, reamed me out, and ordered me to pull the men's' liberty cards. With the war on, I knew they may not often have a chance for liberty so I tactfully remonstrated with him. Though I suggested extra duty as a possible substitute, he wouldn't hear of it.

The two men were upset over having their liberty cards pulled. I pointed out that they had brought it on themselves by carelessness, and that the first sergeant had ordered them pulled. I informed them they'd have to talk to him if they wanted liberty privileges restored. I don't know whether they went to see him and if so, what he told them. At any rate, one held me responsible and decided he'd whip me.

I was sitting on the base of a 5-inch .51-caliber gun, in a starboard casemate, shining my shoes, and in a bull session with a Detachment Marine. The Flag Marine stormed up the ladder from the deck below, "Sergeant! I'm going to kick your ass for pulling my liberty card!"

Unless I wanted my name to be mud among the Marines aboard, I knew future discipline, and keeping my self-respect, made it mandatory that I call his hand. I set my shoes on the

U.S.S. New Mexico

deck and unstrapped my watch and handed it to the Marine beside me. Rising to my feet, I hooked my thumbs over my web belt loosely and replied in a calm, and deliberately unemotional, tone of voice, "You're going to have one-hell-of-a-battle before getting the job done. I suppose this may be as good of a place as any to try it." He had size on me but I felt my boxing and hand-to-hand fighting training gave me a better hand than he thought I held. The ladder hatch stood open close behind him so I decided to sucker him into the first swing, duck, and use a hip-roll to send him down the ladder and hopefully settle the issue quickly.

He stared at me for a few moments, changed his mind about what he planned to do and went back down the ladder. I strapped my watch on, sat down on the gun base and resumed shining my shoes. But, with only minutes separating each incident, he stormed up the ladder twice more for replays.

The humiliation for backing down when I called his hand was enough punishment, I felt, so I didn't put him on report. The incident gained me respect from the Flag and Detachment Marines. They now knew that the baby-faced sergeant couldn't be intimidated. Though he gave me no further problems, the Flag Marine tangled with a Detachment Marine a couple days later and took a good beating. By coincidence, the winner of the fight sported the surname of "Wells." But relations between Flag and Detachment Marines improved quickly as each found new buddies in the other group.

In early December 1942, *New Mexico,* several other older battleships, and screening vessels cleared Pearl Harbor and sailed for the South Pacific.

The bow area of *New Mex* was crammed with mail for South Pacific units. She also carried payroll funds rumored to be about four million dollars, stored in a stateroom in officers' country.

The detachment NCOs were given the responsibility of guarding the payroll. With at-sea routine established, no weap-

The Quack Corps

onry battlestation duties, time on my hands and the feeling that I wanted to be more useful, I volunteered to take my share of watches. Each NCO stood a two-hour watch, armed with a Thompson submachine gun, on post outside the stateroom door. The crew humorously questioned whether *New Mex* was a likely target for South Pacific pirates.

The task force crossed the equator 11 December, 1942. The ships' crews were at General Quarters and equator-crossing festivities were not allowed. The longitude and date were stamped "Censored" on my Domain of Neptunus Rex Certificate; I jotted the information on a small scrap of paper and entered it later.

The task force dropped anchor in Nandi Bay, Veti Levu, Fiji Islands, and remained in the bay for most of the next couple of months. The small town of Lautoka was a few miles from the anchorage. After exploring it, a buddy and I rented English bicycles and hitched a pull behind a sugarcane train for a ride into the countryside. We hitched a pull back to town behind the same train. Its cars were hooked together with chains and what a clanging they made when the train started or stopped.

The Marine Corps was using New Zealand as a rest area for combat troops. The men attached to the small New Zealand unit stationed near Lautoka wondered why the Marines would be sent to their homeland while they had to serve in Fiji. I didn't remind them that facilities for large numbers of men, food, recreation and *girls* were much more plentiful in their homeland.

On one of the daytime-only liberties, I paid $1.00 for a five-foot-long stalk of bananas. I conned a buddy into helping me bring them aboard. We had to board by way of the stern boat boom. I hung them in the ship's P-coat locker. Though only two men supposedly had keys, others beat me to most of the ripe bananas and left me with only four. Some 20-plus years later, that stalk of bananas would make a connection

U.S.S. New Mexico

with a former *New Mex* sailor when I mentioned the "The Queen of the Seas." He had been on duty with the Officer-of-the-Deck and remembered the O.D. wondering aloud whether he should allow me to bring them on board.

A buddy joined me in a visit to two nearby native villages. The natives greeted us exuberantly and proudly showed us their thatched buildings. Our questions about the large breadfruit trees, randomly spaced throughout the villages, brought the information that breadfruit was a staple food item for them.

While walking through one of the villages, we heard girls giggling and chattering in their native language. We couldn't see them at first, then discovered they were showering in a roofless, free standing, sheet metal-enclosed shower in the middle of the village. They were peeking through holes in the metal and chattering excitedly, apparently about two khaki-clad American Marines.

The native girls also spoke English and we spent time talking with groups of them while lolling in the shade of a huge breadfruit tree. They were friendly and curious about our life in the United States, and our girls. At the beginning, some of their elders joined us under the tree but they were perceptive enough to understand that they didn't stand much chance against the more comely of their kin and ambled off to do other things.

My buddy smoked cigarettes and, just like many of the girls in the U.S. would do, some of the Fiji girls sneaked puffs whenever they thought their elders wouldn't see them. They appeared to be reasonably well educated and spoke English fairly well, but with a British accent.

We realized just how far the ships were from their home base when a supply ship ran aground somewhere to the northeast of Fiji. Chow aboard was in short supply and conservation measures were taken. To ensure enough for everyone, ration chits were issued to prevent men going through chow

The Quack Corps

lines for seconds. Rice and beans provided subsistence for about two weeks, until another supply ship's arrival. Unfortunately, Lautoka had few restaurants. It had a food shortage of its own so our sporadic liberties didn't give much chance to supplement our rice-bean diet with whatever foods were available in it.

With the hot days and warm nights, it was stifling hot in the compartments. Only hot tea, coffee or tepid water was available for drinking. What I would have paid for a glass of ice-cold water! The ship must have had an abundant supply of tea because it was served so often that I never did re-acquire a liking for it. Sugar would have helped but none was available.

Swimming was permitted off the starboard side of the ship during certain hours. Though watchers were posted, few of the men braved the threat of sharks to take advantage of its cooling effects.

Unfortunately, it appeared to be a time of calm breezes in the Fiji area which compounded the discomfort caused by hot weather. The heat, sporadic liberty and lack of athletic activities, such as softball, had its effect on morale. Surprisingly, the combination of those things didn't seem to cause squabbling among the crew, maybe for a lack of energy because of the heat.

I wondered why the task force of older battleships remained at anchor with American ships being outgunned and taking huge losses in the Solomon Islands area battles. Later, I realized they were probably being held as a last line of defense in case the Japs pushed American forces out of the Solomons and moved against Australia.

Though I was hoping for a different routine, I wasn't enthusiastic about the change promised when I read the captain's message in the ship's daily newssheet shortly after the task force sailed out of Nandi Bay on 6 February, 1943. It read:

U.S.S. New Mexico

Officers and crew of the U.S.S. New Mexico: The Japs are striking at Guadalcanal in force. We are on our way to intercept them. Tomorrow morning (Wednesday) we will be joined by carriers and destroyers. Happy Hunting!

I thought "Happy Hunting" was not a judicious choice of words. The loss of a single American would quickly change the context of those words for the man and his loved ones back in the States.

Tension mounted as the fleet approached the area of the anticipated liquid battlefield--we knew of the many American and Australian ships already lost in the Solomons and felt that whatever we faced in the days ahead would be no picnic. General Quarters stations were manned around the clock and crew fatigue became a serious threat to battle efficiency.

My duties didn't restrict me to any one area during GQ. With the other Flag Marines still standing their usual schedule of watches, I volunteered to captain a 5-inch .25-caliber AA gun (*New Mexico* still had her old prewar 5-inch AA guns in service) and man it with Flag Marines. They enthusiastically volunteered.

I wasn't completely familiar with the workings of the 5-inch AA guns. But, at least we could serve as additional eyes while a crew got badly needed rest. Our first watch was on a pitch-black night—we had to feel our way along the boat deck to reach the gun. The gun crew left the instant we arrived and before I could ask about the location of the air valve; air was used for clearing the barrel of burning powder residue between rounds. I checked with the relief captain on the next gun but he couldn't tell me nor could anyone in fire control. After feeling all over the gun and its mount without success, I told myself: "Aww hell! If anything happens, the regular crew will probably show up before we blow the thing apart!"

The Quack Corps

A couple days later, the crew secured from General Quarters. Later, the ship's news sheet informed us that the Japanese had refused battle after intensive aerial scouting of the fleet. It also added that the only important surface engagement recently had been a Jap night air attack on an American task force, on the 29th of January.

Though on the Flag, I wasn't in the "need to know" category. So, with my desire to know more about what was going on in the battle area, I sneaked reads of confidential battle reports. I remember reading a battle report by the battleship *South Dakota*, amazed at the details given. Not only did she report the numbers of rounds of each AA caliber expended, she reported her speeds and other data. While under attack by Jap torpedo planes, she took evasive action and turned so fast that her outboard main deck was under water and her inboard 5-inch guns couldn't depress low enough to fire at the planes. I visualized that magnificent craft, with her forest of AA guns spitting projectiles at the Jap planes, as she twisted and turned with the sea foaming from the surging caused by her massive screws. She suffered no damage in the engagement.

Even I could guess that the tide had turned because *South Dakota* was one of the forerunners of a massive and modern fleet, gunned and equipped with the speed for what had become a different type of battle.

Shortly after the Japs refused to challenge the fleet, deciding not to reinforce but instead to withdraw from Guadalcanal, the task force of older battleships sailed through a winding, narrow, and jungle-bordered channel to anchorage in Havannah Harbor, Efate, New Hebrides. And, again we waited!

With no villages or towns near *New Mexico's* anchorage, two buddies joined me in a leg-stretching trip ashore. We walked to a nearby jungle airstrip for a look at bullet-riddled carcasses of Marine SBD planes. The air units to which they had belonged had moved on to Guadalcanal and other Solomon Island areas. The rear-gunner's section on one of the car-

U.S.S. New Mexico

casses had been shredded by Japanese small-caliber shells. I couldn't help thinking of how helpless he and the pilot must have felt when the Jap pilot made a run on their slow and lumbering plane. An airman still at the strip informed us that the gunner's body had been nearly cut in half by the shells.

On another leg-stretching trip ashore, the same two buddies and I hired a native guide for a wild boar hunt. He assured us that he knew exactly where the boars could be found. After following him down a jungle path for a couple of hours without even hearing an oink in the distance, we quit the hunt in disgust. We didn't feel that the buck paid for guide service had been well spent.

The waiting routine was interrupted when *New Mex* joined a small task force and escorted a heavy cruiser toward Pearl Harbor. She had lost part of her bow in the Solomons and a temporary stub allowed her to proceed under power, at slow speed. She listed heavily to port and I hoped the seas would stay calm. Other ships met the task force just north of the equator and took over escorting duties. *New Mex* and another older battleship, *Tennessee* as I recall, headed for and dropped anchor again in Nandi Bay in Fiji.

This time the stay in Nandi Bay was short and the ships sailed in a northeasterly direction with the next stop at Pago Pago, American Samoa, arriving 11 March, 1943.

On the approach to the harbor, *New Mex* sailed parallel to the shore for several miles. The huge ground swells offshore caused a drastic heeling over, the most I had ever encountered aboard ship. In stormy weather, I had seen battleships' screws exposed but never heeling to match that at Samoa.

The area surrounding the harbor entrance was beautiful; to starboard towered a mountain with a rain cloud enveloping its peak and to port the terrain was flat with another mountain rising skyward in the distance. Vegetation was lush and Samoa was what I had envisioned a South Seas island should look like.

The Quack Corps

My curiosity about the natives' living quarters and daily activities led me to a Samoan village. One of my sisters had asked for a Hawaiian grass skirt. Those sold in stores in Honolulu were made with cellophane so I hadn't yet filled her order. A Samoan woman was weaving skirts in front of a thatched hut and I approached to ask about buying one from her. Americans had been in and out of and stationed on the island long enough for the natives to know that they could quote almost any price and get it. I felt that $7.00 was too much but decided to buy one without haggling for a price reduction. I parcel posted it to my sister when the ship arrived in Pearl Harbor a few days later.

Chapter 6
Palmyra Island

I transferred off *New Mexico* 23 March, 1943, and to "C" Company, Marine Barracks, Navy Yard, Pearl Harbor.

My first duty was as assistant mail censor, which meant that I scanned letters for forbidden material, cut it out, and then passed them on to the bonded censor for stamping. I felt like an intruder reading letters written to wives and sweethearts by men with whom I had daily contact. The Japanese were well aware of the barrack's location so censorship was not as restrictive as on the ships and at certain other stations. As a result, the men could write about Honolulu liberties, Hawaiian scenery and about some of their daily activities. They couldn't mention anything of a military nature, such as other units, ships, planes, damage for example during the attack on 7 December, 1941, and so forth.

As I gained censoring experience, I learned to quickly scan for certain words, numbers and phrases. Some of the men repeatedly included forbidden material; their names on envelopes triggered more careful scrutiny. If excessive razor-blading of forbidden subjects was necessary, I returned the letter to the man responsible to rewrite and lectured him about the danger he may cause to his buddies-in-arms in all service branches.

Most of the men wrote letters that were much alike. However, a few penned polished letters which probably made each girl receiving one feel like she was the most beautiful, loved and talented girl on the face of the earth ... I did learn a few things censoring mail!

The company first sergeant was promoted to sergeant major and transferred. My censoring chore ended when the com-

The Quack Corps

pany commander requested that I take over the job; it was more interesting than censoring. It soon ended when I opened a messenger-delivered packet and discovered transfer orders for me inside. The orders were apparently delayed in the chain-of-command because I was to be a passenger on a small ship scheduled to sail in just one hour. I rushed into the company commander's office to inform him of my plight. Though he empathized with me, he didn't feel there was enough time for him try to get the orders changed. So I hastily packed my gear and dumped it into the back of a waiting jeep for a speedy trip to 10-10 Dock. Except for *U.S.S. Sabine*, the oil tanker that brought me to Pearl Harbor to board *Pennsylvania* in April 1941, and berthing by Ford Island, every move I made at Pearl Harbor was over 10-10 Dock. I hurried up the *USAIT Comet*'s gangway only moments before it was hoisted away.

Added to the shock of the sudden transfer was an even greater one because instead of sailing to the States, I was heading in the opposite direction. With almost three years in the Corps, I had yet to have a furlough. My morale nose-dived when *Comet* set course for Palmyra Island, laying 1100-miles southwest of the Hawaiian Islands.

In peacetime, Palmyra had been privately owned by an individual living in the Hawaiian area. It joined Johnston and the Midway Islands, also Wake before its capture by the Japanese in 1941, as an important buffer ring to help protect the Hawaiian Islands. An airstrip had been built on it in 1939. Possession of Palmyra was also important to the U.S. for protecting supply lines to Australia and other South Pacific areas. The island has only one square mile of dry land and its shape is long and narrow. Though some Marines opined they could spit across it, others used a coarser term—piss across—at its narrowest point.

Comet was lightly armed. The ship had limited troop quarters, so a few other Marines and I slept topside. The ship would be almost helpless in a match with an enemy subma-

Palmyra Island

rine. A sub wouldn't waste torpedoes but would use the boat's deck gun to finish her off. I felt the chances of confronting a submarine were remote and relaxed to enjoy the cruise as much as possible.

While basking in the warm sun watching flying fish and porpoises, my thoughts roved over past experiences and about my family. I also wondered what the future held for me. My liberties in Honolulu hadn't been of the nature to give much food for thought except that I now had a diploma to prove that I was a bona fide ballroom dancer, thanks to the diligent efforts of a tiny Japanese woman, a teacher at the Albert Dance Studios in Honolulu. It could be a long time before I had the chance to utilize the results of her teaching.

The days at sea without duties to occupy thoughts and attention gave me the chance to reflect on decisions that had brought me to my present status. Influenced by the depressed economic conditions in the central section of Missouri, and the enthusiasm shown by a brother, Bill, who had previously enlisted, I became a Marine on 5 July, 1940.

After boot camp and a short tour with Bill in "C" Company, 1st Battalion, 6th Marine Regiment, I followed the advice of PlSgt. Harold Reeves and went seagoing with the intention of attending the U.S. Naval Academy, Annapolis, Maryland; nine months of duty on a naval ship was required of enlisted men prior to attending.

The Japanese attack had altered my plans and now *Comet* was delivering me to "C" Battery, 1st Defense Battalion. The battery was about midway up island from Palmyra's tiny harbor.

The battery used 5-inch .51-caliber guns like those on the older battleships. My experience with them, and in offices, was apparently the key to my transfer. I served as senior NCO at the battery and also as a gun captain until I had trained a replacement. The guns sat on a spit of land projecting toward the coral reef encircling the island. The gun crews lived in

The Quack Corps

quarters beneath the built-up gun emplacements. While at the guns, I could see the ocean on the opposite side of Palmyra because the emplacements were the highest land on the island.

"C" Battery had only two pieces of rolling stock, a jeep and a small trac-layer tractor. The tractor had a top speed of probably no more than two miles per hour. It was so slow that even to someone as cab happy, as Marines called those who liked to drive, as me, it wasn't any fun to operate.

Only a few hundred military personnel were stationed on Palmyra. That, coupled with the island's remoteness, made any happening that changed the daily routine and reduced boredom heartily welcome. As a result, the reaction of new men to the hordes of "sidewinder" crabs populating the island was awaited with anticipation. The crabs moved ashore and out of holes at night; they had been known to trigger wild firing by sentries. With one pincer huge and the other unusually small, they moved sideways and were comical to watch. They reminded me of a boxer in a classic stance.

The battery's plotter, a staff sergeant, bunked with me in quarters built by piling dirt on three sides. A blackout curtain covered the entrance and sheet metal the roof. Shortly after dark my first night on Palmyra, a loud scraping began on the sloping roof. Startled, I glanced at my bunkie but he continued with plotting work and didn't look my way. I grabbed a flashlight, dashed outside and discovered a sidewinder crawling on the roof. When I returned inside, he laughed hilariously about my first confrontation with a sidewinder.

The battery's head was about 50 yards from shore and on pilings a few feet above the water. A narrow wooden catwalk built just over the water provided access to it. The water under the outhouse was shallow and so clear that it was like looking through a sparkling-clean window glass. I spent more time than necessary in the outhouse watching the sidewinders movements on the ocean floor.

Palmyra Island

Part of Palmyra's reef was about 50 yards from shore; it teemed with many varieties of brilliantly colored tropical waters' fish. Using a face mask, I spent many of my free hours swimming about the reef admiring the beautiful fish.

The battery's fire control spotter tub was about 50 feet high and supported by four metal legs. The unit's commanding officer, Captain Raymond H. White, apparently had never been in the tub during firing practice. He acted unaware of the effect caused by the concussion from the long-barrelled guns. He left his command post and joined the spotter during a night firing practice.

Firing across the island, the guns traversed to a predetermined compass heading, then ceased fire while traversing by the tower. My gun was firing at a target mounted on a tug-towed sled. "Cease fire!" came almost as a scream in my soundpower headset. A moment later, the question, "What are you trying to do, sergeant, shoot the tower down?"

I was giving close attention to the gun trainer's dail, which showed compass degrees, and answered, "No, Sir! We still have 7° to go."

At night, the shaking and quivering of the tower felt even more pronounced. He didn't climb to it again for firing practice! His tub experience did give the battery's personnel a good laugh.

During my time on Palmyra, it rained almost every night. As a result, the days were hot and humid. The combination of heat and humidity caused the climbing vines, growing over chicken wire stretched above the gun emplacements and camp paths for camouflage, to replenish themselves in three or four days after muzzle blasts demolished them. The humid heat made it mandatory to use a box, painted white inside and with a hanging light bulb to provide dryness, so clothing and shoes wouldn't mildew. Leather shoes turned green if left out of the box overnight.

The Quack Corps

Red Cochrane, World Welterweight Boxing Champion, was on Palmyra with the Navy. He organized and refereed the boxing matches between island units. I had fun, many laughs and beneficial exercise while training the battery's boxing team. The effect of professional boxing on the Champ's speech and features caused me to change my earlier intentions of becoming a pro. I felt that if anyone good enough to be champion still showed the scars and speech effects that he did, then there must be a smarter way to make money.

On 4 July, Captain Marvin P. Schaikoski took command of "C" Battery. He had played professional football with the Green Bay Packers. His thighs were larger in circumference than my waist. The enlisted men watched in awe as he, seemingly without effort, trotted up a ramp with a cement filled wheelbarrow during construction of a partially above ground command post. It was a struggle for two of them to wheel the barrow up the ramp. They teased that he should continue demonstrating its ease, but he laughingly commented that pushing the barrow would get them in shape.

A Japanese submarine had shelled Palmyra before my time on the island. And, increased U.S. naval activity and the Solomons' area fighting decreased the chances that Palmyra would be shelled again, so high command made the decision to move the gun crews into Quonset hut living quarters. I assumed construction foreman duties though I had never helped put one together. But, neither had the commanding officer nor any of the men.

It rained the night after roof insulation had been installed. The next morning, I climbed the framework to check whether it had dried enough for the sheet-metal roof to go on. My foot slipped and I gashed my knee across the kneecap, requiring several stitches. The doctor advised me to walk stiff-legged for several days to avoid tearing out the stitches. As a result, my thigh and calf muscles became extremely sore and stiff; that would have some bearing on future events.

Palmyra Island

The *Daily Eagle,* a mimeographed newssheet was distributed on Palmyra by the First Defense Battalion. In early June, it published an order by the battalion C.O. that any man who hadn't received a Purple Heart for wounds received in action to report to his commanding officer. The Purple Heart wasn't given for heroism and due to the circumstances entitling me to it, being awarded the medal wasn't very important to me. But, it might be valued by my family if I didn't survive the war so I had informed Captain White. Even a Purple Heart presentation would be big news on Palmyra and the Corps decided to make the most of the opportunity.

In a letter dated 3 July, 1943, the commandant of the Marine Corps' aide sent the ribbon bar and informed the First Defense Battalion C.O. that the medal was being engraved with my name. It would be forwarded to me later. The ribbon bar would be sufficient for what the island commander had in mind.

The July 20th issue of the *Daily Eagle,* a legal size sheet mimeographed on both sides, informed island personnel of how the war was going in Italy, Russia, and in the Solomons area. It printed a report by Radio Tokyo that Japanese women would receive military training, gave major league baseball scores, and that the evening movie was "Hold Back the Dawn," with Olivia DeHaviland and C. Boyer. That information filled the front page. The editor had sent a combat correspondent to "C" Battery to draw a sketch of me. It and the story about the presentation filled the second page. His article had a number of misquotes and language not usual for me—I felt he should restrict his activities to sketching!

Lt. Col. E. H. Phillips, C.O., Depot of Supplies, Pearl Harbor, flew to the island. As a supply officer, I suspected that he hadn't had many opportunities to review troops or to pin ribbons on chests and he too was going to make the most of it.

I assumed the Purple Heart would be presented in the island commander's office. A jeep was sent to pick me up at the

The Quack Corps

battery, and it surprised me to be taken to the airstrip where units were mustered in ranks. It was only a few days after my fall so I could only hobble when a detail of Marines escorted me to my place in the reviewing line. The men were probably empathetic, thinking: "What is that poor bastard doing out here in the Pacific? He should be stateside!" I completely agreed with anyone who thought that way! They didn't realize that I felt sorry for them, too, because they had to stand on the coral-surface strip under searing sun.

After Colonel Phillips informed the men why I was receiving the Purple Heart and pinned the ribbon bar to my shirt, the units passed in review. I thought the activity worthy enough for at least a Silver Star!

A few days later, I received orders to return to the United States for a 30-day furlough. After it, I was to report in at Camp Elliott, near San Diego, for reassignment.

The shortwave radio I had bought from the man I relieved helped prevent the stay on Palmyra from becoming overly boring. Sometimes, the music beamed across the Pacific by a San Francisco station made me very homesick for the States. Other days and nights, it faded in and out so much I turned it off. I had paid $90.00 for it but my relief pleaded that he had only $75.00 to his name so I sold it for that amount. In any event, it was so bulky that I planned to leave it behind, even if I couldn't find anyone with the money to buy it. I've wondered how many hands the radio passed through before the heat and humidity made it a worthless piece of junk.

On 31 July, I boarded *Arrow*, another of the small ships used for inter-island supply. As they had on my cruise to Palmyra Island, porpoises, flying fish, and thinking helped pass the time during the *Arrow*'s return to Pearl Harbor. Fortunately the *Rainier*, a diesel-powered Swedish ship under Navy charter for the duration, was in Pearl Harbor ready to sail for the United States and I transferred aboard her. The efficiently run and super-clean ship made my trip to the States fast, comfortable, and well-fed because the three-other Marines aboard and I ate with the crew.

Chapter 7
Furlough and Camp Elliott

Hardly aware of the rise and fall of the ship's bow, I stood with feet spread and eyes straining for the first glimpse of the Golden Gate Bridge. When it rose out of the mist, exhilaration and excitement surged through me because I had returned to my country and would soon see my father, brothers, and sisters for the first time in over three years.

The *Rainier* proceeded to Treasure Island and docked at the naval station. I would stay on the island until my furlough papers were ready.

After taking dubs on a bunk and getting it squared away, I made train reservations. I left Oakland the next morning for Missouri, via way of Galveston, Texas, where three of my sisters lived. After a week's stay with them, I headed for my old home area, near Waynesville, Missouri.

Upon enlistment in July 1940, I stood at 5-foot 7-inches in height and weighed 127 pounds. During the three years of absence, I added 4-1/2 inches to my height and was 25 pounds heavier. My appearance had changed so much that a brother wondered who was that stranger his wife was so joyously hugging and kissing. It took the two of us several minutes to convince him that I really was his brother.

My boyhood pals were away, involved in the war in a branch of the armed services or working in defense plants, but visiting relatives and dating local girls kept me fully occupied.

One night, I returned a former schoolmate to the apartment she shared with a girlfriend who had been trying to breakup with a boyfriend. He wasn't taking it very well. When we entered, he was sitting on a table in the middle of the room. The roommate was pleading desperately for her life, staring

Furlough and Camp Elliott

into the bore of the pistol in his hand, while he raged that he was going to kill her. He didn't acknowledge our arrival. My date sized up the situation at a glance, placed her hand on my arm, and calmly said, "Go sit down. I'll handle him."

Tensely, I eyeballed him while making my way to a chair off to one side and across the room. Still eyeing him, I gingerly eased myself down. I planted my feet and grasped the chair's arms firmly so I could propel myself out fast, if need be.

In a soothing voice, my date began talking to him and I marveled at her courage and calmness. A wrong word might set him off and I was trying to decide the best course of action, if it should happen. I also felt a little embarrassed that I, a Marine, was doing nothing while a girl confronted the big, curly haired, former classmate of mine.

After listening to my date's talk for several minutes, he calmed and handed the pistol to her. Then, dropping his head, he covered his face with his hands and sobbed convulsively. After a few minutes, he rose to his feet and left without saying another word. My date still had the pistol, lessening the chances that he might barge back through the door and shoot whomever might move.

I felt relieved that it hadn't been necessary to test the disarming and hand-to-hand combat techniques I had learned as a part of my training. After the many months in the war zone, I thought it would have been almost funny to be shot while home on furlough.

But, there was another incident that I could laugh about: Fort Leonard Wood had been built in my absence. With a brother living in base civilian housing, I passed through the main gate several times. Apparently, the majority of the sentries had never seen a Marine in dress blues close up because almost every time I passed through the gate, they saluted. They must have thought that anyone in a uniform like that must be an officer of something!

The Quack Corps

At the end of my Missouri stay, I caught a train heading for San Francisco. My Marine brother, Bill, was stationed at Moffit Field, a few miles south of the city.

We double-dated with his girl and her sister. While dancing with my date in a nightclub, a woman of about 70 years of age stopped us. She wondered what I was and I couldn't make her understand that I was a Marine. Apparently the Army lieutenant with her, who I took to be her son, hadn't been able to explain it to her either. Among her many questions was, "Are you in the Italian Air Force?" I felt insulted enough that she didn't know what a United States Marine was, but for her to intimate that I was wearing the uniform of an enemy made holding my temper difficult. But, because of her age, I kept my cool and patiently tried again to define a Marine.

After more talk, she wanted to dance with me. My date didn't object. At the end of the number, the elderly woman wanted to kiss me. I leaned down and she kissed me on the cheek. I returned her to the lieutenant and rejoined my date.

About an hour later, I saw the woman, with the lieutenant under tow, heading for our table. She stopped to talk again and several minutes later, she decided to leave and wanted to kiss me goodbye. So, I leaned down for a kiss on my *other* cheek. My date and her sister were having trouble stifling laughter. Later, Bill commented that they were daughters of the former Italian Consul in San Francisco who had changed to the American side when Italy declared war on the United States. Bill hadn't told me before the date for fear I'd refuse to go. With that incident to remember and laugh about, I reported to Camp Elliott.

Duty at Camp Elliott brought back memories of my time there while a member of "C" Company, 1st Battalion, 6th Marine Regiment, the latter part of 1940 and early 1941. The company alternated duty at the camp on Kearney Mesa, about 12 miles from San Diego, and the barracks adjacent to the parade ground on the Marine Base in San Diego.

Furlough and Camp Elliott

During my first go-around at Elliott, the United States had been drawing closer and closer to war. The Marine Corps had called up reserves to expand its manpower. The seriousness of the situation was dramatically brought to my attention while on guard duty at the naval radio station near Point Loma. The posts at the station were challenge posts, which meant that anyone approaching a sentry was to be challenged.

My post was along a high chain-link fence bordering a path cut through the manzanita bushes. The previous night, an intruder had cut a hole in the fence and entered the compound. The Marine on the post had fired a few rounds but missed his target.

I was armed with a .45-caliber automatic pistol. It caught when about halfway out of its leather holster. Because of the previous night's events, I didn't want any delays if necessary to draw quickly so I tried eliminating the catching by slipping the pistol in and out of the holster as I walked.

About midway through my watch, I heard noises inside the compound and rustling of bushes as if someone was making their way through them. I stopped to hear better, continuing to slip the .45 up and down in the holster. The rustling noise continued and advanced toward me. When I judged it to be the proper distance for challenging, I made my move. I wasn't able to say, "Halt!" nor even, "Stop!" but did manage "Hah!" Whatever was in the bushes stopped, momentarily, then began to advance. I tugged desperately at the .45 but it caught halfway out of the holster. Before I could get it loose, a huge bob-tailed dog stepped out into a cleared spot. I felt very relieved but my legs were rubbery the rest of the watch. A short time later, the Officer of the Day made his rounds—he didn't get very close before being challenged.

The radio station was the first guard duty I'd had with a loaded weapon; it made me more aware that the world situation was becoming more dangerous for the United States. Other moves had reinforced the feeling, such as in late 1940

The Quack Corps

the Marine Corps calling for volunteers to form paratroop units.

My brother and I were in the same squad. We passed up the opportunity to jump out of airplanes but our platoon leader, 2dLt. W. S. Osipoff, "jumped" at the chance and volunteered. He was gung-ho, slender of body, and relished putting us through our paces physically during field maneuvers on Kearney Mesa.

The men liked the lieutenant well enough but still had to think, "That's good enough for you for running our legs off on Kearney Mesa," when hearing about one of his early experiences as a paratrooper. On a practice jump at Kearney Mesa, he was the last man out of the plane and his chute caught on its tail. In time, the pilot learned that he had a paratrooper hanging from his plane's tail assembly. He knew that, if he landed, the paratrooper would be killed or seriously injured, so he remained airborne while courses of action were considered. Eventually, a Navy pilot at the North Island Naval Air Station volunteered to take a two-seater, with another volunteer to man the rear seat, and try to save the paratrooper. He was able to maneuver so his plane's rear-seat occupant could get the lieutenant into the seat with him. The shroud lines were then cut. Lieutenant Osipoff was unconscious but recovered from his ordeal—what a feat of flying by the naval aviator to rescue him!

Once we learned that he was okay, we enjoyed a chuckle about his experience. I never knew whether he remained in paratroops or decided he'd had enough of parachute jumping. That incident reportedly triggered the use of jumpmasters by all paratroop units.

It was a different time at Camp Elliott and barracks now covered the soil where our tents had been. Instead of racing over the rough terrain of Kearney Mesa as company runner and semaphore signalman, I supervised a night crew in the camp's main office. That duty gave me a jump on others when

Furlough and Camp Elliott

a slot opened up in the camp's Western Union office; manned by civilians daytimes and by a single Marine at night. It was the "cushion" duty in camp and much sought after by qualified and "in the know" men.

Proficient use of a typewriter was definitely a plus since a requirement of the job was the use of a teletype machine. Another plus was to know just who would make the final decision, and then use the necessary connections and tact to land a duty classed as "cushion" or "snap." A pretty, red-haired, high school typing teacher and duty in various Marine unit offices helped me clear the first hurdle without effort. Other duties in over three years of service, involving close daily contact with officers of all ranks, put me in better position to clear the second hurdle than others striving for the job.

Two other Marines, PFC George Tolar and Sgt. Estes Bass, alternated Western Union duties with me. The result was one night on duty then three days and two nights free between watches.

The office stayed open until midnight, then the accumulated telegrams were teletyped to the main office in San Diego. After getting them on their way, I spent time talking via teletype with the girl at the other end of the wire. One was an exceptionally good conversationalist and we made those machines chatter! On slow nights at her end, we sometimes kept it up for a couple of hours. Many mornings, the wastebasket by my machine was running over with discarded teletype tape.

I appreciated a girl who was well read and could keep up her end of a conversation and I thought she would be fun to date. The night before our scheduled date she teletyped that her fiancé, stationed at a San Diego area Army base, was getting an unexpected liberty and she had to cancel. She hadn't mentioned a fiancé. To my knowledge she hadn't seen me or knew anyone who had, so she may have just lost her nerve.

A few days later, the manager of the main office invited the Marines in the Camp Elliott office for a tour. It would have

The Quack Corps

taken a platoon of men to keep me away because now I'd get to see the girl. I was dumbfounded upon meeting her. The terrific over-the-wire conversationalist was totally lacking in in-person personality. Her extremely freckled face, stringy sandy-colored hair, and matchstick thinness added to my disappointment. Her lack of beauty wasn't of over-riding concern but I didn't want to spend the time, or money, dating a girl who didn't have a pleasing personality. Though we kept up the teletype chatter, I shied away from another date by using her engagement as an excuse.

I had read about them but I hadn't seen a woman dressed in green, with the Marine globe and anchor insignia on collar and cap, until arriving at Camp Elliott. Male Marines referred to them as *BAMs*, short for broad-ass Marines. Their barracks was adjacent to the male barracks area. When a clean-cut male Marine passed, some of them leaned out windows to catcall and whistle. Though secretly pleased when a target, it did destroy my sergeant's dignity! When meeting or passing a woman officer, I usually changed course to avoid the required salute even though it was to pay respect to the rank, not the individual. Most of the other men with long service or combat time pulled the same stunt. It would take a while before we became accustomed to saluting women with bars on their shoulders, and, in a position of authority in the Marine Corps.

I respected the women in service for their patriotism and their desire to aid in the war effort, and I treated them with courtesy and consideration.

Though I never made a conscious effort to date a woman Marine, one night I got two for the price of one, as the saying goes. With a date-free night, I decided to look in at the U. S. Grant Hotel, though it unofficially was officers' country. When I entered the main bar area, it was jammed with shoulder-to-shoulder officers. But, I noticed two enlisted women Marines standing near one end of the bar. Rather than nudge an officer aside to order a drink, I approached the women and they made

Furlough and Camp Elliott

room for me. Shortly, we decided there was too much brass present to suit us so we left to cruise the city in my car, purchased shortly after my arrival in camp.

One, a private first class, was a brunette and the other, a corporal, a strikingly beautiful blonde. Later, I learned that she had been a model and was a colonel's daughter. After a fun evening, we headed back to Camp Elliott. En route, the blonde asked if she could drive. I hadn't allowed anyone to drive my car. Like most males of the time, I doubted her ability to use the stick shift without stripping transmission gears. But, she pleaded so prettily that I couldn't resist. After she had driven for only a short distance, I leaned back against the seat and relaxed because I realized my car was in the hands of an expert!

After reaching Camp Elliott, we parted with plans to do it again but coming events precluded it happening.

With no other in-camp duties and bored with the excess free time, Sergeant Estes Bass, PFC George Tolar and I began part-time work in a San Diego aircraft plant. The pay was 75¢ per hour and the total hours we could work per day restricted to four hours. We learned that a Point Loma tuna packing plant paid 90¢ per hour. Also, we could work an unrestricted number of hours so we switched jobs.

December 15th was payday and we took time off from the job to return to camp to draw pay. While inching forward in the pay line, I strained my ears to hear the orders issued, by an officer sitting at the pay table, to certain men after they drew pay. I guessed they were receiving transfer orders. After I had received my pay, he spoke, "Sergeant Wells, report to the main office, at once!" The urgency in his voice made me apprehensive because I felt it was an omen of bad news. As I walked toward the office, I suspected that my "snap" duty in the Western Union office was about to end. Sure enough, transfer orders were waiting. They not only ended my cushion duty but also nipped my tuna-packing career in the bud. The apprehension was further heightened when the office personnel couldn't tell me anything about my new unit, other than it being something new for the Marine Corps.

I knew my varied service experience could land me in almost any kind of unit, and the news that a second lieutenant was coming for me gave ominous overtones—it would be the first time an officer performed taxi service for me. My orders were to pack my gear without delay and wait at the barrack's porch for him. Frequent transfers had made me a proficient packer so only minutes had passed before my seabag was setting near the porch's top step.

Chapter 8
A Quack Marine

Though ordered to hurry with my packing, I didn't know how long the wait would be before the second lieutenant showed, so I sat on the porch rail. Even before sitting on it became uncomfortable, I noticed a jeep heading my way with an officer behind the wheel. He stopped it by the steps, "Sergeant Wells?"

I jumped off the rail, saluted, "Yes, Sir!"

While returning my salute, he ordered, "Toss your gear in back! Let's go!" He seemed in a hurry so I hastily dumped my gear in and made a move for the passenger seat. Before I even settled in, he engaged the clutch and the jeep began moving. *Take it easy, lieutenant! We're not going to any fire!* I mentally reprimanded.

He headed the jeep for Camp Linda Vista, adjacent to Camp Elliott's northern border. En route he offered, "Sergeant, I'm 2dLt. James B. Blackburn," in a typical Southern accent. "I'm the platoon leader of the first platoon and you're going to be my platoon sergeant."

"Aye, aye, Sir." I replied. After twice before performing duties up through first sergeant rate, I hoped this time the Marine Corps would see fit to bless me with a rocker stripe. But, by now, I'd learned that the Corps didn't always follow the book.

With the ice broken by his comments, I asked, "Sir, what kind of outfit is this?"

"A duck company."

"A duck company? They told me in the office that this outfit was something new for the Marine Corps but they didn't tell me that the Corps is forming companies of ducks. What in hell are we going to use ducks for?"

"They're Amphibian Trucks," he replied, with a laugh. "It's spelled D-U-K-W but it's pronounced 'duck,' just like the waterfowl."

The lieutenant handled the jeep in an aggressive manner. I chuckled inwardly at his method for signaling a left turn— raising his left arm, with elbow bent and index finger pointing skyward, he suddenly thrust his arm outward with a straight-arm motion jabbing the finger in the direction of the turn. It was a different technique than any I'd seen in my home state of Missouri or anyplace else for that matter.

Upon arriving at Camp Linda Vista, where the First and Second Amphibian Truck (DUKW) Companies were forming, 15 December, 1943, I grabbed my gear and he walked along to show me the 1st platoon tent area. The lieutenant and 31 enlisted men would make up the platoon. Henceforth, the companies would be referred to by their personnel as First and Second DUKW.

Camp Linda Vista was a tent camp. While walking to the platoon's tents, I noted turmoil in camp and commented, "Sir, everything and everybody seems to be moving at a rush, rush pace. What's going on?"

"The company's making preparations to ship out for overseas in a few days," he answered. That really caught me by surprise. By now, I had learned to make quick adjustments and to conceal emotions and feelings so I quickly recovered.

"Sir, I've already cancelled a date for tonight but I have a car and no one to take care of it while I'm gone. I need to make arrangements for storage in San Diego. Do you think I can get a pass so I can take care of it?"

"I'm sorry, Sergeant, but everyone is restricted from liberty. Orders are that no one is to leave camp, even to take care of emergency matters. You'll just have to leave it set." His re-

A Quack Marine

mark filled me with desperation because I wouldn't be allowed to leave the car at Camp Elliott.

Strange, I thought, that a newly formed company with new and untried vehicles would be shipped overseas without stateside training. So the scuttlebutt floating in Camp Elliott that men back from overseas were guaranteed six months stateside before being shipped back over was, as so often happened with scuttlebutt, untrue. Upon learning of my transfer and anticipating that it might be at least partially correct, I had expected the company to stay stateside for training because it had many overseas veterans with little time back in the States.

Although forming a new company and preparations for shipping overseas took many hours of work, it appeared to be overreaction for those in command to prevent passes for men to take care of emergencies. I didn't feel the forming of two DUKW companies would have any earthshaking effect on the Japanese, even if they learned of it.

One of the men manning the Western Union office with me also joined the company. Private First Class George Tolar had hit Guadalcanal on his 16th birthday. His experiences there had quickly taught him to live life to the fullest whenever opportunities arose. With the war on, regulations forbidding fraternizing between NCOs and subordinates were ignored so we had become good buddies. Though he hadn't been assigned to the 1st platoon, we soon made connections at Camp Linda Vista.

He told me that he planned going AWOL to keep a date with his girl. I cautioned him about the penalty if he got caught but he was adamant, even if it meant I'd put him on report. He offered to put my car in storage if he could use it for his date. At first, I turned him down but after my second request for a pass was refused, I was in the mood to accept his offer. He didn't get caught and gave me the key and storage claim check next morning.

The Quack Corps

I had hoped for enough time off base to put the car in storage, and to sneak a visit with Dolores Alden, a girl I'd met while working at the aircraft plant. With my hopes for liberty dashed, I wondered how I'd manage to get in touch with her because I hadn't spotted any phones in camp. Later, Tolar informed me he had seen phone booths just outside the main gate.

In what I knew would be our last conversation, Dolores asked about my destination. She had relatives in the Navy so she must have been aware that, even if I knew, I couldn't tell her. I informed her that I'd write just as soon as I knew my return address.

The first platoon mustered seemingly every hour so information could be passed on to the men. We also lined up for inoculations and served as guinea pigs for a young navy corpsman giving them. It apparently was his first experience giving shots. He was having a terrible time and I watched as he struggled with the needle. He tossed the instrument like a dart, from several inches away. The body of the instrument sagged while the point of the needle remained in the flesh. It struck me as being funny and I began to laugh, so hard that the other men in line stared as if they thought I'd lost my marbles. My laughter embarrassed the corpsman but I couldn't stop and I was still giggling when my turn came. Though I apologized for laughing, it didn't appear to lessen his embarrassment.

December 22, after a week of hectic preparations and without sighting a single DUKW, the personnel of 2d DUKW embarked on *U.S.S. Corrigedor,* a small aircraft carrier used primarily for escort duty.

That night, I spent many hours leaning against the ship's rail by myself facing the darkened silhouette of San Diego. This time, I felt that I wouldn't make it back. I mentally pictured the face of a Japanese woman frowning in concentration as she bent over a bench assembling the shell with my name

A Quack Marine

on it. It seemed my fate and I accepted it and wondered when, where, and how.

In some ways, I felt much older than my 21 years but in other ways ... so young. The awareness that I was heading back overseas as a platoon sergeant in a unit that would undoubtedly land on enemy beaches made the responsibilities with and to the first platoon's 30 other men weigh heavy on my shoulders. The knowledge that the decisions I'd make and the orders I'd give could mean life or death for some of them had a sobering effect. I'd do my best to be a good platoon sergeant and I'd look after the men to the best of my ability. The knowledge I'd gained I'd pass on so those just out of boot camp and other short-timers in the Corps would have the best chance of surviving in battle. Fortunately, the platoon's other experienced NCO's would also do their part to train the others.

I didn't leave the rail until the wee hours of the morning of 23 December—I had mentally said goodbyes.

Corrigedor left her berth at North Island after daylight on the 23rd. It was always depressing to see the coastline receding over a ship's stern but even more so with Christmas so near. I watched until Point Loma faded from view. The men with previous overseas duty were quiet but most making their first trip over acted as if they were on a pleasure cruise ... they knew not what they were to face.

At this stage of the war, many of the prewar Marines already were death statistics. So it was unusual for a unit to form with the unusually large percentage of prewar and combat veterans boasted of by this company. Some had been bloodied during the Japanese attack on the Hawaiian Islands, and others at Guadalcanal or other Pacific battles. They were joined by men drawn from units at the San Diego Marine Base, Camp Elliott, Camp Pendleton and other nearby areas. Included were fresh-out-of-boot-camp Marines, who would draw on the experience of the veterans to make life in the future more certain.

The Quack Corps

At sea, I engaged Lieutenant Blackburn at length in bull sessions and learned more about him. Knowing what my superior officers were like governed my relations with them on a day-to-day basis.

The lieutenant was a tall, slender, dark-haired man from Louisiana, with the southern accent typical of the south. He was a graduate of Louisiana State University, attended Officers' Candidate School, and came to the company from duty at the Recruit Depot on the San Diego Marine Base. He had spent little time in the Marine Corps and this was to be his first overseas tour. His movements leaned to the languid side. He was gung-ho about the Marine Corps and that he was going overseas to fight Japs; I wondered how long that enthusiasm would last.

With things so hectic at Camp Linda Vista, I had seen little of the company commander, Captain James L. George. During a short conversation aboard ship, I sized him up as a man of few words. One of the men informed me that he had been in auto finance and had played professional baseball, at the Triple-AAA level. He revealed little about himself during our conversation but I later learned that it was his first command. What I had pegged as reserved was due, probably, to an unsure feeling about how friendly he should be with the men under his command.

Captain George leaned a little to the chubby side, with facial skin as smooth and unblemished as that on a baby's ass. I speculated whether he'd cut the mustard in battle, just as I suspected some of the men in the first platoon speculated about me. Because I pegged him as a man who was all business, I decided to keep my contacts formal and arms' length.

I liked serving under a commanding officer who had no patience with inefficiency, who believed in strict discipline, and adhered to Navy and Marine Corps Regulations. I had been in the Corps long enough to judge, even before I saw him, whether a unit had a good commanding officer by the attitude and actions of the junior officers and enlisted men. With this new company, patterns hadn't yet been established.

Though pre-enlistment service station work may have had some bearing, it was surprising because of my line rate to find myself in what usually might be classed as a motor transport unit. I learned there were others who were in the same predicament, because in its haste to get the company formed the Marine Corps grabbed bodies regardless of time back stateside or whether line or motor transport rates. Future events would make me feel that high command had been smarter than I had given it credit for being, when I had first learned the number of line rates in 2d DUKW.

Warrant Officer George Unterkoefler led the 2d platoon, with Sgt. Thomas Black acting as platoon sergeant. Warrant Officer Patrick H. Lassitor headed the 3rd platoon, with Sgt. Edward F. Dewey acting platoon sergeant. Warrant Officer Curtis Bush ram-rodded the maintenance platoon, with Sgt. James Hines second in command. Second Lieutenant Victor Sellers was the company's executive officer. Other company officers, without specific duty titles, were 2dLts. Richard Mangnall, William McAdams, Robert Patrick, George Raleigh and Fredrick Winker. Gunnery Sergeant Robert McClelland was acting as company first sergeant. A malaria victim, he would have a reoccurrence in early January 1944 and be replaced by 1stSgt. Harold Pohlad. With few exceptions, the company's NCOs with line rates had enlisted prewar and claimed combat time.

After *Corrigedor* sailed into Pearl Harbor 30 December, Second DUKW debarked and was transported to Camp Catlin, a tent camp located between the harbor and Honolulu. Pending arrival of the DUKWs, we spent time getting acquainted; on conditioning hikes with packs on our backs; listening to the usual loudmouthed arguments between Yanks and Rebs as they refought the Civil War; and other arguments about almost every known subject; the strumming on guitars

The Quack Corps

and forlorn sounds of harmonicas; on and off-key singing voices, and gum beating about the Marine Corps and being overseas. Gripes also could be heard because we were a DUKW company with wheeled vehicles but still had to walk to get anyplace.

Though permitted liberty, I had seen enough of wartime Honolulu during previous stops at the island. Occasionally, I accompanied Tolar and another buddy, Corp. Harry Mefford, on a Honolulu liberty. Sometimes we'd split because I didn't always agree with what they wanted to do. Invariably, they'd get in some kind of hassle or trouble while separated. Once I rejoined them to discover Mefford with a black eye and Tolar also bearing marks of battle. They had boarded a bus and Tolar dropped a slug in the fare box. The driver, a native Hawaiian, objected and the three ended up in a scrap on the sidewalk. The Hawaiian must have been some man because he apparently won the fight.

Fortunately, a few days after arriving at Catlin the company's vehicles arrived. For my first contact with a DUKW, I stood a few feet away and spent several minutes letting my eyes rove over hull-configuration details of this cross between a boat and a truck. It measured 31 feet in length and I judged its height, at the cargo space, to be about six and one-half feet, with the top of its windshield about a foot and a-half higher.

After eyeballing to my satisfaction, I proceeded to the bow for a close-up look at the tow harness, headlights and fold-down splashboard. Then, I made my way to the stern and squatted down for a look at the propeller and rudder in the tunnel underneath. I raised up and inspected the stern winch and cable, the brackets for holding three 5-gallon gas cans, and the spare tire. I also noted that a gas filler pipe extended above the stern deck about six inches, which tipped me that the gas tank was located in the stern of the vehicle.

Retracing my steps to amidships of this strange hybrid, I placed a foot on one of the three horizontal reinforcing ribs

A Quack Marine

and both hands on the gunwale to hoist myself into the cargo space. Next, I catwalked the gunwale to the bow, opened the steel hatches to take a look at the air compressor located forward of the radiator, and the six cylinder, 93 H.P., General Motors Corporation motor.

In the open cab, I sat in the driver's seat to read the dashboard decals, take note of the usual expected gauges and the tire pressure indicator, the center-mounted compass, and the first aid kit. I shifted the transmission gears and those in the transfer case, and manipulated the lever for inflating and deflating the tires from inside the cab.

Then, I stood up, released the windshield catches, folded the side wings inward and lowered the three-piece windshield. To finish my inspection, I looked at the tarp bows and the tarpaulins for covering the cargo space and cab.

After looking it over, I inquired of Lieutenant Blackburn standing near the DUKW whether we had training manuals. After he informed me that we didn't, I asked about getting some from First DUKW; he felt it was in the same boat. So, we would learn about the vehicles on our own. We were pioneering the use of the hybrid craft/vehicle by the Marine Corps. I stood for a moment before debarking from the DUKW and let my eyes rove back over it. *What will man think of next?* I wondered.

Developed for the Army, the 2-1/2 ton, 6 x 6, amphibian truck was built upon the model KW cargo truck chassis. The letters, DUKW, reportedly meant the following: D-General Motors Corporation designation for 1942 model year; U-amphibian; K-designation for front-axle drive and W for tandem rear-axles drive. The wheeled amphibian was revealed to the American public in late 1942 newsreels.

The DUKW was designed for use in water or on land. Its six wheels were all-drive. The governors on the vehicles' motors allowed a maximum speed of 6.4 mph in water and 50 mph on land. The men quickly learned how to bypass the gov-

The Quack Corps

ernors. With full power available, I drove one at over 60 mph on an Oahu highway. It would have moved faster but I shut it down when it began bouncing toward the shoulder of a washboard curve. Soft springing and specially compounded rubber helped reduce the ripping of tires on sharp coral reefs encountered in the Pacific. The propeller was disengaged on land, as were the wheels when the DUKW was waterborne. I estimated the ungoverned water speed at nearly 10 mph.

The hybrid vehicles proved to be safer than the LVTs (AmTracs) when entering or exiting the ocean through heavy surf. DUKWs entered the tank decks of Landing Ship Tanks (LSTs) at sea without assistance. They could operate in stormier seas than the LVTs and proved to be extremely beneficial in the Marine Corps Central Pacific invasions.

Chapter 9
Hitting Hawaiian Surf

Inner-company organization was completed at Camp Catlin. It included organizing each of the first, second, and third platoons into three sections consisting of four DUKWs each, with a sergeant or senior corporal as section leader. Now, the company was prepared to knuckle down for serious training. So after a week at Camp Catlin, we loaded our gear and headed for a training beach near Waianae, Oahu, T.H, many miles from Honolulu. The new camp was a short distance inland from the ocean in a grove of trees bordering the road running from the Honolulu area to Waianae.

Immediately after settling in, Captain George issued orders for training activities to begin. First priority was given to familiarizing company personnel with the proper maintenance of the vehicles. The men quickly learned how to scrape scratched or rusted spots on the hulls, the proper application of a red lead primer coat first, and then paint to prevent metal deterioration. Constant attention would be necessary once the vehicles were immersed in saltwater. Second priority was given to the DUKW's handling characteristics on land. In-camp schooling took care of the first priority and short trips over varied terrain, the second.

In the muggy heat, the men soon became bored with scraping, painting and lubricating but they retained high enthusiasm for the second training priority; like most young men, they were "cab happy."

A platoon sergeant is the buffer between the platoon leader and enlisted members of a platoon. I likened the position to that of a mother with several children, who bears the brunt of the kids griping about dad and visa versa. I had fore-

The Quack Corps

seen that Lieutenant Blackburn's inexperience was going to cause problems unless he changed his methods in dealing with enlisted men. Overzealous about concerning himself with every little detail of the platoon's daily activities, he hadn't yet learned to utilize his NCOs in the proper manner. Though he treated me with courtesy and consideration, he had the other men in an uproar.

When I realized that real problems were coming, my first inclination was to try for a transfer out of the company. Overseas duty was taxing enough without the additional strains I foresaw.

I pegged the lieutenant as having the potential to be a good officer because he didn't have the arrogance of so many of the right-out-of-college newly commissioned. That, a feeling of responsibility to the men in the platoon, and my personal and Marine pride combined to make me decide to stick it out. The lieutenant was trying to do a good job. He was told how to command in Officers' Candidate School but he hadn't yet learned how to *lead*.

I made the mistake, while serving in the *U.S.S. Pennsylvania*, of criticizing a new Navy ensign in a letter to a sister. It was censored by the wrong officer resulting in my appearance before the ship's skipper, Captain T. S. King. His only punishment was a fatherly talk. He made me feel like an old salt when he told me: "Those of us with more time in service should bear with new officers and men until they gain experience." I passed his advice on to the men of the first platoon bolstering it with mine that they should give the lieutenant time to get his feet on the ground. But those with previous overseas and combat time were not in any mood for patience. They continued to bitch in such strong terms that I knew it was only a matter of time before someone got into serious trouble.

I now wore the stripes of a platoon sergeant. But the men didn't seem to realize that the extra stripe didn't give me enough authority to go to a second lieutenant and order him to mend his ways. I didn't want Captain George involved unless it became absolutely necessary so I decided to try to influence the lieutenant by talking with him. I realized it might boomerang but I took pride in trying to solve problems without involving superiors or causing embarrassment to the principals. It would be the first time I had tried to *educate* an officer by using a direct and head-on method.

By now, I had dealt with him enough to know that he was intelligent with personal and fierce pride in his rank. He seemed to be an officer who might listen and be amenable to change if put to him in a tactful and courteous way. His actions indicated that it was a matter of his Marine pride that his platoon would be second to none. But, our service together hadn't been long enough for me to peg how he'd react if he felt his authority challenged. Hopefully, he would be responsive to what I planned to say.

His officer bunkies left the tent after evening chow and, with a purposeful stride to help overcome nervousness, I walked to the tent opening. He was sitting at a small table writing a letter. When he had apparently completed a sentence, I spoke in a toned-down voice, "Lieutenant Blackburn."

He raised his head, "Yes, Sergeant."

"I'm sorry to interrupt your letter writing, Sir, but there is a matter that I feel I should talk to you about, in private."

"Come in, Sergeant, and sit on my cot," he directed.

"Thank you, Sir." I entered and sat down. I stared at the tent deck while bolstering my nerve and having last thoughts about the approach I had decided to take.

"Go ahead, Sergeant," he prompted.

I raised my eyes and, using a respectful tone of voice said, "Lieutenant, I hope you will understand that what I am about to say is not, in any way, meant to question your authority or to be disrespectful. The men have been bitching in strong terms and I felt it best to come and talk with you about it."

When I hesitated for a moment, he prompted, "Continue."

The Quack Corps

Carefully choosing my words, and speaking slowly, I resumed, "Sir, some of the men have served overseas and have been in combat. A few have been wounded in action. They feel they've earned their spurs and deserve to be treated with consideration and respect. They also have become accustomed to the less G.I. way of doing things overseas."

When I again hesitated he interjected, "What are you trying to tell me, Sergeant?"

I hadn't wanted to, nor felt that I should, walk in and without softening him up by laying some groundwork blurt out what the men were bitching about. He seemed impatient for me to get on with it so I plunged ahead with the remark that might blow the top right off his tent: "Sir, the men are complaining in strong terms that the way you talk to and treat them, makes them feel as if they're back in boot camp. Lieutenant, we will have a better platoon if the men are kept as happy as possible. I hope I haven't offended you, Sir, but I felt that I must try to get them calmed down."

I had been keying on his facial expressions as I talked and he appeared to be thinking about what I was saying. After my last comment, he gazed at the tent deck and I sensed that he was stifling the urge to explode with anger. After gazing at it for a few moments, he raised his eyes and in a calm voice, "Thank you, Sergeant, for coming to me about it. I hadn't realized that we had a problem. I'm not offended that you came to me about it."

I breathed an inaudible "Whew!" and quickly changed the subject to general platoon activities. A few minutes later, I thanked him for his time and left the tent. As I walked away, I hoped that I hadn't worsened the problem. But he *had* listened to the end without exploding in anger and ordering me out of his tent.

The next day, he began using a softer and less-ordering tone of voice and more care in his choice of words and methods in dealing with the men. Though they took a wait-see attitude, their response was favorable and morale improved.

By now, drivers, assistant drivers, section leaders, *and* platoon sergeants had become adept at handling the DUKWs on land and they were anxious to try their hands in the water. Their first chance came on a day when the surf was light. By experimenting, they learned that the proper and best way to enter the water was to goose the motor and go through the wave just as it began breaking. They also learned to come ashore by riding waves in as one does with a surfboard. If they timed them correctly and then floor-boarded the throttle, the waves carried the DUKWs well up onto the beach.

The cab lever for changing tire air pressure proved very beneficial. Tire pressures could be lowered to about 10 pounds, for sandy beach operations, without the necessity of stopping the DUKW to deflate each tire separately. The wheel hubs were airtight with a short air hose connecting to the outside of them. What luxury we had until sand wore the hubs and air wouldn't stay in the tires. Then, we disconnected them and used a long hose attached to a nipple in the cab to inflate each tire separately. Pressure in each tire also had to be lowered manually.

Only a few days after water training had begun, the platoon leader of the 3rd platoon adamantly insisted on taking his platoon into the water despite a huge surf. One of his drivers misjudged a wave and the 14,800-pound DUKW flipped over, crushing PFC Lester Reams; he died before reaching a hospital. He was the only man 2d DUKW ever lost in an accident.

With Reams' death, the mood in camp was somber. I boiled about the incident—to me it was an unnecessary loss of a man, caused by a lack of good judgment. Some good did come of it because the men were more acutely aware of the perils faced entering and exiting the surf in an angry sea. Thereafter, they were even more attentive to their actions as they practiced to become adept at judging the surf. After ac-

The Quack Corps

quainting themselves thoroughly with the DUKW's water-handling characteristics, the men were able to and did take their vehicles through even higher surf.

After daily DUKW training activities ended, we improved physical condition by playing volleyball in the sand, tag football and other physical games. We also improved combat preparedness by practicing modified *Ju-jitsu*. Corporal Orval C. Smith, a tall, lean Arkansasan and a Guadalcanal vet, and I usually paired off because we both had had considerable practice. Dust boiled into the air whenever one of us threw the other violently, drawing Lieutenant Blackburn's caution that one of us was likely to get hurt. Of course, we had learned how to fall and knew the chance of injury was slight.

Scuttlebutt floated that wild boars could be found in some of the canyons back of camp. One evening a man did bring his kill in but Captain George forbid eating it. He felt it'd be wormy in the warm climate. I decided to try my hand with the boars even if we couldn't eat the meat.

Alone, I headed up the canyon nearest the back of camp. After hiking for a few hundred yards, I spotted something ahead—just behind the crest of a little knoll on the canyon floor was what appeared to be a wild boar. To edge closer, I used the infantryman's crawl, with the .30-caliber carbine cradled in my arms. When I felt the range was just right, I drew a bead on the boar. In a moment, I saw an ear move. Although I had never seen one, it didn't look like I thought a wild boar should. So I crept closer for a better look. My boar turned out to be a reddish-colored cow, standing just behind the knoll's crest with only the top of her shoulders and part of her back visible. Since I had also drawn a blank in the earlier boar hunt in New Hebrides, I decided that I may as well call it quits on boar hunting.

The luck-of-the-draw had provided a winning hand for the Second Marine Amphibian Truck Company. The abundance of experienced NCOs had provided a balance for the lack of

Hitting Hawaiian Surf

overseas and combat experience by some of the company's officers.

Even though 2d DUKW was Captain James L. George's first command, he commanded with a firm and even hand. His leadership, combined with the company's personnel mix, resulted in 2d DUKW melding quickly into a cohesive unit with esprit de corps. Training progressed faster than expected and the company was ready to begin finding its niche in the scheme of things by the end of February.

Second DUKW was self-sustaining and a location move was quick and easy. So after loading gear and men into the DUKWs, the company boarded *U.S.S. Henry Clay* for the short hop to Maui where it joined the Fourth Marine Division, 2 March, 1944, at the division camp on the lower slope of Haleakala Mountain.

A few days after arrival on Maui, Second DUKW moved to a windy beach at Maalaea Bay, near Lahaina, for even more training. At times, the wind whistled through camp so hard that we had to get behind a tent to prevent sand blowing into our chow. The high wind did enable the men to get more experience in battling heavy surf and choppy seas.

Several days later, the DUKWs were offshore and two humpback whales appeared and became their escorts. When a DUKW neared, they nonchalantly swam away but only fast enough to keep clear of the hybrid craft. After we secured for the day, the whales approached the beach and lay looking us over as if holding inspection. The next morning they were there as if waiting for us to come play with them again. The humpbacks were escorts, off and on, for the remaining time we bivouacked on the beach. The superstitious men in the company wondered if the whales were our guardian angels.

In April, Second DUKW moved back to the 4th Division area. Our tents were across a small canyon from the division's main camp because the area had enough level ground for parking the company's 50 DUKWs.

The Quack Corps

Bivouacking across the canyon made us feel as if we were hardly a part of the division because it was a long walk to the showers. Fortunately, we had our own mess hall and generator for lights. Camp water was piped from higher up on the mountain and it was icy cold. In preference to the long walk and super-cold shower's water, most of us filled our steel helmet shells with hot water and took what servicemen called a "whore's" bath.

Preparations were underway for the division to sail for an invasion. With in-camp preparations completed, we were granted a last liberty. James Hines, now sporting a technical sergeant's rate, and Sgts. Eugene Kalain and James Crawford, all from the maintenance platoon, and I decided that the nearby towns would be jammed with other Marines so we copped the recon car and went to Hana, about 40 miles away, for the daytime-only liberty.

After exploring Hana and finding little to do, we played tennis for a while on the public courts. None of us were good with the racquet so we spent most of the day talking to girls we met there. Our liberty was due to end at 1800 but we guessed that it'd probably be a long, long time before our eyes gazed on real-live pretty girls. So we decided to extend the liberty. Three of us managed to make dates for the evening. Though none of us had ever been absent over leave, we realized it could well be our last ever liberty.

We discussed whether it was worthwhile to try getting off the hook for being AOL and agreed to at least make an attempt to avoid being charged with the offence. So, we decided to call the first sergeant with the tale that the recon had broken down and we didn't know how long it'd take to fix it. The three of them voted that I should make the call. It seemed far-fetched that he'd swallow that tale with three maintenance platoon men present but he gave the impression that it'd be okay for us to be late.

Hitting Hawaiian Surf

I got badgered into driving the 40 miles of winding and narrow road back to camp, under blackout conditions. The others slept most of the way which made the slow drive even longer. But, I preferred doing the driving so I didn't feel imposed upon.

We thought we were in the clear for being AOL but the first sergeant reported our after-midnight return to Captain George next day. When the captain sent for us, we gathered near his tent but still far enough away that we couldn't hear the conversation inside. I was the last one called. Without an opportunity to check the others' stories, I decided that I'd better tell the truth and take whatever medicine he dished out. Hines and Kalain were fun-loving individuals and did a lot of in-camp grabassing. So, even though Hines had a stripe on me, Captain George apparently felt that I should have made sure we got back on time and restricted me from liberty for 30-days; a restriction that never took effect, because it had been my last liberty as a Marine. The others contended they didn't receive any punishment but I wondered whether they were only ribbing.

A day or so before we were due to board ships, one of the company's men claimed that he was a conscientious objector. He became unpopular very quickly. The men felt that it was a little too much to expect anyone to believe that he didn't know his feelings until only two days before heading for combat. They could understand his feelings that he didn't want to kill anyone but, in his case, they felt it was probably cowardice because others in similar circumstances had volunteered to perform medical services.

The company received 15 additional DUKWs a short time before the division sailed. It formed a 4th platoon using extra personnel already in the company and a few replacements to provide manpower for it.

After joining the company and guessing that the DUKWs would be used only as supply vehicles, I had thought it was my

The Quack Corps

destiny to be relegated to the peripheral side of the war ... in the war zone and near the fighting but still not actively firing at the enemy. Being stuck in a supply unit wasn't my idea of a fighting Marine though I had no real desire for frontline battle. I didn't like the feeling that I wasn't doing my part in killing Japs. After reaching Maui, I felt better when I learned that the Marine Corps planned to use the unarmored DUKWs almost like assault vehicles by hauling 14th Marine howitzers ashore in them during a forthcoming invasion.

With our last liberty now behind us, the 14th Marine 105mm howitzers, several clusters of ammunition and the gun crews were loaded into the DUKWs. When loaded, the drivers drove to Kahului Harbor, at Maui, and into the tank decks of beached *LST-23, LST-121, LST-340* and *LST-354*.

Eight DUKWs in each of the 1st, 2d and 3rd platoons were loaded with guns and crews and the other four vehicles in each platoon hauled howitzer ammunition. The 4th platoon hauled ammunition and other 14th Marine gear. The maintenance platoon worried about company supplies for repairs and maintenance. The headquarters platoon had responsibility for company office and mess hall supplies.

After boarding was completed, the LSTs practiced formation maneuvers and then headed into Maalaea Bay. The 1st platoon was aboard *LST-354*. After her huge bow doors opened and the ramp lowered beneath the water, the drivers backed the DUKWs down it for a last practice landing.

It was shortly after mid-day and the ocean had become very rough just off the beach where 2d DUKW had had the training camp at Maalaea Bay. Number-8 DUKW was bobbing in the water causing the assistant driver and the 14th Marine gun crew to become seasick. The waves were breaking over the gunwales. I decided to shield the 105mm from the saltwater and keep some of the water out of the DUKW by covering the gun and ammunition with the vehicle's tarpaulin. The driver had to maintain control of the vehicle and none of

Hitting Hawaiian Surf

the others were in condition to help me. By catwalking the gunwale down the side of the bucking DUKW, I managed to get the cover over the cargo space. I returned to the cab and moments later vomited my K-ration lunch; the first and only time I ever became seasick.

As the driver eased his DUKW into position so Lieutenant Blackburn could jump onto the LST's partially raised ramp, a huge wave hurled it into a corner, punching a massive hole in the vehicle's side. It headed for the bottom very quickly but the men aboard were saved. A specially equipped maintenance platoon DUKW, the pride of Warrant Officer Curtis W. Bush, maintenance officer, also went to the bottom that day. Someone had failed to replace the gas cap after gassing it, allowing water to surge into the gas tank when the DUKW backed out of the LST. With the motor not running to operate the automatic bilge pumps, the emergency hand pump couldn't handle the volume of water shipping over the sides and the DUKW sank; all hands were rescued. It had been a costly day for 2d DUKW.

With the practice landings completed, the LSTs hauling 2d DUKW pulled anchors and departed Maalaea Bay.

Chapter 10
Fire Storm in West Loch!

Some had floating pontoons lashed to sides, others had LCTs riding piggy-back topside and topsides so packed with supplies and vehicles for war that they were almost shapeless and unrecognizable as ships, the flotilla of LSTs carrying 2d DUKW entered Pearl Harbor on 20 May. Each was so heavily laden that bows pushed a wall of water ahead as they sailed through the harbor channel like a flock of birds coming in to roost, one after the other, then veered to port to enter the channel to the shallow anchorage in West Loch.

The LSTs berthed in nests, beam-to-beam, cross channel from the West Loch Naval Ammunition Depot. Personnel crossed from one to the other by walking planks placed across the narrow gap between them.

The four LSTs hauling the 204 men and 65 vehicles of 2d DUKW had ammunition layered in their tank decks with heavy beams laid on top for the wheels of the DUKWs to rest on. The ships' top decks were crammed with land vehicles, supplies, and 55-gallon barrels of gasoline.

On the morning of 21 May, 1944, most of the company's DUKWs loaded with 105mms had debarked from the ships and were ashore for servicing and other maintenance after the saltwater dousing off Maui.

The first platoon was in a flat spot on Waipio Peninsula between a dirt road paralleling the Loch and the water's edge. It was only a few yards from *LST-205*, the first ship from shore in Tare 8 berth. The other company DUKWs were ashore on Hanaloa Point astern of the last nest of LSTs. The 105mms had been unloaded so grease points in the DUKWs' drive trains were accessible.

Firestorm in West Loch!

Photo: Robert L. Dennebaum (Navy) *LST-272*
West Loch (Pearl Harbor)—LST explosions 21 May, 1944—Saipan invasion forces.

Photo: Robert L. Dennebaum (Navy) *LST-272*
West Loch (Pearl Harbor)—LST explosions May 21, 1944—Saipan invasion forces.

The Quack Corps

Like Sundays can be in Hawaii, the afternoon of the 21st was hot for those who had to work in the sun. The men still aboard ships in the Loch were dozing in the shade of vehicles or ship projections playing cards, rapping in bull sessions, or sitting in thought while watching activities around them.

The DUKW men were restricted to the area. Several first platoon men expressed wishes for a cold drink, water or whatever, because the afternoon was hot and humid. So I checked with Lieutenant Blackburn for permission to take a DUKW to a small store nearby to buy cases of Coca Cola® for the men. He reminded me of the restriction order but gave permission when I suggested that, if stopped, I could use the excuse that we had been working on the DUKW's motor and were taking it for a test run.

I ordered Corp. Harold Reynolds to grab his assistant and crank up his DUKW for the run. They enthusiastically welcomed the errand and in moments, we were underway.

A dirt road, just wide enough for a single vehicle, was atop the levee separating the bordering canefields and Walker Bay. After traveling some 200-yards or so, I felt the DUKW shudder and heard an explosion aft. I swiveled around and saw a huge mushrooming cloud of smoke boiling above one of the LSTs in Tare 8.

The road banks were steep. I quickly scanned ahead for a place to park until I knew what was happening. A flat area in a clump of trees about 100-yards ahead drew my attention and I ordered Reynolds to pull off there. Fires had leapfrogged to other LSTs and explosions hurled slabs of metal and other debris high into the air.

The conflagration quickly appeared to be turning into a catastrophe. After watching for several minutes, I realized that the DUKWs could be used for hauling casualties. Several other men had arrived in a couple of DUKWs to join us, some from 2d DUKW and others whom I didn't know. I called for volunteers to return to the 1st platoon area with me but only

Firestorm in West Loch!

Reynolds stepped forward. I decided to leave the DUKWs there because other vehicles might need to exit the LST area via the levee road.

Reynolds and I began double-timing back to the area. About halfway there, we were stopped by two MP'S, a very young Army 2d lieutenant and an enlisted Marine. The lieutenant informed us that no one was allowed to go into the area. I explained that we were with a DUKW company and our vehicles were on shore by the LSTs. We were going back to drive them to haul casualties to hospitals, and, that only DUKW men could be expected to know how to operate the vehicles.

After some discussion that progressively became more heated, he emphatically stated, "You're not going in!"

"Lieutenant, my unit is right in the middle of that and we're going in!" I retorted just as emphatically. I wasn't trying to make like a hero but I felt I'd be deserting my platoon if I didn't go back.

"I said you are not going into the area!" he repeated. I stood my ground.

It was the first time I'd locked horns with an officer or an MP but he was being unrealistic by trying to keep us away from our unit. I also knew there must be many dead and injured men on the LSTs and even more would die if they didn't get quick medical attention. Throwing caution to the winds, I stated, "We're going in!"

He jerked his pistol from its holster, "I told you that you're not!"

The lieutenant was acting panicked. The enlisted Marine was standing close behind him and apparently thought the young officer had lost his judgment and might shoot me. So, yanking his .45 from its holster, he pointed it at the officer and in a commanding tone of voice said, "Lieutenant! If they're willing to go, let them! It's their necks they're risking. Now put that damned pistol away!"

The Quack Corps

After a few moments of hesitation, the lieutenant dropped the muzzle of the pistol and reholstered it. "All right, you can go." I didn't answer but silently signaled Reynolds with a nod and we hurried on.

Massive explosions were hurling huge chunks of steel, vehicle parts and other debris our way. We ducked behind the road bank until the mammoth pieces had passed over head and then leaped to our feet and ran until the next explosion.

When we reached the 1st platoon area, most of the DUKWs were gone and I saw only Captain George standing forlornly by himself apparently wondering what had happened to his men. He was very calm and seemingly oblivious to the danger. His demeanor indicated that he'd stand muster in trying circumstances. I didn't see any casualties in the area. When I approached him, he ordered: "Get the vehicles cleared out!"

"But Sir," I said in a respectful tone of voice, "if any casualties come in, the DUKWs can be used to run them to hospitals. That is the reason Reynolds and I came back, Sir."

He changed his mind, "Leave the DUKWs but get those AmTracs [LVTs] out!" A few of them had also been brought ashore.

"Aye, aye, Sir!" I ran to the nearest AmTrac and hoisted myself over its side and entered the driver's compartment—I had never even been inside an AmTrac! I looked at the multitude of switches and other gear in the compartment but didn't spot a starter button. I didn't relish trying to steer one of the things down the levee road. But, if I managed to get it running, the little experience I'd gained on the small trac-layer tractor during the short hitch on Palmyra Island might be of benefit. I rechecked the compartment but still couldn't figure out how to start it. After spending a few short minutes fooling with switches, I gave up, hoisted myself out, and ran back to Captain George, "Sir, I can't figure out how to start those damned AmTracs!"

Firestorm in West Loch!

"Then leave them set, Sergeant." Moments later he added, "Don't worry about it."

The nearest LST was about a hundred or so feet away and each time an explosion erupted the captain and I dived under the same DUKW. I was smaller and quicker so usually beat him under. Once, he landed on top of me. It gave us a laugh and lessened some of the tension but soon, the concussion from a large explosion brought it back.

With the worst of the force generated by the explosions going upward, our greatest danger was from falling debris. Peering from under the DUKW, I could see huge pieces of debris falling far inland.

The Loch was a melee and LSTs bumped as captains tried desperately to get their ships away from those burning and into safer places. Some made it to open sea, while others beached in a cove or in another area of the Loch. I also could see smaller craft scurrying about in the Loch with men aboard pulling survivors from the oil-scummed water. Others wouldn't be saved for they were pulled under by the spinning screws of ships getting under way, while others drowned because they were injured, were poor swimmers or couldn't swim at all.

I saw a burning LST in mid-channel floating inexorably toward the ammunition depot piers. Fortunately, a tug arrived in time to push it away. Most of my attention dwelled on the nearest LSTs. The platoon had come ashore just off the bows of the LSTs in Tare 8. With several burning in that nest, it was impossible to take DUKWs into the water from the platoon's position. Captain George and I just waited for casualties who might make it ashore on their own.

As evening approached, a Navy tug, equipped for fire fighting, approached an LST in Tare 8. The captain nestled the tug's bow against that of the LST right where her bow doors met in the center. Shortly after the tug began pouring torrents of water on the raging fires aboard, a tremendous explosion

The Quack Corps

erupted. I dived behind a DUKW and crouched there until the concussion and shrapnel passed. Then I cautiously edged forward and peered under the DUKW's bow. I stared in astonishment because the tug's superstructure was in shambles! The LST's bow doors had blown open right where the tug had nestled against them. Every man topside on the tug had disappeared. I carefully scanned the water near the tug and some distance forward of the LST but not a single man or body was visible. The tug was floating slowly and silently away. The tug's superstructure destruction had been caused by the last of the most-violent explosions.

A few men had swum to shore before the tug was demolished. None appeared to be seriously injured and as soon as their feet touched solid ground they began running and quickly disappeared inland. Captain George and I wondered about other casualties because we knew there must be many. After things settled down, we learned that many had swum or been taken to Hanaloa Point. Company DUKWs, including some from the 1st platoon, made many runs to area hospitals. The Hanaloa Point area wasn't visible to us because of vegetation along the shoreline.

The commander of the LST group hauling 2d DUKW was aboard *LST-354*. He apparently had used his command privileges and had his ship moved to Tare 3, in the channel leading out of the Loch, after the 1st platoon had debarked. *LST-121* with 2d DUKW's 3rd platoon aboard was berthed in Tare 5 near Intrepid Point, up-channel from *-354's* berth.

LST-340, with the company's 2d platoon and *-23*, with the 4th platoon were in Tare 9, the nest immediately astern of Tare 8. The other company personnel were distributed among the four ships. *LST-23* made it to open sea with an 8-inch hawser wrapped around a screw shaft. Though it bent the shaft, she would tag along when the flotilla eventually sailed. *LST-340* managed to clear the nest and backed into shallows in another part of the Loch.

Firestorm in West Loch!

On one of the company's LSTs, a DUKW man was on the fo'c'sle with his feet bare. As white-hot pieces of metal landed on barrels of gasoline stored there, he kicked them overboard! Possibly, his action prevented that LST catching fire.

Later, I learned that six of the 1600 ton, 328 feet long LSTs, five in Tare 8 and one in Tare 9, were destroyed along with three LCTs. A Naval Court of Inquiry concluded that carelessness in handling or a defective fuse in 4.2 mortar ammo being off-loaded on *LST-353* was the probable cause—LCTs especially equipped to serve as floating platforms for the mortars had been lost in heavy weather off Maui. Sergeant Edgar Bacon, of 2d DUKW's Maintenance platoon, told me later: "I saw a man welding on an LST near barrels of gas stored on the top deck. One of them must have been leaking because they exploded." Other men also contended that welding was being done near the point where the first explosion had occurred.

It had been a costly few hours because in addition to the loss of critically needed ships, weapons, and supplies, it had caused death or injury to 559 men. Second DUKW had only one man injured, a perforated eardrum, and none killed. But the catastrophe had taken its toll of the Second and Fourth Marine Divisions because their losses totaled 207 men.

The catastrophe was one of WWII's best-kept secrets. So little official information was divulged that one news service even reported it as another Japanese attack on Pearl Harbor. And, official photos were not de-classified until 1962.

Shortly before dark, the 105s were reloaded into the DUKWs. The first platoon entered the waters of Walker Bay, just forward of the remains of the ships in Tare 8, and proceeded through the oil-scummed water to *LST-354's* berth. In the now calm Loch water, it was a snap for the drivers to judge the ramp's depth and gun the motors for the front tires to grab and pull the vehicles up it into the tank deck. Force of habit caused me to caution the Marine posted on tank-deck fire watch to be especially alert. But, after the events of that day, he didn't need any cautions.

I felt edgy because the disaster had brought back vivid mental pictures of another day in Pearl Harbor. The meeting with the bomb in *Pennsylvania's* casemate, 7 December, 1941, had not only dramatically shown me the destructiveness of explosives, it had also created a great deal of fear because of the horrible flash burns and shrapnel-shredded bodies. Now gun-shy of the harbor, I was anxious to leave before another catastrophe ensued, though I knew the next stop was probably an invasion beach.

The disaster had caused only a one-day delay in the LST fleet's departure because replacement ships, men, and equipment were quickly assembled.

On 25 May, *LST-354* moved from her Tare 3 berth and proceeded down channel to leave Pearl Harbor. I joined the two Marine officers and 47 other DUKW men topside and watched the familiar shoreline slip by as the ship left the main channel to enter the open sea. She joined the rest of the flotilla in the waters outside the entrance to Pearl Harbor.

The bows of the LSTs pointed westward and the men speculated where the next stop would be. And, everyone aboard became one-day older when the flotilla crossed the International Dateline on 31 May.

Each day could be expected to be just like the day before with hours spent by the Marines in bull sessions, sacking out in quarters in the stern of the ship, or in the shade of a vehicle or ship projection top side. Physical drill would have been beneficial but there wasn't enough room to muster the platoon for it. Other than occasional tours of the tank deck to check that everything was secure, reminding the men to keep their weapons in good order, and assigning fire watches, I had little to keep me busy. I spent many hours topside by myself thinking of what lay ahead, of my best girl back in San Diego, and

Firestorm in West Loch!

of my family. Each turn of the ship's screws was taking me farther and farther away.

The boring daily routine was broken when at 0515, 7 June, 1944, word spread like wild fire that land loomed on the horizon. *LST-354's* PA system passed the word that we were going to stop at Eniwetok Atoll, in the Marshall Islands, to wait for the rest of the invasion fleet.

Shortly after 0700, the ship entered the now calm and peaceful lagoon at Eniwetok, 2100 nautical miles southwest of Pearl Harbor. The men were not allowed to go ashore, but I planted my feet on what only short months before had been enemy territory on official business. I rode a Higgins boat in to pick up documents relating to the forthcoming invasion.

It was in the Marshalls where events occurred that may have determined just how the Marine Corps would use "The Quack Corps", as other Marines called the men in DUKW companies.

Official documents in the U.S. Marine Corps Historical Center Files reveal:

> *The attack on Namur in the Marshalls 1 February, 1944, pointed up to the Marines the definite need for the DUKW. Colonel William W. Rogers, Chief of Staff of the 4th Marine Division, reported: One of the main things we learned from this operation was the value of the DUKW, which the Army had and we did not. If we had the DUKWs to land ammunition and save the tractors [AmTracs], I firmly believe the Namur attack would have been over in a few hours. The attack was seriously hampered by the failure of the tractors to get to the line of departure on time.*

The colonel may have been unaware that the Marine Corps already had plans for the DUKW and that two Marine DUKW companies had been formed prior to his observations.

The Quack Corps

His comments may have changed the intended use of DUKWs by the Corps.

The flotilla of LSTs carrying 2d DUKW hoisted anchor, at about 2000, and sailed out of the lagoon on 9 June.

I unrolled the map and recognition flashed ... it's Saipan! The island had been included in our speculative guesses but I knew little about this small blob on a map of the Pacific Ocean.

Poring over the map, I learned that Saipan had 47 square miles of land and that Mt. Tapotchau's peak towered about 1500 feet into the air. Also, Saipan was about 1600 miles southeast of Tokyo. The coral barrier reef that we would have to cross was starkly outlined but there was much the map didn't show.

After firming a mental picture of Saipan, I spent most of the daylight hours topside reading a tattered paperback book or magazine, or gazing out over the ocean with unseeing eyes and with thoughts of far away places. Many hours were also whiled away in bull sessions with the men or Lieutenant Blackburn. The lieutenant and I were becoming accustomed to working as a team and our relationship was becoming more than just a platoon leader and his platoon sergeant. While reminiscing, we relived many opossum and other hunting trips and a multitude of fish were caught. He had learned that one didn't deal with men heading into combat the same as those at boot camp.

When by myself, I wondered whether I'd come through the battle okay. Also, whether my fear of burns and shrapnel would eventually become more than my nerves could take. There was also danger from small caliber fire but I took a somewhat fatalistic attitude; either it would kill me outright or chances would be I'd survive without being crippled.

Though this would be my first landing on an enemy beach, conversations with battle-tested buddies, watching newsreels, reading Combat Correspondents' accounts, and my

Firestorm in West Loch!

own training helped prepare me for what I'd face. But, I knew that one had to *make* a landing to know what the real thing was really like.

Some of the hours were spent sacked out in my bunk. Boredom was temporarily relieved when my reverie was interrupted by Private First Class Mac, an assistant driver, who rushed to my bunk. Breathlessly, he said, "Sergeant, some bastard has stolen my Thompson (.45-caliber submachine gun)."

He was very agitated so I replied, "Calm down, Mac. We'll get it back." I questioned, "Where did you have it?"'

"Leaning against my seat in the DUKW."

"Relax. If necessary, the entire ship will be searched. We'll find the Thompson." Ship captains usually cooperated in situations of this type and I had no doubts that this captain would too. The weapon would probably be found unless it had been thrown overboard by a thief who got cold feet after realizing what he had done.. I wanted to do some checking before reporting the loss to Lieutenant Blackburn.

At this stage of the war, some of the men being inducted into the services had been prone to thievery as civilians. Though a known thief was not allowed in the Marine Corps or Navy pre-war, bodies were needed and standards had been drastically lowered. Both services had been stymied since they could no longer take the pick of the draftees. Even with the lower requirements, I wondered how any man could justify stealing the weapon of a man heading for a beach invasion. It could cost the man his life.

I went to the tank deck to check with the Marine fire watch. He assured me that he had been alert and hadn't seen or heard anything. I checked the DUKW and discovered the ammunition clips for the Thompson and the clip belt were still on the floorboards of the cab. Presumably, whomever had stolen the weapon either didn't know it required the use of a clip or intended to return later for the items.

The Quack Corps

En route back to quarters, I checked with the sailors in the compartment nearest the tank deck hatch but they hadn't seen anyone carry the weapon out. Because of the wartime circumstances, I felt it unlikely they would lie to me, so I headed for my bunk to lay down while mulling it over. If the sailors hadn't seen someone carry it out, then it must be somewhere on the tank deck or nearby. I began to visualize how I would have stolen the Thompson, then I pictured how it had probably been done. "Mac," I bellowed, "Go down and check behind that coil of rope I noticed in the small compartment between crew's quarters and the tank deck!"

He raced away and quickly returned with his face *beaming*, carrying the Thompson. I felt very smug over solving the case in a way that would have done credit to Sherlock Holmes!

When I began thinking about how I'd steal the Thompson, I visualized that it would be easy enough to slip into the tank deck, walk bent over between the bulkhead and the outside row of DUKWs, cautiously check the direction of the fire sentry's attention, and then carefully reach in and ease the weapon over the side without banging against metal. The thief apparently had figured he could return and get the weapon from behind the coil of rope before it was missed.

The LST had a determined thief aboard. We had to post a watch over our K-rations because they began disappearing.

The theft of the Thompson had broken the routine of another boring day at sea and its disappearance, with the added K-ration thievery, had created tension among the men. But, it was low key compared to that created when we were apprised of the scheduled date of the Saipan landing.

Some of the men wrote letters to stick in their packs for later mailing or to tear to shreds after realizing they had survived the landing. I didn't write any letters because it could be weeks before shore units sent mail out.

Chapter 11
Saipan!

Smoke hovered over Saipan as daylight broke on 15 June, 1944. I stood topside on the LST watching warships hurling tons of steel onto the island; most of the ships' silhouettes were familiar to me from my seagoing days. Columns of smoke rose into the air whenever a barrage of shells hit an ammunition or fuel storage dump. Navy planes and ships had bombarded the island steadily for the past few days. How could anyone or anything survive under that pounding, I wondered.

The invasion beaches were designated by colors: blue, yellow, red and green. Red ... what an apt name for an invasion beach!

The 4th Marine Division would land on beaches Yellow One, Two and Three, and Blue One and Two, located from the north edge of and to the south of Charan Kanoa (presently known as Chalan Kanoa).

As time drew near to man the DUKWs, tension tightened the men's faces. Some continued to watch the bombardment while others talked with buddies in low voices. Then, "DUKW crews! Man your DUKWs! Howitzer Crews! Board DUKWs!" blared raucously from the PA system.

Earlier, I had taken my gear topside. One of the men volunteered to take my pack to the tank deck while I made one last check through quarters to make sure nothing was left behind. After checking quarters, I took up position with Lieutenant Blackburn near the LST's ramp.

The bow doors opened, the ramp lowered into the water and the first DUKW began backing to the head of the ramp. It stopped and Lieutenant Blackburn climbed aboard. At 0846,

The Quack Corps

the vehicle backed down the ramp into the water, then it turned away to head for the platoon's assembly point.

The first assault units of the 4th Division were scheduled to leave the line of departure at 0815 but were delayed in heading for the beaches.

Number-8 DUKW backed up and stopped. I grabbed the edge of the cargo space with both hands, placed a foot on a reinforcing rib and hoisted myself aboard. As the DUKW headed for the assembly point off Blue Beach Two, I looked back to make sure the four ammunition loaded DUKWs had cleared the LST and were following us. Number-8 was the last DUKW hauling a gun. The last ammo DUKW left the LST at 0920.

Number-8 reached the assembly point and Corp. Donald J. Shults, its driver, maneuvered it into the large circle of hybrid craft which were bobbing in the gentle waves with motors turned off.

Units of the assault forces needed to secure the beaches and far enough inland to make it reasonably safe for the 105mms to come ashore and be protected from small arms fire. The word was passed that the wait might be long because progress of the first assault waves had been slow. Then, unexpectedly, I saw Lieutenant Blackburn giving the crank up signal by twirling his arm in a circular motion above his head.

Later, scuttlebutt was that the 105s had landed much earlier than planned, supposedly in the 3rd wave. Whether it was true and who gave the order to head in was never clarified.

White water boiled behind Number-1 DUKW, as the driver gave heavy throttle and the vehicle began to move toward the line of departure. Things must have improved immensely on the beach for us to move in so unexpectedly. Number-1 didn't slow at the line of departure but continued toward the beach under heavy throttle. The white line of the low surf breaking on the reef was only faintly visible, because we were still quite far out.

Saipan!

Water surged behind the DUKWs as the drivers gave more throttle to maintain positions of about 25 yards behind the DUKW ahead.

I sat on the rim of the cargo space just behind the assistant driver and periodically checked the line of DUKWs ahead of and behind Number-8. Though I could hear the roar of the DUKW's exhaust and dull booms of explosions on the beach or inland, we seemed isolated and almost alone in our own little world.

As we neared the island, details of palm tree remnants and the sandy beach appeared. I could see the hazy outline of the sugar mill smokestack at Charan Kanoa and planes as they dived and soared above the island. The noise level became a thundering din, at times, then quietened and individual explosions could be heard.

The bulk of Number-1 DUKW became more prominent as the front tires caught and pulled the vehicle up onto the coral reef. At almost the same moment, I saw geysers of water rise high into the air when Jap shells hit the water a few yards to starboard of -2, then, geysers of white rose to port. I knew from my experience with the 5-inch .51-caliber guns on Palmyra Island and aboard battlewagons that the next salvo could mean disaster for men and DUKWs because, if their spotters were good, the optimum was for the third salvo to be on when firing at waterborne targets. I also suspected that the Japs had preregistered their guns and were laying a barrage with the expectation that a craft would run under a shell. It's doubtful they knew that *these craft* wouldn't stop at the reef. Maybe we'd surprise them by crossing it and barging forward until reaching the beach.

The men in the DUKWs ahead hunkered down in the thin skin vehicles as each approached and plowed into and through the geysers of water now rising on each side of them. I felt grateful for the low freeboard because it'd take an almost direct hit to sink a vehicle.

The Quack Corps

As Number-8 neared the spurting geysers, I crouched on my haunches with only my head and shoulders above the cargo space so I could continue checking the 1st platoon's DUKWs. Then, a geyser of water! Explosion! A DUKW slowed and stopped in the water. A shell had hit near its port side and flying shrapnel had wounded most of the men and damaged the vehicle.

Corporal Shults headed Number-8 toward the disabled DUKW. The men were on their feet and it wasn't on fire so I yelled at Shults, "Head for the beach! The ammos will get them!" He spun the steering wheel to the right and the DUKW swung to starboard of the disabled vehicle. I rose to my feet and signaled the tailing ammo drivers to swing by the disabled craft; if a DUKW got hit they had orders to pick up the men.

The vehicles hauling 14th Marine Howitzers, gun crews and several rounds of ammunition were already grossly overloaded so they didn't have load capacity or room for the additional men. The DUKWs were rated for 5000 pounds but Captain George computed that the vehicles hauling guns were carrying over 8000 pounds. In any event, it was necessary that we tie a rubberized ditty bag over the gas tank cap to prevent saltwater surging in because the sterns were almost awash.

As Number-8 passed the disabled DUKW, its driver, PFC Phillip Chapman, was standing in the driver's seat with blood streaming from his face. Possibly his wounds were caused by the shattering of the windshield wing. All the men were frantically yelling and motioning to us. Their mouths were opening and closing but I couldn't hear what they were saying. None appeared to be seriously wounded.

I checked that the ammo DUKW drivers had responded to my signal, then returned to the action ahead. In a short while, I rechecked to make certain the rescue was underway.

When the shells exploded in the water, I could hear a sharp c-r-a-c-k-i-n-g noise. The shelling slackened as we neared the reef.

Saipan!

The front tires clawed, slipped and then gripped the coral and the DUKW's bow raised as it climbed onto the reef. Shults floorboarded the throttle and the DUKW accelerated in the shallows, pushing a wall of water ahead until we reached the beach. Shells were plastering it and we dived for protection the moment the vehicle stopped. Vehicles were burning up and down the beach but I couldn't tell whether AmTracs or DUKWs.

While waiting for the shelling to decrease, concern for the men on the hit DUKW flitted across my mind. It had been hard to pass them by, even though I knew the ammos would be there in moments. The drivers of DUKWs with 105s aboard had orders to continue to their objective, unless hit craft were afire or in imminent danger of sinking, because it was of extreme importance that the guns get ashore.

After shelling decreased, I located Lieutenant Blackburn. The noise level was high and we had to talk loudly. "Did all of the DUKWs make shore?" he inquired.

"One got hit! The ammo drivers rescued the men! None looked to be seriously wounded!"

"Did it sink?"

"It was still afloat when I passed, Sir!"

"Do you think you can salvage it?"

"I'll give it a try just as soon as a DUKW is unloaded, Sir!"

The waves had probably carried the DUKW to the reef. I didn't relish trying to hook onto it to pull it ashore with the Japs trying to drop shells down my throat. Glancing seaward, I tried to locate the vehicle but didn't spot it so assumed it had sunk. Later, I learned that the crew of a small Navy craft had observed the events, rushed in, attached a line and began towing the DUKW to a ship but it sank before it could be hoisted aboard.

Some of the DUKWs were equipped with fold-down A-frames mounted on the stern for use in loading and unloading other vehicles. After the howitzers had been taken to the area where they would be set up and unloading had begun, Lieutenant Blackburn informed me that he was going to return to the LST on the first DUKW to supervise unloading in the tank deck. He would send word by a driver when he wanted me to relieve him so he could return to the beach.

After howitzer unloading was completed, Corp. Lee D. Smallwood approached me, "Hey, Sarge! You missed all the excitement!"

"I did? Didn't you see me peeking over the gunwale of the DUKW ahead of you on our way in to the beach?" I retorted.

"I don't mean that excitement! When I backed into position [he drove an A-frame ammo DUKW] to unload the guns, the DUKW ran over a tunnel. Eighteen Japs boiled out. We had a turkey shoot and killed all of them!"

"I suppose the weight of the DUKW caused the tunnel to begin collapsing. They probably were scared of smothering and preferred to take their chances outside," I observed.

After the DUKWs began making runs to the LSTs to bring in ammunition and other supplies, I noticed Captain George standing on the beach. He was watching the company's activities while smoking a big cigar, seemingly oblivious to the shell bursts kicking up sand. His conduct set a good example for the men under his command but he didn't have to be that exposed to the shrapnel to do it I thought. Later, I learned that another company officer, who also smoked cigars, had brought four boxes ashore with him but *he forgot to bring ammunition for his carbine!*

About every three hours, Lieutenant Blackburn sent word for me to come to the LST and relieve him. I stayed aboard until he returned to the ship. The hot coffee and chow on the ship helped make the day a little better than it otherwise would have been.

As the hours passed, the DUKWs were shelled less as they made their way through the surf to the reef but the surf was be-

Saipan!

coming higher and higher as the day waned. I had judged that the AmTracs would be a death trap in heavy surf. My judgment was confirmed, I felt, when a DUKW driver told me that he counted 22 capsized or swamped on our section of the reef—it was becoming increasingly difficult for the drivers to find sufficient clear space between them as the DUKWs continued making runs.

During spare moments, I'd walk to the head of the LST's ramp and scan the reef and island. I could see white frothing water boil up when the waves broke on the reef. The DUKW drivers expressed concern and wondered when they'd get to knock off for the day. The supplies were vitally needed on shore so they had to take their chances in the surf.

As dusk approached, PFC Arthur Stover brought word that his DUKW would be the last for the day. Though I would have preferred spending the night on the LST, I was aboard the DUKW when he backed it down the ramp—I felt I should be with the platoon and face with the men whatever the night might bring. In all probability I would have lost whatever respect I had gained from them if I had stayed aboard the ship.

A Marine captain on board a Navy control ship stationed some distance from the reef was supervising the tallying of supplies going ashore and directing reef activities. Each driver was required to swing by and report his load. When Private First Class Stover swung by, the captain ordered, "The AmTracs are having problems in the surf. Use the channel!" The channel was one the Japs had blasted through the reef to provide access to Charan Kanoa.

"Aye, aye, Sir!" I answered for the crew. Stover swung the DUKW away to head for the channel entrance, which was to the north of us.

When about halfway to the channel mouth, I noticed an LCM between the reef and the beach desperately maneuvering to evade a barrage of Jap shells. *Oh! Damn!* I mulled over what to do, because we had been ordered to use the channel. I

The Quack Corps

felt it was almost certain that the Japs would get us as we entered. They were persistent in trying to get the LCM. After watching a few moments longer, I decided that our chances of living were better by challenging the surf. So I decided to ignore the captain's order.

I had confidence in Stover's ability. "Take the surf!" I yelled. He also had been eyeballing the LCM's evasive maneuvers and, without hesitation, swung the wheel to starboard.

Standing up, I could see better than Stover so I scanned for an opening between the capsized and swamped AmTracs on the reef that appeared wide enough to give us a good chance of getting through. The DUKW was heading south, paralleling the beach. We were almost to the southern extremity of the Yellow beaches before I noted an opening that looked wide enough to maneuver through. After reaching a point directly seaward of the opening, Stover spun the steering wheel left and the DUKW responded.

As we neared the reef, the wave tops towered high above us when the DUKW dropped into the troughs between them. I hadn't driven or ridden in a DUKW through surf that massive. Maybe I had made an error in judgment by ignoring the captain's order. But, the decision was made and it was too late to turn back. I tightened my grip on the tarp rail across the back of the cab and prayed that Stover wouldn't misjudge the wave he chose to surfboard. He glanced frequently to his left. Suddenly, I felt the DUKW surge forward. We were committed!

The huge wave lifted the DUKW high. Stover pushed desperately on the already wide-open throttle as he tried to nurse more rpm from the straining motor. The bow angled sharply downward as the DUKW sped toward the reef. I prayed that the vehicle wouldn't tumble over stern first. Then, the spinning tires caught. We had made it!

I eyeballed the surf. *Oh, God!* I implored, because a huge towering wave was racing toward us! "Stover! Put your foot

Saipan!

in it!" I bellowed. My body tensed and my hands riveted to the tarp rail. The DUKW lurched forward and the wave crashed onto the reef an instant before reaching the stern and dumped hundreds of gallons of frothing water over us and into the vehicle. The motor continued to roar as Stover headed for shore. The automatic bilge pumps were still squirting water even after we had reached the sandy beach.

Stover turned off the motor and we sat for several moments looking at each other with relieved grins and in agreement that even the scare and soaking by the wave was better than dodging Jap shells. My admiration for the capabilities of the DUKW had reached even greater heights.

Darkness was coming on and I suggested that Stover and his assistant find a hole while I located the platoon. I turned northward after noting where they holed up because I planned to return for them. But, I didn't find any DUKW men. Light was fading and I didn't feel it would last long enough for me to return to the general area of the DUKW. Everyone had become moles so I began to look for an unoccupied hole or one with room for another man, because my intrenching shovel had gone to the bottom with the sunken DUKW.

A check at a nearby first aid station for a shovel drew a blank. As I was the only one still above ground, I decided I hadn't better waste any time getting under cover. No one in the area offered to make room in their hole so I removed the steel shell from my helmet and scooped out a shallow hole, long enough to stretch out in, at the beach's tree line. My body was barely below the sandy surface.

Of course, I knew it was a *no-no* for a man to foxhole by himself on an enemy beach but I felt it was better that than get shot by a trigger-happy Marine while trying to find company. I also didn't relish having to stay awake all night so I wouldn't have my throat slit while sleeping. But the tension of the day had been too much and, fatigued, I fell asleep not long after settling in for the night.

The Quack Corps

Occasionally, the Navy fired a starshell to light the beach area. The noise made by the small explosive used to eject the small parachute and light out of the canister awakened me. Each time, I raised my head and quickly scanned the area around my hole—I had memorized the terrain features before sacking out—then grabbed the helmet shell and dug deeper. After awakening off and on during the night, my hole was large enough for two men and halfway to China by morning! Even with the fatigue, I wondered how I could let myself fall asleep because I knew the extreme danger of occupying the hole alone.

During one of my awake periods, I heard what I took to be a goat kid bleating. I guessed that it wouldn't live long because of a Marine's itchy trigger finger. The cry pierced the darkness again. I strained to hear better because it could be a Jap trick to draw fire, thereby disclosing Marine positions. I heard low voices but in a language that I couldn't understand, and I realized that the bleat I had assumed was a goat kid was in actuality a baby. When the infant wailed, a soft female voice quietened it with a soothing, cooing tone. *Oh, God, it's hard enough on grown men, how terrifying it must be for that poor little baby,* I reflected. Then, I realized that, when it grew up, if it did, the infant would not even remember this night.

After daylight, I saw an elderly woman, a young woman cradling a baby in her arms, and a man leaving a Marine AmTrac parked a short distance down the beach from my hole; they were Saipan natives.

Sporadic firing during the night just forward of my position didn't cause me much concern because I knew that flitting shadows, trees waving in a breeze, and nervousness or imagination often caused indiscriminate firing by unseasoned men in combat. After daylight I learned that artillerymen, a short distance inland from my position, had killed several infiltrating Japanese.

Saipan!

At dawn, the Japanese began laying mortar and artillery barrages on the beach area. Big guns, hidden in caves, were rolled out on rails and, after firing a few rounds, were rolled back inside before counter fire could be brought to bear. After the first few barrages, we noted that the shells came south on the beach to a certain spot and then moved inland. After determining their firing patterns, we merely walked ahead of the barrages as they moved south toward the spot. The Japs didn't seem to ever vary the pattern and could have created more havoc had they reversed it because it would have caught us by surprise.

The Japanese apparently didn't expect that the landings would be made across the reef after the lesson of Tarawa, and if so, small caliber weapons could dispose of men wading ashore after disembarking from landing craft. So the southern portions of Yellow Beaches were shelled mostly by mortars and field guns. The barrages were not as intense as those to the north and didn't cover as much area.

The 14th Marine 105mm Howitzer unit serviced by the 3rd platoon took a severe beating during the big gun barrages. When the barrage angled inland, it caught part of the guns serviced by the 2d platoon and then walked a line forward of those serviced by the 1st platoon.

I located the platoon at daybreak and found that I would have been successful in my search if I had continued north for only a short distance. DUKWs parked on the beach were obscured by AmTracs. The men had made it through the night without severe problems.

Guns in a battery serviced by one of the other platoons had run short of ammunition during the night and two DUKWs made a run to an LST just after midnight for replenishment ammo. Fortunately, the surf had calmed by that time.

While eating a K-ration breakfast my mind roved over D-Day activities. I didn't know how the other platoons had fared but the 1st platoon had been blessed, considering the circum-

The Quack Corps

stances. In addition to the few men wounded and the DUKW sunk on the first run in, Corp. William H. W. Carr's DUKW was also sunk. He had delivered casualties to an offshore ship and was heading back to *LST-354* for another load of 14th Marine supplies when a shell took the stern off his DUKW; neither he nor his assistant were wounded. They inflated their Navy life belts and floated out as the DUKW plunged to the ocean floor beneath them. A small craft gave them a ride to the LST where they picked up another DUKW and resumed making runs.

The men resumed work at daylight and, as on D-Day, loaded casualties at first aid stations for delivery to ships offshore. Stretcher cases were laid crosswise with the stretcher handles resting on the cargo space rims. Four ambulatory casualties sat on the stern of the DUKW with their feet inside the cargo space.

When I had occasion to go to the LST, I leaned against the cab-cover rail and watched the wounded men while the DUKW knifed through the surf. The surf increased in size as the day wore on and men could be washed overboard by the large volume of water breaking over the vehicles. I kept an eye on the ambulatory casualties in case they panicked and bailed out when they saw the wall of water relentlessly coming toward the DUKW. Though I assured them that we'd make it okay, most eyed the surf with a dubious look. After we reached calmer water seaward of the reef, most broke out in smiles of relief. They, too, had learned about the capabilities of the hybrid truck. I doubted if ever again would they derisively quack like a duck when one of the vehicles passed by them.

On one of my trips, I boarded a DUKW containing a young Marine with a severe head wound; it appeared that the entire back of his head was shattered. He lay on his stomach, moaning and attempting to move at times. I placed my hand on his shoulder in hopes the feel of it would comfort and quiet him and left it there while the DUKW knifed through the surf.

Saipan!

I worried that he wouldn't receive expert medical care soon enough since it took several minutes to reach the ships offshore.

Though I tried to shield my mind and emotions against the suffering of wounded men, the young Marine with that terrible head wound pierced that shield. I assumed that his brain was damaged and felt heartsick and near to tears. I seethed at the inhumanity of men to other men.

As the DUKW neared the closest LST equipped for handling casualties, I stood on the bow and used a cardboard megaphone to communicate with an officer standing by the ship's gangway. He informed me that the ship had all the wounded she could handle. Though I stressed the critical condition of the Marine with the head wound, he refused to take him, remarking, "The only empty bunks on the ship are in officers' quarters."

His remark was the match that lit my fuse. I exploded and, for the first and only time, cursed an officer to his face and with every curse word in my vocabulary. I ended my tirade with, "Sir! You can take those bunks in officers' quarters and stick them up your ass!"

He didn't reply but stood with a startled look and mouth agape. The temptation to shoot him was strong so I yelled at the driver to get out of there before I killed the bastard.

To me, no bunk was sacrosanct under those circumstances. I just couldn't stomach that he wasn't willing to give his bunk to the young Marine, to whom a few minutes might make the difference between living or dying.

Quickly scanning the anchorage, I didn't spot any hospital ships but did notice a huge APA (transport) near the seaward edge of the anchored ships and decided that she might be the best chance, because I suspected that the close-in ships were in the same situation as the LST.

As the DUKW neared the APA, I hailed the bridge and was told to come alongside and the DUKW would be lifted

The Quack Corps

aboard. The main deck of the ship was far above us, the DUKW probably looked like a toy bobbing in the water to those above.

The driver, Corp. Lee D. Smallwood, maneuvered the vehicle into position alongside the ship. The davit operator lowered the sling so we could hook it to the DUKW. With the danger of the metal sling further injuring the casualties, he couldn't give us enough slack to fully compensate for the bouncing of the DUKW. With the assistant driver, Corp. Paul H. Fluegel, Jr., on the stern and me on the bow, each of us grabbed the sling's bridle and after several attempts to try and accurately time the rise and fall of the vehicle, managed to hook it to the four metal lifting eyes on the DUKW.

Before raising it out of the water, someone yelled to inquire whether the crew wanted to use a Jacob's Ladder to come aboard. Smallwood and Fluegel decided to remain in the DUKW—they were not about to climb the ladder up the side of the huge ship. I didn't trust the ship's davit cable that much and didn't want to dangle high over the water in the vehicle. After climbing the ladder to the rail, two sailors grabbed my arms and helped me the rest of the way on board. Later, I learned that 2d DUKW had received notice of faulty welds on lifting eyes. The company apparently didn't receive any vehicles with them because no DUKWs were dropped because of breaking welds.

Climbing a rope ladder up the side of a huge ship is no small feat, particularly with a carbine, binoculars, handheld walkie-talkie radio and gas mask slung over one's shoulders. My prewar net climbing practice back in San Diego during my hitch with the 6th Marine Regiment had paid off.

The moment the DUKW's tires touched the deck, ship crew members climbed aboard and passed the casualties to waiting hands. The stretcher bearers took off at a run for the vessel's medical facilities.

Saipan!

Appreciative of the treatment afforded the casualties, I hailed the bridge to thank those responsible for taking them aboard.

The concern and actions of the officers and men on the APA helped to lessen the anger I felt over the LST incident. I realized that it was an isolated case and didn't damn the entire Navy, or all officers, because of it. To my knowledge, it was the only time that the platoon's DUKW crews were not given cooperation and consideration by personnel on Navy ships.

The davit operator dropped the DUKW to the water. I descended the ladder and helped Fluegel unhook the sling bridle. Smallwood spun the steering wheel to clear the APA and headed for *LST-354*. I casually saluted as the DUKW pulled away and men aboard the APA waved in return.

The Navy began using whatever ships with medical facilities were available to help handle the larger than expected numbers of casualties. We had received word earlier that the hospital ships were full. The warships usually didn't accept beach casualties because they were either moving, bombarding or could be called into action at any moment. Also, if hit, they would need their medical facilities to take care of their own men.

Usually, many weapons were stacked around first aid stations but I noted that the one on our beach had none. Later, I learned that a casualty went berserk, had grabbed an automatic rifle and sprayed the area with a hail of bullets. After that, weapons were taken from the wounded before they reached the station.

After daylight on D+1, I walked inland from the beach and noticed a Marine sprawled on his stomach. His helmet was still on his head and his rifle was grasped in his outstretched right hand. His left arm was also stretched out. He appeared to be sleeping or that he had stumbled and fell, stunning himself. I walked over to check him. As I bent down to ask if he was okay, I saw a bullet hole in the center of his fore-

The Quack Corps

head. Startled! I straightened up. After hesitating for a few moments, I went on with my errand.

The image of that Marine lying there, as if asleep, continued to bother me. Though realizing there wasn't anything I could do for him, I hoped his body wasn't left until it bloated beyond recognition in the heat. I returned later to see if he was still there. I felt relieved when I found that Graves Registration had collected his body. The thought crossed my mind that the big strapping Marine was now nothing but a memory to his loved ones ... the result of one apparently well-aimed Japanese small-caliber bullet.

Dodging a Marine's body floating offshore occasionally didn't leave the vivid mental impression that particular man did—most didn't look that peaceful in death.

On D+1, the Japanese were shelling the beach again and I crouched behind an Army armored AmTrac. It and its crew rode our LST to Saipan. Its commander, an Army sergeant, was an arrogant braggart. During a bull session, he told a group of us, "We are going to show you Marines how to really fight."

"I'm from Missouri and you'll have to show me," I retorted.

One gun on the first fairly high hill inland from the beach had been giving us fits. Navy ships had made a stab at it, dive bombers and fighters had worked the position over, but the gun continued harassing us. The Army sergeant kept muttering, "Why doesn't somebody get that gun?"

Here was my chance to see whether his backbone matched his mouth, because we had heard far too much of it on the ship. To my knowledge, his AmTrac hadn't turned a tread since hitting the beach. So I turned to him, "Why in hell did you bring that tank ashore if you didn't intend to use it? Why don't *you* take your crew and go get that gun yourself?"

He looked at me with a startled expression for a moment and then replied, "I think I will." He gathered his crew and

Saipan!

they climbed into the armored AmTrac and took off. I didn't know where they went but they didn't get the gun—it continued harassing us for several more hours.

The gun was finally put out of action late that day or very early the next morning. Later, while DUKWs were being unloaded near its site, I walked up the rest of the hill to take a look at the emplacement. The Japanese had dug a hole just below the crest of the hill, on the beach side, taking advantage of a small grove of trees to help provide camouflage. Dirt was piled up around the emplacement. Setting on the edge of the gun pit was a Marine armored AmTrac, its gun pointed directly at the Jap gun. The barrel of the Jap gun was pointing at the AmTrac; the vehicle had a huge hole in its side. I judged that the guns had fired simultaneously because both were demolished.

D+1, I again caught the last shift on the LST. This time, the driver of the last DUKW loaded either didn't know he was to be the last or forgot to pass the word to me. I fumed when I realized that I had been left aboard. Sometime after dark, I was leaning against the rail and a huge explosion erupted north of Charan Kanoa. A gale force wind hit the ship. The elation caused by the belief that a friendly gun had taken out a Jap ammo dump was deflated when I later learned that the shoe had been on the other foot, because it was an American dump in the 2d Marine Division area.

As night approached on D+2, Army personnel moved just inland from my beach position. The Army 27th Division had been held in reserve during the initial landing. Resistance was tougher than expected and was taking its toll on the Marine divisions so the Army units were moving ashore.

Shortly after dark, I heard small-caliber fire in the area where I had seen the Army personnel. The next morning I learned that the soldiers had been moving above ground in the dark and were fired on by friendly forces, resulting in several casualties among the Army personnel. A Marine informed me

The Quack Corps

that the soldiers had used the previous day's password when challenged. The Japs attempted infiltration sometimes by using our previous day's password. To help forestall its use, the password was changed every day.

The same afternoon that the Army units came ashore, Corp. Harry Mefford, PFC George Tolar and I dug a circular foxhole on the ocean side of the beach tree line. We felt a round hole would give us better protection, since Jap planes filtering through our defenses could come from any direction to bomb or strafe the beach area. We laid one row of sandbags around the rim to help prevent sand from filtering back into the hole.

When we secured for the night, Tolar was on the left, Mefford in the center and I was on the right. I stuck the tip of my KaBar knife into the sand by my right hip; that position enabled me to grab it quickly if needed during the night. The firing at the Army personnel made us edgy because we didn't know but what the Japs were trying to infiltrate to the beach. In the faint light, we could barely see the remnants of palm trees that were still standing and silhouetted against the sky.

Several minutes after the firing had occurred, I felt something fall on my feet. Carefully, I slipped my hand to the handle of the KaBar and grasped it snugly, and as Colonel Biddle (a famous Marine knife expert) had taught back in my 6th Regiment days, with the top edge of the blade snuggled against my forearm and its point towards my elbow. Trying not to tip off our visitor with even a twitch in my feet or legs, I cautiously raised my upper body. At first, I couldn't see anything but, as my eyes adjusted to the darkness inside the hole, I could see that a sandbag had fallen off the rim. I glanced at Mefford. He was laying rigidly with the whites of his wide-open eyes glistening in the light reflected from the sky. "It was just a sandbag fell down, Mefford," I whispered. He chuckled once but didn't make any reply.

Saipan!

A Jap could have knocked it off the edge crawling by so I carefully scanned the area around the hole. I didn't see anything to confirm it and after listening carefully for several minutes, reached down and replaced the sandbag. Relaxing after the scare, I too could chuckle because neither Tolar nor Mefford had moved a muscle until after I whispered about the sandbag.

The next day Corp. Stanley Donham, of the maintenance platoon, and I were in a bull session sitting on the sand at the beach tree line. He was leaning back against a palm tree stump smoking his pipe. The Japs began another barrage and I rolled into a shell hole beside me. When he didn't join me, I raised my head to check on him. He was still relaxing against the stump calmly puffing on his pipe. "Donham! Damn't! It's a hell of a lot safer in this hole!" He continued gazing out over the ocean. He had been on Guadalcanal during that invasion and must have become fatalistic about artillery fire—I wondered if he really had that much courage or had an unconscious desire to die.

Fear of shrapnel didn't affect most men nearly as much as the awesome fright and almost panic caused when word flashed through the beach area, "The Japs are using Gas!" I was in a DUKW approaching the beach and about halfway in from the coral reef, when I noticed men scurrying frantically about on the beach; I wondered if the Japs had broken through our lines. AmTracs and DUKWs along the beach headed out to sea, and as one of the DUKWs passed its crew yelled, "Gas! Gas!" I had given thought to the possibility that Japan, in its desperate attempt to stop American advances, might turn to its use. But, I had discounted the possibility because they had much more to lose. After all, we had ships to take us away and they were trapped on the islands.

"Head for the ships offshore!" I yelled to the driver. After reaching the nearest ship with any size, I hailed the bridge, explained the situation on the beach, and requested every spare

The Quack Corps

mask they had aboard. The hastily accumulated pile on the DUKW's floorboards was pitifully small. With time of the essence and the next ship too far out, I decided to take what we had to the beach. Part way in, word came over my radio that it had been a false alarm. We returned the masks to the ship, with our profuse thanks.

Gas, the weapon of war that most of us feared the most, prompted a frantic search for working gas masks. Despite all of the many amphibious landing exercises we'd undergone, apparently no one had learned what saltwater would do to an unprotected gas mask. The masks issued to 2d DUKW's personnel for the Marianas invasion were not sealed in waterproof pouches. In subsequent invasions, our masks were in sealed pouches but I don't know whether other units had them prior to the Saipan invasion. In any event, many of the men had discarded or lost their masks. Few serviceable masks could be found on the beach because I made it a point to test several after getting ashore. A man had two choices: breathe deadly gases or smother because no air could be sucked through the filters. After that incident, *all* kept their gas masks handy.

The false alarm had occurred when Japanese photography chemicals stored in a cave exploded. The Marines satchel charging the cave didn't recognize the odor. They took no chances and passed the word.

In addition to shrapnel and gas scares, a Jap sniper got in the act. He'd fire a round and then remain quiet while many pairs of eyes searched for him. He couldn't be in a tree for shelling had shredded the foliage from them. It was well into the next day before anyone discovered his hiding place. He had climbed to a hole near the top of the sugar mill smokestack in Charan Kanoa and sniped from it. Once his hiding place was discovered, he was quickly eliminated.

The stresses of war often caused men to pick up bad habits and cure some as well. As a fingernail biter, my extreme

Saipan!

nervousness on the invasion beach only added to my habit. I was sitting on a fallen palm tree eating a K-ration when I looked at the ground and saw little pieces of a human body mixed with the sandy dirt. The body had been between two palm tree stumps and the vehicles had to go between them when moving inland from the beach. Afterwards, whenever I got the urge to bite my nails, I remembered the incident and stopped because I didn't know what might be mixed with the dirt under them. By the time the island was secured, I had conquered that habit.

With the unloading of 14th Marine supplies completed, Second DUKW became jacks-of-all-trades. The company hauled ammunition, water, rations and other supplies to infantry units; supplied the 75mm batteries; kept the tanks in gas and ran other errands.

As a result of their diverse activities, the DUKW men had a better overall picture of how the battle was going than most. They were a pipeline of information for the men aboard the supply ships who could only watch from afar and wonder what it was like on the beach and how the battle was going.

I rode along when two DUKWs took loads for dumping on the hill below the emplacement where the Jap gun had harassed us the first couple of days. During unloading, a sniper opened fire and we hit a nearby ditch. Stretched out and scanning higher on the hill to try to locate him, I glanced into the sky. American and Jap fighter planes were having a free-for-all over the ocean beyond Aslito Airfield. I rolled over onto my back to watch as they turned, dived, climbed and performed various other drastic maneuvers while striving for the kill or to avoid it. They were too far away for me to identify whether a particular plane was Japanese or American.

Smoke streamed behind one of the planes. It went into a long curving dive, headed in my direction, then banked away. I felt elated when I noted a red ball under its wing. A huge ball of flame and smoke erupted when it crashed near Aslito. The

The Quack Corps

fight was fast and furious. I saw only one parachute floating down. It wasn't the usual white. The distance was too great for me to see its color but it appeared to be black.

I knew who had won that fight when a flight of planes formed up and headed in the general direction of Tinian. I recognized the silhouettes of Hellcats and Corsairs, as they appeared to be disdainfully departing in triumph from the air space of battle.

Since Marine DUKWs were involved in their first invasion, combat photographers made frequent appearances. As the platoon passed a side road, one had his jeep parked and was snapping pictures as the DUKWs passed on the dusty road. As usual, the men on Number-8 were laughingly coaxing each other to "smile at the birdie." A picture of Number-8 later appeared in *Life* magazine and it's also in *Collier's Photographic History of World War II*.

The infantry had advanced far enough that the 75mms could move forward. Preparations to move them with the DUKWs were underway. A Marine was fouling up the detail by driving around in the area in what appeared to be a Jap copy of a 1937 Ford. He was having a ball until all the tires went flat and the car got stuck, blocking the road. It was shoved out of the way and Lieutenant Blackburn ordered him to let it set.

As we moved out, I saw a Marine sitting on a dud 14 or 16-inch battleship's projectile while eating a K-ration. The shell hadn't been defused and I wondered if he realized just one more jar or bump might be all it needed to trigger an explosion. "One thing for sure, you dumb bastard, if it explodes, you'll never know about it," I mused.

Delivering supplies to varied units gave the DUKW men the chance for a variety of experiences. Two had an experience they wouldn't forget for awhile. When making a delivery to a frontline unit, one of the Marines in the unit pointed, without being specific, in the direction the supplies were to be taken.

Saipan!

Photo by Lt. Anthony Tesori (Navy)—executive officer *LST–340*
The first DUKW leaving *LST–340* D-Day, Saipan 15 June, 1944.

Photo by Lt. Anthony Tesori (Navy)—executive officer *LST–340*
The first DUKW returning to *LST–340* D-Day, Saipan 15 June, 1944.

The Quack Corps

U.S. Marine Corps photo
Moving 75mms forward—Saipan. No. 8 DUKW 1st platoon. Corp. Donald Shults driver

U.S. Marine Corps photo
Destroyed city of Garapan—Saipan. July 1944.

Saipan!

U.S. Marine Corps photo
DUKWs alongside off-loading cargo ship—Saipan. June 1944

U.S. Navy photo
Charan Kanoa (note sugar mill smokestack)—Blue and Yellow Beaches—Tinian in background.

The Quack Corps

The DUKW moved forward and its crew unloaded it in a small draw. As they headed for the rear, a lieutenant in the unit stopped the driver and wanted to know exactly where the crew had unloaded. After the driver described the location, the lieutenant exploded, "Hell! We haven't taken that ground yet! You dropped it in enemy territory!" In later trips, the driver made absolutely certain that he knew which was enemy and which was friendly territory.

Corporal Vernon Bowman and his assistant would long remember a delivery they made to a frontline infantry platoon. Four members of the platoon had been killed. Their buddies hadn't been able to take or send their bodies to the rear. As a result, the bodies had lain on stretchers putrefying in the heat. The platoon leader requested that the DUKW crew take them back. They laid the stretchers across the cargo space. The smell was overpowering so Bowman rode on the bow with his assistant doing the driving. As they headed for the rear, a noise drew their attention skyward and they found themselves staring into the bores of a strafing Zero's winking guns. The DUKW skidded to a quick stop. Bowman dived off the bow into a Japanese foxhole with his assistant piling in on top of him. The Jap holes were smaller than ours so it made for a tight squeeze. Fortunately, the quick stop didn't dump the bodies off the stretchers, nevertheless, it took many scrubbings to deodorize the DUKW.

One of the DUKW men had a buddy in Intelligence who kept us up to date in that field. He passed the word, and asked us to spread it, that Intelligence was desperate for Jap prisoners to interrogate. Only a day or so later, the grapevine flashed the word that the bodies of two Marines were found on Mt. Tapotchau with arms and legs cut off and laid across their chests. The deadly anger permeating the air seemed thick enough that it could be cut with a knife—we didn't hear any requests for Jap prisoners for awhile.

Saipan!

Later, he told us of a conversation he had had with a Jap prisoner. The prisoner related his impressions of the landing. One of his most vivid impressions was of the big ships arriving offshore, their fronts opening and little ships coming out of them, sailing to shore and, without stopping, coming right up on land. Then the little ships sailed back out to the big ships and again, without stopping, went inside them. His description of the little ships made it obvious that he was talking about DUKWs.

Chapter 12
Moving forward on Saipan

After moving the 75mms forward, the 1st platoon also moved up. The platoon's new bivouac was on the hill where I had watched the aerial dogfight. The 75mms were about 100 yards to the north and northeast in the tree line bordering a sloping sugarcane field. The field wasn't level, but it at least gave enough room for the DUKWs to disperse better than they had in the beach area. Without vegetation for concealment, they were completely exposed to the eyes of any Japs looking our way, particularly those on Tinian.

The first night after the platoon's move, I decided to sleep in something other than my filthy dungarees; my spare pair had gone down when the 1st platoon DUKW had sunk on our first run to the beach. As darkness fell, I stripped to skivvies and stretched out on my blanket on the floorboards of a DUKW. My sack wasn't as soft as the dirt of my foxhole a few yards away but the surroundings were cleaner.

Tinian lay to the south, about four miles of open water separated it from Saipan. At times, Tinian's gunners added the projectiles from their guns to those spewing from Jap guns on Saipan.

Shortly after dark the first night in the new bivouac, I heard the moan of incoming rounds; they appeared to be coming from Tinian. As they neared, I heard the now familiar wuffle as some passed just overhead, then the sharp crack as they hit cane stalks still standing in the field.

Oh, God! They're really going to work us over now, I thought, because the rounds were hitting all around and in the 1st platoon's bivouac. Instinctively, I tried imbedding my body through the DUKW's wooden floorboards to more safety on

Moving Forward on Saipan

the ground below. More *splats!* as projectiles hit cane stalks. My body tensed awaiting the explosions but ... the noise of explosions and the whistle of shrapnel didn't come. The waiting was even more nerve wracking than exploding shells.

I searched frantically in the darkness for my dungarees. I would be completely exposed to shrapnel as I went over the gunwale and without dungarees, I'd really be caught with my pants down! I didn't find them so grabbed my blanket and went over the side at the first lull. *It was the only night I ever spent in a foxhole in skivvies.*

The Jap gunners were using armor piercing, or had failed to set the fuses, or they were using faulty ammunition because not one of those shells exploded.

I knew I'd be ribbed unmercifully by the men for bailing out of the DUKW in skivvies. So, at the break of dawn, I wrapped in a blanket and slunk back to the DUKW. I sat on the floorboards while donning the dungarees.

In a bull session with one of the 75mm Marines that morning, he laughingly told me about the unit's C.O. boiling out of his foxhole when a dud landed between his outstretched legs.

A couple of days later, enough of the most critically needed supplies had been brought ashore and we knocked off shortly after mid-afternoons because of the progressively higher surf. It gave us time to catch our breath, rest, and explore the area.

I was more interested in checking out Japanese equipment and buildings than looking for the usual souvenirs of war, nevertheless, some would be accumulated.

Shortly after its capture, Corp. Darwin "Nick" Nicholson and Corp. Donald "Dutch" Shults accompanied me to take a look at Aslito Airfield. American planes had begun using it right away. We looked at the demolished buildings and disabled Japanese airplanes. While checking out a building some distance from the runway, we found a Japanese three-wheel

The Quack Corps

motorcycle. I wondered why some playful Marine hadn't already "captured" it.

The motorcycle was designed for fire fighting, with a siren, bell, and a rack over the motor for coiled hose. A step at the rear allowed a couple of firemen to ride on back. The motor looked like a Straight-8 Oldsmobile engine [I was later advised that it was probably a Continental].

Nick was a happy-go-lucky little man who had boxed professionally in civilian life. He had owned a motorcycle and because he had cycle experience, Dutch and I decided to let him drive.

We checked it thoroughly for booby traps and then pushed it off the hill to try to start it. The motor turned over and began purring after a short distance and we were on our way.

Dutch and I hung on as Nick sped down the road. Part way back to camp we met a tank and infantry unit moving to the front. We realized that we didn't stand a chance in a game of chicken with the tanks and pulled off the road, parked, and waited for them to pass.

While waiting, we talked to the Marines who were walking single file on each side of the road. They had been pulled off the front for a rest and now were heading back to battle. At first, they were reluctant to talk for most front line men felt disdain for men whose duties kept them in rear areas. I knew they thought we were rear echelon'ers out copping the goodies while they did the dirty work. Apparently, they had been supplied by 2d DUKW because they loosened up after learning we were DUKW men.

I had a soft spot for Marines in infantry because they had the toughest lot. Also, many of them had little time to live.

Though we hadn't been buddies, one of the walking Marines recognized me from 6th Regiment days, in 1940/41. He had a good memory for faces because mine was partly concealed by my helmet but, maybe, he recognized my voice.

Moving Forward on Saipan

After the tanks had passed, we resumed our trip back to the bivouac turning on the siren and ringing the bell while bouncing across the cane field to the DUKW parking area. The men gathered around to inspect our prize.

The motorcycle was heavy and the rough terrain caused the front wheel spring forks to break quite often. This happened at least a half-dozen times and each time, we headed for the maintenance platoon area so the welders could repair them.

Lieutenant Blackburn liked to use our cycle, supposedly to run official errands. He borrowed it so many times that we accused him of hiring out for messenger duty.

The motorcycle fit easily into a DUKW's cargo space and we planned to take it along, wherever we went.

I wheeled into camp one day and the downhill wheel hit a wet spot where a DUKW's radiator had been drained. The cycle turned over with me underneath it. Several men ran from their foxholes to check whether I was okay. I crawled, unhurt, from under it. Luckily the handle bars and hose rack had kept the bike from crushing me. The men helped me set it back on its wheels. The mishap didn't cause any damage but, after that, I crossed the cane field at a much slower speed. I also kept my eyes peeled for muddy spots.

Only a few days after the landing on Saipan, the Army Island Administration unit moved in. Its C.O. immediately began issuing orders, including one that all captured Japanese vehicles and equipment were to be turned in. Nick, Dutch and I decided the doggies wouldn't get to enjoy our prize and we began to consider ways to keep it out of their hands. I returned to the bivouac one day to discover Nick and Dutch had taken the cycle to the deepest canyon they could find in the secured portion of the island. Nick dismounted, opened the throttle, popped the clutch and the cycle tumbled end-over-end to the bottom. The possibility that American forces could use the cycle for fire fighting didn't cross our minds.

The Quack Corps

On D+4, a new-to-the-island Army unit bivouacked adjacent to the 1st platoon. Dutch, Nick and I thought there must be some way we could have fun at the soldiers' expense and our opportunity came the day after they had settled in.

While scouting a mile or so forward of our bivouac, we ran across a farmhouse and spread out to approach it, with carbines cocked and ready. Japs didn't contest our advance and, carefully eyeballing for booby traps, we checked out the building. It was packed with Japanese goods; the military was using it as a storehouse. Among the goods were about two dozen cases of sake, with each bottle encased in straw; huge cartons of Jap Marine shoes, with about 50 pairs loose-packed in each; and stacks of large cardboard cartons filled with Japanese cigarettes.

We began choosing goods to take to the bivouac. We were very selective; if a case of Sake had even one bottle broken, we tossed it aside. Three cases were enough for me and Nick and Dutch took several. Nick and I stood guard over the booty so others wouldn't appropriate it while Dutch returned to camp for a DUKW.

Nick suggested that the Army unit might like some souvenirs. We knew they hadn't had the chance to get any of their own. But, the souvenirs should show our disdain for the Army. The shoes were extra-wide widths and extremely small sizes so we decided to take one case along. We'd soften the blow just a little by taking them cigarettes. Chances were they wouldn't guess that we thought smoking Japanese cigarettes probably tasted like smoking horse manure.

Dutch stopped the DUKW at the edge of the Army's bivouac and Nick yelled, "Hey! Do you guys want some souvenirs?" Many of the soldiers stopped what they were doing and headed for the DUKW. Nick and I each grabbed a carton and heaved it over the side. Dutch shoved the DUKW in gear and sped away, since we were not sure how they would react when they saw what we had delivered.

Moving Forward on Saipan

We had taken things that no longer had an owner but others didn't operate that way. Our seabags were left on the LSTs when the company debarked. The ships had to leave, because of a possible Jap sea-air attack, so the Navy brought the seabags ashore and stacked them on the beach. When a company work detail picked them up, they found many had been slit open and keepsakes and valuables stolen. Apparently, the thieves were scared off before getting to the 1st platoon's stack since its seabags were not molested.

As the Americans secured more of the island, the first platoon moved to the top of a little hill almost midway up the island. By now, some of us had finagled canvas folding cots because we could stash them in the sterns of the DUKWs. If we felt a bivouac might be in use for some time, we dug our foxholes large enough for two cots. A DUKW tarp served as a roof so we'd stay dry during rains. We trenched under the drip edge of the tarp, but sometimes it rained so hard that water ran into our holes, almost reaching the canvas bottoms of the cots. In any event, we were fighting the war in style because not many combat units could brag about having their seabags along and also sleeping on cots in foxholes.

A Japanese storage dump was across the canyon from our bivouac. Nick and Dutch crossed the canyon to see what the Japs had stored there. I could see them picking up gear and either throwing it aside or into a pile, which I assumed they intended to bring to the bivouac. When they started back across the canyon, I walked to the edge and waited for them. "Nick, what are you lugging back to camp now?" I called.

"Parachutes!"

"Parachutes! What the hell are you going to do with them? They're too bulky for souvenirs and we're sure not going to jump out of any airplanes."

"If nothing else, we'll throw them in our holes to soak up some of the mud," he countered. Apparently, they were made

The Quack Corps

of silk because they didn't soak up much of the mud and water in our hole.

We thought the terrain bordering our bivouac looked interesting and decided to scout it. Rough, high terrain bordered the south edge and we headed for it first. Dutch and I were on the lower slope of a hill and Nick was about 50 yards higher in a steep area. "Hey! Come up here!" he yelled.

"Why?" I asked.

"There's a big cave opening! Come on up and let's check it out!"

"Nick, it's too dangerous for us to go sticking our noses in caves!"

"Come on up and take a look!" he replied.

Dutch and I resisted Nick's urging that we enter the cave with him. The risks were high because Japs may still be in it or they may have entered after the Marine infantry units pushed through.

"Nick, Japs may be in there. It's too dangerous and I think we'd be foolish to go in," I forcefully reminded him.

"I'm going in whether you guys go with me or not," he replied. He was a nervy little man but at times foolhardy.

Hoping that he might not enter alone, Dutch and I informed him that we were going back to camp. "Go ahead. I'm still going to check it out," he stated. With that statement, I figured it wouldn't do any good to order him not to enter, because he'd just secretly return to check it out. Dutch and I decided we would try to give him some protection and took up positions behind large rocks in front of the 15-foot high opening. Both of us knew there was little we could do to help if Japs *were* in the cave.

The entrance showed no evidence of shelling or the use of other explosives. That heightened my fears as Nick began making his way down the slope to the entrance, periodically climbing over clusters of three and four foot high rock piles, until reaching the bottom of the slope about 25 yards from us.

Moving Forward on Saipan

He turned and looked back then waved and entered the darkness.

Dutch and I waited ... tense, barely breathing, our carbines aimed at the dark opening with fingers on the triggers. I breathed a prayer that he wouldn't be shot. Silhouetted against the light, it would have been impossible to rescue him if he got hit without the loss of other men.

Time stretched into minutes ... then we saw movement in the light filtering into the cave entrance. We became even more tense until we saw that it was Nick emerging from the darkness. He was lugging a large leather valise in each hand. Dutch and I kept our positions while he slowly made his way up the rocky slope to us.

He had found the bodies of a Japanese officer, a woman and two enlisted men in the cave depths. Based on the appearance of their bodies, Nick felt that they had committed *hari-kari*.

Apparently, the cave was used by the island paymaster because each valise was bulging with sen and yen. In addition to the money, one of the valises contained maps and a few Japanese military medals, including one Order of the Rising Sun. The other valise also contained pornographic photographs. Nick had also removed a fancy, obviously expensive, watch off an enlisted man's wrist.

The Order of the Rising Sun was beautiful, with three rubies, each about the size of a dime, mounted in silver ... It was appraised about 30 years later by a Chicago, Illinois, jeweler at $1,800.00.

The maps showed fortifications and another island. Even though we couldn't read Japanese, we knew that one map was of Saipan because we recognized the locations of certain gun emplacements. Though we had seen Tinian only from a distance, we felt that another map must be of it. We realized that Nick had made an important find and felt elated. The map of Saipan was valuable because it showed fortifications in the

The Quack Corps

uncaptured portion. The one we thought was Tinian would be of extreme value when and if American forces invaded it. Upon returning to camp, I ordered Nick to take them to Lieutenant Blackburn at once. The lieutenant assured him that he'd deliver them to Intelligence immediately.

I felt better about the risks Nick had taken. Nevertheless, I'd make every effort to keep our little scouting force away from areas that gave him opportunities to enter caves.

American forces used currency good only for use in Pacific areas and we assumed that the Japanese money was good only in the Marianas. Later, I learned that it was the same as the currency used in the Japanese home islands.

With our assumption that it was worthless, except for souvenirs, we lined our foxhole with the currency. It didn't soak up mud and water any better than the parachutes had. One valise was still almost full so Dutch and I each took a small quantity and Nick kept the rest.

Our first-priority duty was to prime move the 105mm batteries, and sometimes the 75mms, and to keep them supplied so each of the operating platoons bivouacked near the battery it was servicing. While not busy with those units, the platoons performed jacks-of-all-trades duties. Each operating platoon worked independently and usually bivouacked by itself so each was responsible for its own defense. Higher command's assignment of experienced line-rate NCOs to the company proved of much benefit in setting up defense perimeters.

Scuttlebutt spread the word that the Army took *everything* along on an invasion. Accustomed to the sparseness and basicness of Marine supplies, the men were flabbergasted when they saw the quantities of goodies destined for certain U.S. Army units, though their front line units lived and ate like the Marine units. Food destined for medical facilities was out of bounds, but the men made a practice of taking a share when hauling for the Island Administration and the Army Air Corps.

Moving Forward on Saipan

When the 1st platoon had moved to the bivouac on the little hill, the supply of appropriated food almost filled a DUKW's cargo space. The cache included fruit cocktail, canned roast beef and other tasty foods not supplied in our field rations. So, to supplement the usual K or C-rations, I ate over half a Number-10 can of fruit cocktail in one setting.

We had to wolf the roast beef, even though piping hot, because the huge green-bodied flies swarmed like bees around our mess kits; we had to keep one hand in constant motion to keep them off the beef. We also had to be certain that the beef went from mess kit to mouth quickly, otherwise, the flies attacked it en route. Though we called them sugarcane flies, we had seen them swarm over dead bodies—the thought of that would have usually made me squeamish but, by now unless the smell was overpowering, I ate near dead bodies but with my back turned.

Possibly the diet supplements helped prevent the 1st platoon men from being wracked with diarrhea because none reported suffering with it. In my case, I didn't have to use a can in the hole or crawl away from it in the darkness even one night to answer an *urgent* call of nature.

Later, the pickings became slimmer because the platoon wasn't hauling many of the goodies. But some of the men kept our supply in good shape by using a damaged DUKW from one of the other platoons for food raids on an Army dump.

The rear wheels on one side of the DUKW had caught in a coral reef crevice during the early stages of the landing so it had to be abandoned. Later, an enemy shell blew a large hole in its starboard bow, destroying the air compressor but causing surprisingly little damage to the radiator. After salvaging and restoring it to running order, we used the DUKW on land only, since the hole in its bow obviously made it unseaworthy.

Second DUKW had some imaginative and ingenious men and one of them devised a system for using the DUKW for food raids. While one man distracted the supply dump sentry,

The Quack Corps

the driver made a slow turn around the heaped-up supplies and a man posted in the bow took a share of whatever he felt the Army had in surplus. Marines could usually find a way to justify any action and, this time, used the excuse that the dump might be destroyed in an air raid and the food wouldn't benefit anybody!

The front had moved forward so the 1st platoon moved farther north. The new area had only enough room for part of the 14th Marine 105mm batteries so the others took up positions farther back.

Only once since leaving the beach area had the 1st platoon bivouacked adjacent to one of 2d DUKW's other platoons. This time, the 1st was again alone in a bivouac located to the northeast of Mt. Tapotchau and near Magicienne Bay.

The bivouac was bordered on the south by a small cane field, on the west by a dirt road along the edge of a large canyon, on the north by a large Jap-excavated pit and on the east by the 105mm battery.

Word was passed that the Japs had infiltrated some of the rear-area units the previous night and appeared to be moving north. As an extra precaution, three men occupied each of the 1st platoon's foxholes. Sergeant Mac, who usually didn't join in group bull sessions and who the men considered to be a loner, began digging his hole in a small ditch under a coconut tree; it also was a few yards outside our defense perimeter. I cautioned him about being outside the perimeter but he insisted that he planned to hole up there. Assuming he'd have second thoughts, I went on with my duties and didn't give it any more thought. When darkness approached, I noted that he had ignored my strong warning.

Shortly after falling asleep, I was awakened by a loud noise. Nick had the first watch so I whispered, "Nick, what was that?"

"I don't know but it came from the direction of Mac's hole," he whispered a reply.

Moving Forward on Saipan

I strained to hear in the darkness but didn't hear anything indicating a struggle. Mac, damn you! I fumed, you may be laying there hurt and unable to call for help and a man could die coming to check because you didn't listen to me.

I felt certain that a Jap had paid him a visit. Worried that he had been bayoneted or knifed and could be bleeding to death, my conscience got the best of my judgment so I decided to check on him, though I had given orders for everyone to stay in their holes after dark, regardless. I grasped my KaBar but before I could whisper to the nearest hole that I was coming out, I heard a rustling in the little ditch; it sounded like it was heading toward a perimeter hole. If Jap, I felt some satisfaction because I knew that the men in the hole had him outnumbered. I continued to listen and shortly the rustling stopped at where I judged the perimeter hole to be, but I couldn't hear any sounds of a struggle.

I crouched in the hole and speculated about the rustling noise. Moments later, I heard loud whispering and stifled laughter in the perimeter hole. I decided I'd better quiet them down and then check on Mac. After passing the word that I was coming out, I made my way to the perimeter hole and gave the proper password. "What's going on? You men be quiet. I could hear you clear over in my hole," I reprimanded.

"Mac's here. I'll tell you about it in the morning," came a whispered reply.

The next day, I learned that a coconut had fallen off the tree and hit Mac's steel helmet. Startled, he had bailed out of his hole and scrabbled down the ditch looking for friendly company. The men had been laughing because as he crawled down the ditch, he kept repeating, "It's me, Mac! It's me, Mac!" in whispers. He didn't need to be cautioned again about loneing it in a hole.

In addition to Nick, Corp. Orval "Smitty" Smith had shared the night with me in the hole. At dawn, small arms fire awakened me. Nick had disappeared and Smitty was sitting on the bottom of the foxhole, peering out the end of the DUKW tarp. "Smitty, what's going on?" I asked.

"There are Japs in the area," he replied, without turning his head.

I grabbed my carbine, jammed my helmet on my head, attached a bag of hand grenades to my belt, and dashed up the slope to where men were firing into the canyon. "What's happening?" I asked the first man I encountered.

"We've got a bunch of Japs cornered in the canyon," he answered. Edging forward cautiously, I peered into it and saw several 1st platoon men slipping and sliding down the canyon wall, firing at several Japs who were desperately scrambling ahead of them. In moments, the Japs were cut down by the hail of bullets ... some bodies rolled down the steep slope until stopped by rocks or trees.

I glanced across the canyon and saw a lone Jap frantically scrambling up the other side. A skirmish line of Marines had appeared at the top of the far canyon wall. The Jap was about a third of the way up the wall when he spotted them. He reversed course and headed back toward the bottom, running from tree to tree as he searched for a place to hide. He crouched momentarily behind a big rock. Apparently, he decided that it didn't hide him well enough and began to search for a better place.

I estimated the range at about 300 yards and braced my carbine against a tree to draw a bead on him. The carbine was notoriously inaccurate at over 200 yards. He appeared to be unarmed and I knew he wasn't going any place. So I decided not to fire. I probably wouldn't hit him but I'd still have to clean the damned carbine again. I had requalified in 1943 as a sharpshooter with the M-1 Garand but the little carbine was a different kettle of fish. In the meantime, Corp. Harold Reynolds, a BAR man [Browning Automatic Rifle], had braced his weapon against the other side of the tree trunk. "Let him have

Moving Forward on Saipan

it!" I commanded. The BAR chattered in a short burst and the Jap tumbled to the ground and lay still.

The DUKW men were checking to insure that all the Japs were dead, so my attention switched back to the Marines advancing down the opposite canyon wall. One of them stopped by the Jap that Reynolds had shot, rolled him over with his foot, looked at the body for a few moments and then resumed advancing with his unit to the canyon floor.

One of the Marines making the sweep walked off from the others. He stopped and looked down at something. He retreated for a few yards and threw a grenade at the object. A large explosion erupted, hurling him through the air. He lay where he landed, motionless, and I couldn't tell from my vantage point whether he was dead or merely stunned. His buddies carried him out of the canyon on a stretcher. He had thrown the grenade into a hole filled with other explosives because the explosion was far larger than that caused by a grenade. He was with an infantry unit bivouacked across the canyon from us. Sounds of the firefight had drawn their attention.

The Jap had reminded me of a cornered animal as he scurried frantically to find a safe place to hide. Surprising to me, I momentarily felt compassion for him. Realistically, I didn't doubt that he would have killed me had he had the chance.

I waited at the edge of the canyon, watching, while some of the men searched dead Japs for whatever information and souvenirs they could find. Several climbed the canyon wall waving Japanese battle flags with big grins on their faces. And Corp. William H. W. Carr had added to his collection two sabers taken off Japanese officers.

Fortunately, the enemy soldiers were not heavily armed because the charge down the canyon wall by the men had been undisciplined. The Japs appeared to be more interested in escaping rather than making a stand for a fight to the death. They had died anyway because 72 fell in that canyon, without a single DUKW man being killed or wounded. They may have

The Quack Corps

been service troops who had been cut off south of Aslito Airfield and headed north to rejoin the Japanese forces there. Probably, they had accidentally stumbled into our bivouac.

The men felt they had become Marines to kill Japs and they hadn't had many chances, so they took advantage of the opportunity. They were also getting revenge for the many snipers' bullets fired at them, Zero strafings, and for the time spent cringing in holes while mortar or artillery shells, or bombs, sought to find them.

At dawn, one of the men had walked across the road to the edge of the canyon to urinate. He spotted the Japs looking for cover for the daylight hours. He passed the word to the nearest foxholes and the battle began. But, it hadn't been a battle, it had been a slaughter.

I felt disturbed that the enemy could get so close without the men on watch detecting them. After things calmed down, I asked some questions. Corporal Harry Mefford commanded the men in a DUKW with a .50-caliber machine gun mounted on the ring over the assistant driver's seat, at a perimeter post in the cane field bordering the south edge of our bivouac. I learned that four of the Japs were spotted walking boldly down the dirt road. He judged it best to not disclose his post's position so didn't open fire.

When I checked with other perimeter hole men, Sgt. Eugene Kalain, a Guadalcanal vet with maintenance but assigned to be with the 1st platoon during the invasion, told me: "I saw one of them. He walked by my hole but at first I thought it was one of our men. When he neared the edge of the pit and was silhouetted against the sky, I could tell he was Jap by the shape of his cap." He hadn't opened fire either because he feared, if he missed, the Jap would jump over the edge of the pit and throw grenades into our holes. As it turned out, Kalain and Mefford made the right decisions.

That afternoon, Lieutenant Blackburn informed me that the platoon was moving in with the 105mm men for the night,

Moving Forward on Saipan

with one DUKW man joining the artillery men in each of the unit's holes. He also advised that Intelligence had passed the word that bypassed Japanese were apparently making a concerted effort to join the main forces in the north.

That night, I occupied a perimeter hole between the 105s and the Japanese lines. After dark, what I took to be a phosphorus shell hit about 25 yards in front of the hole. Phosphorus continues to burn into the flesh after landing on the skin. My fear of burns and the anticipation of more phosphorus shelling got to me because my body began shaking as if with chills. One of my foxhole companions threw me a blanket to add to mine. The second blanket did the trick and the shaking stopped. Later, I had reason to think the onslaught of dengue fever may have been the cause of my reaction, because shellfire or bombing hadn't affected me that way before, nor did it after. The night passed without further incident.

Next morning, I checked where the shell hit and discovered that my phosphorus shell was a starshell that hit the ground before igniting.

As the front moved farther north, the platoon moved forward. By this time, the men had become expert foxhole diggers.

Lieutenant Blackburn sometimes arrived late at the bivouac after a move and we ribbed him that he just didn't like digging holes. Smitty and I finished our hole just before dusk and were settling in for the night when the lieutenant appeared. Traditionally, Lieutenant Blackburn and I had made it a practice to not hole up together since platoon command could be wiped out by one shell. "Do you have room for one more?" he asked. "I just got in and haven't had time to dig my hole," he explained. Then, he tried bribery. "I got my liquor ration today."

"We sure have, Lieutenant!" Smitty responded instantly. By morning, the bottle's contents had disappeared!

The Quack Corps

Smitty and I decided the night had been more pleasant than usual so we made it a practice to make our hole extra wide from then on, just in case. He was a very tall, dark-haired Marine, with an infectious and boisterous laugh, and we always had to dig an extra-long hole anyway.

We moved the 75mms forward and dug our last foxhole when the island was almost secured. The bivouac was adjacent to the rear of the 75mm's perimeter in a relatively flat sugar-cane field.

Smitty and I had borrowed extra shovels from machine gunners adjacent to our bivouac. We returned the shovels and were ambling across the field to our hole. Automatic fire began kicking up dirt around us and we sprinted across the field. Instinctively, I knew the bullets were coming in from higher up, which made the cement wall of a house at the far edge of the field look more promising than the hole. As I sprinted by the hole, I felt something hit my left heel. I didn't break stride but headed for the wall at a speed that would make a track coach feel ecstatic. After belly flopping behind the wall, I caught my breath and checked my heel but didn't find any evidence of a bullet hitting it. Checking later, Smitty and I saw that hundreds of small caliber shells had sprayed the area surrounding our foxhole.

Smitty hadn't joined me behind the wall so I asked, "Where did you go? I didn't look back to check on you. I felt certain a bullet had hit my heel but I didn't even slow down."

"I dived for the hole. As I cut across behind you I hit your heel with my foot," he replied, laughing.

We were positive the automatic fire could have come only from Jap gunners in the high ground ahead of us. But, the next day we learned that a Marine fighter had been strafing into a cave and the pilot didn't cutoff his guns soon enough. He sent his apologies. Miraculously, no DUKW men had been hit nor were any of the DUKWs seriously damaged. And, there were no reports of men being hit in the adjacent units.

Moving Forward on Saipan

During the battle for Saipan, I took advantage of every opportunity to eat hot meals on ships. One small ship in particular is remembered very well. I boarded over the stern by reaching up and grasping a sailor's hand to be hauled aboard; the DUKW crew remained in the vehicle. As I set foot on deck, the captain called from the bridge to inquire whether we were hungry. My answer, that we hadn't had a hot meal for several days, was truthful. The galley was just under the bridge. He yelled down to order the cook to fix each of us a steak with all the trimmings.

I thanked him and walked into the galley and began to talk with the cook. "I don't want to impose on you to cook steaks. You've already cleaned up after morning chow and you'll get the range greasy. Do you have other chow already prepared that you can just heat up for us?" I offered.

"Sergeant, what are you trying to do, insult me? I become very insulted when someone thinks I don't know how to fry steaks without getting the range greasy." he joshed.

"Sailor, this is one sergeant who doesn't believe in insulting people," I bantered in reply.

He proceeded to cook the steaks and added whole eggs and potatoes to the menu. I was accustomed by now to eating only powdered eggs, and I felt the captain must really have drag to have whole eggs on his small ship. I guessed they had been obtained from a cargo ship that was heading stateside. After eating, I hailed the bridge, "Thank you, sir. It was a delicious treat."

"I'm glad you enjoyed it, Sergeant. Good luck on the beach." I snapped a casual salute in his direction and re-boarded the DUKW.

I boarded small Navy ships in a non-G.I. way but stuck to regulations when boarding warships. I boarded the heavy cruiser *Indianapolis* in hopes that I could get a clean pair of dungarees from a member of her Marine Detachment. With

The Quack Corps

my spare pair on the ocean floor off Saipan, by now I was feeling, and no doubt smelling, very raunchy.

When the DUKW neared the ship, I hailed the bridge through a cardboard megaphone for permission to come alongside and stated my purpose when questioned. Boarding by way of a small at-anchor gangway forward, I saluted the Colors, then the officer standing at the head of the gangway and requested permission to come aboard. He granted permission. A Marine platoon sergeant on deck took me in tow and we headed for the Marine Compartment.

After reaching the compartment, a Marine of about my size dug a new set of dungarees out of his locker. I pointed out that he should keep those and give me his old set by kidding, "I don't want it to look like I'm just landing when I return to the beach." With the deal made, the platoon sergeant loaned me a towel so I could take a shower before changing. "It's chow time. Come on and I'll get you to the head of the line." Unless Corporal or Sergeant of the Guard while seagoing, I hadn't dragged a chow line. This time, the long line of sailors just looked me over with curiosity. Undoubtedly, as I had learned seagoing, the grapevine had spread the word that a Marine had come aboard from the hell hole of Saipan.

The detachment Marine hadn't wanted anything for the dungarees. Though it had a broken stem, I insisted that he take my watch, a 21-jewel Bulova, I had bought on *Pennsylvania*. My name was engraved on the back. In peacetime, he wouldn't have dared have anything with another's name on it without his service record showing that he had permission to have it. I knew he could probably get it repaired on the ship. He was reluctant to take it but I pointed out that I'd eventually lose it out of my pocket. The watch reflected light if worn on my wrist, heightening my chances to be wounded or killed. I've always wondered whether that watch went to the bottom with *Indianapolis* when she was sunk some 14 months later.

Moving Forward on Saipan

While aboard, I looked the ship over with interest because I could have had a berth in her after Sea School graduation, in the spring of 1941. I had also felt nostalgia for the cleanliness of shipboard living.

When the battle for Saipan ended on 9 July, 1944, the platoon joined the rest of 2d DUKW in a bivouac on the hill where the dud shelling had occurred. This time, the company was on the other side of the crest, in a flat spot near the top.

For the first time since leaving Maui, Second DUKW's personnel were in the same camp. Now, the company could take inventory of its total losses during the campaign. Maybe the superstitious men in the company had been right in feeling that the humpback whales at Maui had been our guardian angels, because the company's losses were miraculously light ... only two men killed and 13 wounded. Also, 2d DUKW had had a substantial number of vehicles destroyed or put out of action, some of which were salvaged and put back into service.

Killed in Action:
    PFC John B. Ray, Jr.
    Pvt. Harold A. Reed

Wounded in Action:
Corp. Fred Bay, Sr.	PFC Harlow M. Lunney
Corp. Adrian T. Best., Jr.	Corp. Earl G. Murphy
PFC Phillip P. Chapman	Corp. Orville Podoll
Pvt. Clarence E. Hawkins	Sgt. Edward Sanders
PFC Donald C. Laitsch	PFC Sam H. Threatt, Jr.
PFC Edgar H. Looney	Sgt. Keith H. Walker
Corp. Everett H. Lorenz	

It had been easy for me to tally the 1st platoon's losses. Though I had heard of some, I didn't know the total for the rest of the company. Now, I would hear the details, and have some laughs while listening to the men's tales.

The Quack Corps

Added to the two 1st platoon DUKWs sunk offshore D-Day, June 15, Captain George's and a maintenance platoon DUKW were hit on the beach by enemy shells only moments after the men had bailed out to take cover. Later, Sgt. Edgar Bacon, maintenance platoon, sent a couple of men to salvage what they could. When they returned towing the captain's DUKW, Bacon wondered why they hadn't driven it in. Unbelieving upon being informed that it didn't have a motor, he climbed aboard and opened the motor compartment hatch to see for himself—for fast removal, someone had used a cutting torch to cut motor mounts and other metal connections.

In addition to the DUKW with the hole in its bow, three others had swamped when wheels caught in reef crevices. Two were winched out and put back in use, but only the hull of the other reached shore because the undercarriage had torn loose when an AmTrac jerked the DUKW off the reef.

On D-Day, Pvt. Odis Batey was refueling his DUKW alongside an LST when the Japanese began shelling the ship. The LST got underway before the DUKW crew could cast off or get the gas cap on, causing water to surge over the stern and into the gas tank. The motor ran for a while then stopped but restarted after the crew drained the carburetor sediment bowl. Shell fragments had damaged the vehicle and it was settling lower and lower into the water. The assistant driver pumped frantically with the emergency hand pump each time the motor stopped but he couldn't keep up with the in-rushing water.

After restarting the motor, the crew pursued the LST while yelling for the ship to stop because the DUKW was sinking. Eventually, the captain agreed but the ship would lay to for only a couple minutes. He passed the word to be ready to bring the DUKW aboard the moment the LST's ramp was down. The DUKW's front wheels caught and pulled the bow onto the ramp but water rushed to the stern causing the undercarriage to catch on the lip of the ramp. An AmTrac was aboard the LST and a cable was hooked to the DUKW. On the first at-

Moving Forward on Saipan

tempt to pull it up the ramp, the LVT'S driver used too high a gear, stalling the motor. On the second try, he gave too much throttle and the tow cable snapped. The DUKW slipped off the ramp and, with its cargo, quickly disappeared beneath the surface.

Also on D-Day, Corp. William Jensen headed his hole-filled DUKW, loaded with casualties, for the ships offshore. Jap gunners fired in excess of 20 rounds at it. The DUKW appeared to be traveling faster than its actual speed and the shells walked seaward ahead of it so none caused any damage. After a ship had taken his casualties aboard, he headed for his platoon's LST. The DUKW's motor had been damaged and it wasn't running well enough to pull it up the ramp and into the LST's tank deck without stalling. Working in tandem, Jensen worked the throttle and restarted the motor when necessary and his assistant driver used the foot and emergency brake to try to prevent the DUKW from slipping off the ramp. Despite their efforts, the DUKW began taking on water over the stern and they bailed out over the bow as the vehicle dropped off the ramp lip. After bailing out, they turned just in time to see the DUKW's bow slip beneath the water.

Late on D-Day, the motor of PFC Wilbur Parsons' DUKW stalled and wouldn't restart. The wind and current were carrying the vehicle inexorably toward Tinian. Frantically waving dungaree jackets and skivvy shirts, he and his assistant were unable to attract attention. Dusk was approaching as the DUKW floated by Saipan's Agingan Point and into the waters separating the two islands. Fortunately, a Navy patrol ship's captain got nosy and decided to investigate. The DUKW crew requested either a tow back to Saipan or that the vehicle be taken aboard for the night. Unable to leave her patrol area or to hoist the DUKW aboard, the ship's captain radioed higher authority for instructions. Since the DUKW was loaded with ammunition, orders were given that the vehicle be sunk so it

The Quack Corps

wouldn't be a hazard to ships or end up at Tinian. The crew used an axe to chop holes in its side causing it to quickly sink.

Many other DUKWs had hull holes caused by small-caliber shells or shrapnel. The crews had stuffed socks or rags into them and continued making runs until they could be patched.

Second DUKW was the first full company to set Marine DUKW wheels on enemy soil when it landed D-Day on Saipan—the First Amphibian Truck Company, attached to the 2d Marine Division, landed on D+1. DUKWs carved their niche in Marine Corps annals during the invasion and, henceforth, they would be a vital part of the Pacific fighting. Their use saved uncountable man-hours of supply handling and relieved beach and rear-area congestion. Often, emergency runs from ship directly to fighting unit had forestalled lack of ammunition with which to fight, water to quench thirst, and gas for thirsty tank motors. Even more important, the versatile hybrids meant quicker and more comfortable transport to better medical care facilities for thousands.

Chapter 13
Rest and Tinian

With the battle for Saipan over, the men set up tents, dug foxholes for use during air raids and cleaned up and burned the trash in the camp area.

Near the new camp, dozens of used condoms were scattered over a small flat area under a tree near the top of the hill. A Japanese prostitute had apparently set up an open-air brothel. I thought it was an odd location and assumed she closed up shop during rains.

I noticed a banana tree alongside a partially demolished building at the edge of camp. During boyhood, almost every nickel or dime I had acquired was spent to buy bananas at the nearest grocery store. Mainly my desire had gone unsatisfied because I seldom came in possession of a silver coin. I waited anxiously for the very small size fruit to ripen—I did get to eat a few before moving from that camp.

With the company in a semi-permanent camp and a daily routine established, the maintenance platoon gave the DUKWs a thorough servicing and made put-off repairs. Men took each vehicle to the area where the mechanics had set up shop. But, the men in the operating platoons did the scraping and painting of the hulls' rust spots.

When I had returned with the three cases of sake during the previous stay on the hill, I had distributed two cases among the men in the 1st platoon. My remaining case was stored in the stern of a DUKW and I locked the hatch cover, but another way to reach the storage area was to remove the wooden floorboards in the cargo space. When that DUKW was returned from maintenance, all but one of the bottles of sake had disappeared. Though investigating over a long period of time, I never found out who had appropriated the others.

The days were rather routine and filled with maintenance work but we could almost always count on some excitement during the night, causing us to dive into foxholes, but not always as the result of Japanese actions. A friendly plane caused interruption of our sleep one night when a C-46 flew over the island. After a dive into my hole before the sirens quit howling, I watched the searchlights pick it up in their brilliant shafts of light. Every anti-aircraft gun on the island must have opened fire. The pilot flicked his running lights but the AA fire didn't slacken. My heart was in my throat because I recognized it as American. The pilot turned on the plane's landing lights and the guns quit firing. Word hadn't been passed quick enough that a friendly was coming in. One gun opened up and the others played follow-the-leader. All of us were willing to lay bets that the pilot would never forget Saipan because he received a bang-up welcome.

Even though the days were busy and the Japs and other incidents disrupted the routine at night, the men still found time to write numerous letters. When they ran short of stationery, or such things as shaving cream, I headed for the ships offshore to buy or trade for more. Island Administration had ordered all enemy weapons turned in, along with the vehicles, but we still had a stash of Jap rifles and other goodies. So I threw an armload of rifles in the cargo space when heading out. I knew which ships were most likely to have the wanted items and headed for them first. The cargo ships were usually the best pickings for food. Most headed far to the east, maybe even to the States, when they left the Marianas. Consequently, the cooks were more likely to strip their larders. I couldn't take the rifles on board larger Navy ships, but I purchased most of our stationery needs on them.

On one of my trips, I took several bottles of sake along— I had to be an Indian-giver and bum it back from the men to

Rest and Tinian

whom I had given it. The sake would be good trading bait. There were only a few ships offshore so I headed for an LST on the long chance that the ship's store might have a surplus of stationery.

As the DUKW pulled alongside, I was standing in the cargo space with a bottle of sake, still encased in straw, under my arm. The ship's captain came out on the bridge and asked an officer by the gangway what I had under my arm. I overheard his question and volunteered the information that it was sake. The captain told the officer, "Have him bring it aboard."

When the officer informed me that the captain wanted me to bring it on board, I reminded him that Navy Regulations forbid bringing liquor aboard a Navy ship. Conversation followed between the two officers. I heard the captain remark, "Aww hell! Have him stick it under his dungaree jacket." I stuck the bottle under my jacket and climbed the gangway.

The captain invited me into his cabin. He wondered how much I wanted for the sake. I explained that I didn't want to sell it but planned to trade for something my men could use. He was anxious to get the bottle and continued pressing. He was a pleasant individual so, in time, I agreed to trade for some of his liquor stock. I wasn't too happy about trading for liquor but, with so few ships present, I didn't want to return to camp empty handed.

After checking his supply, I selected the brand and type I felt the men would most appreciate. He acted ecstatic over his trade. The bottle of Calvert's bourbon snuggled under my dungaree jacket was hard to come by in the Pacific during the war. The men would think I was really a sharp trader.

While the invasion had been in progress, the Marine Civil Affairs unit had placed the Saipan natives in an internment camp for their safety and to keep them out of the way of the invasion forces.

I had noticed a roped off area in the shallow water near Charan Kanoa and wondered why it was there. I guessed that

The Quack Corps

it might be to keep people away from an unexploded bomb or naval shell. I hadn't seen mixed-sex bathing before and my eyes bugged when I passed the area one day and saw dozens of men, women and children stripped to the bare skin, blithely and unself-consciously washing themselves and frolicking in the water.

The natives appeared happy and apparently welcomed liberation. And, the kids quickly learned about candy bars, chewing gum, and Marine skivvy shirts.

One day, two other Marines and I were talking with a Guam native. He spoke English well and told us: "The Japanese treated us like animals. The men received only one pair of pants per year and the women nothing. We had to steal food at night." A moment later, he added, "You Marines are our friends. You treated us like human beings before the war." He was anxious for the Americans to retake Guam so he could go home.

When and what will be the company's next move, I wondered. Surely it was only a matter of time before American forces invaded Tinian. We could see it from the top of the hill near our camp. Tinian's terrain appeared to be much flatter than Saipan's and like the weight of American explosives had beaten it deeper into the ocean. Undoubtedly, 2d DUKW would participate in its invasion.

Surely, the Japanese on Tinian knew their days were numbered. How hopeless it must feel to be in that situation. Maybe some of them had helped capture Guam, shortly after the war's beginning, and now were learning how the Marines and others had felt while awaiting the certainty of that Japanese attack. I didn't feel any sympathy for them in their untenable position and gloated about their misery.

Shortly before Saipan was secured, I had begun to run a high fever. My stomach wasn't upset but I began losing weight, which I could ill afford to lose. After a few days, I reported to sickbay but the doctor didn't seem to know what was

Rest and Tinian

U.S. Marine Corps photo
Tinian 25 July, 1944. DUKWs making runs. LSTs (Landing Ship, Tanks) offshore.

U.S. Marine Corps photo
DUKW cab interior—invasion fleet in distance. July 1944.

causing it. Nevertheless, he ordered the corpsman assisting him to give me a supply of the pink pills that we seemed to take for everything. They didn't help and the fever continued. Later, I had reason to believe that it was dengue fever because it was prevalent on the island; dengue was transmitted by mosquitoes and the island had hordes of them.

My fever had disappeared but I was feeling unambitious and spent as much time sacking out as possible. My clothes fit as if they were a size too large.

Hopefully, I wouldn't be left behind if and when 2d DUKW went to Tinian. The axe fell when Lieutenant Blackburn informed me that Captain George had decided to leave me on Saipan. He softened the blow by advising that I would serve as liaison with the 14th Marines. It was a shock and I asked the lieutenant if he'd try to get the C.O. to change his mind. He indicated that he had already tried but the captain was adamant and, that I should know, once the C.O. made up his mind, he wasn't likely to change a decision. I dreaded the forthcoming invasion but it was a tremendous blow to my pride to be told, in so many words, that the platoon could do nicely without me. Added to that blow was the feeling that I had failed with the girl back in San Diego. Combining those things made me feel depressed, unneeded and unwanted. Also, I felt concern that the men would feel I had bailed out on them.

An infantry unit wasn't likely to refuse an experienced NCO, especially a volunteer, so I requested a transfer to the 6th Regiment. I could vent my rage and disappointment more directly on the Japs, if with the 6th. Captain George didn't approve the transfer so I was stuck on Saipan.

The DUKWs would haul 75mms ashore in the Tinian landing. After they were loaded, I wished the men good luck then turned quickly to walk away so they wouldn't see the mist in my eyes. Though only 22, I felt a fatherly concern for them, including the man in the platoon who was a grandfather.

Rest and Tinian

Without a backward glance, I climbed into the driver's seat of the DUKW with the hole in its bow and drove away. I puttered along since I was in no hurry to get to the area where the 105s, wheel-to-wheel near Agingan Point on Saipan, had their muzzles pointing at Tinian. With only about four miles of water separating the two islands, they could cover the landing and a good way up the island from their position.

A flat spot about 25 yards behind the line of 105s provided a good spot for my batching quarters. For rain protection, I removed the DUKW tarp bows and set them upon the ground to support the cargo space tarp. With a cot and rations to last for several days, I was self-sufficient. Though still seething about being left behind, I decided to enjoy the stay as much as possible.

The wait began to see how the landing was going 24 July, 1944. I hung close to the artillery CP and felt elated when word was passed that the Marines were ashore, were meeting little early resistance and, apparently, the choice of a landing site had caught Tinian's defenders with their pants down. With the good news, everyone became more relaxed and laughter was again heard as the men talked and grab-assed.

While preparing to sack out the first night, I stretched a mosquito bar over my cot and lay my carbine inside it, with the muzzle pointing toward the foot. The bar would interfere with its use if the weapon was in any other position. I placed my KaBar under the folded clothing that I used for a pillow. Jap stragglers were still on Saipan and I was taking sensible precautions. Well inside the artillery defense perimeter, I had few fears and slept without difficulty the first night, except for the 105s periodic laying of harassment fire on Tinian.

Shortly after dark the second night, I crawled onto my cot and carefully secured the mosquito bar. As I lay back, I caught a glimpse of the tarp flaps fluttering at the foot end and I sensed that someone had entered my quarters. Slipping a hand to my carbine, I raised it to aim where I guessed that someone

The Quack Corps

was crouched, just inside the flaps. Earlier I had heard artillerymen grab-assing and wondered whether they were playing hide-and-go-seek. But, I heard nothing to reinforce that thought. I just couldn't believe, if playing the game, that one of the men would be foolish enough to risk getting killed by entering my quarters in the dark. I didn't want to fire, unless it became absolutely necessary, because a 105mm crew was directly in the line of fire. I didn't reach for my knife because I didn't want to make any movement that could tip off my exact position.

I lay, tensely, with eyes and ears acutely tuned to detect movement. In the momentary flash of light when a 105 fired, I discerned the figure's exact location—it looked to be American! I waited for another gun to fire. In the flash of light, I decided that my first impression had been correct. I didn't move or make any noise and continued aiming the carbine, with my finger ready to squeeze the trigger. *What in hell is going on?* I asked myself and decided it was time to find out. "Who are you?" I challenged.

"I'm American," in a low voice.

"What in hell are you doing in my quarters? What do you want?"

"I thought we could have some fun," a man replied, softly. I had never been propositioned by a homosexual but he didn't need to say more for me to understand what he meant. I blew my stack because he had given me such a terrific scare, and threatened to fill him full of holes if he didn't clear out in about two seconds. "I meant you no harm," he apologized, hastily. "I'm sorry." He quickly slipped through the tarp flaps.

I hadn't seen his face clearly nor did I recognize the voice. The next morning, a machine gunner on the nearby hill informed me that he had also been approached during the night while standing watch. I didn't want the homosexual killed because of his sexual aberration so I cautioned the gunner that if

Rest and Tinian

he knew him, he should either turn him in or encourage the man to do it himself.

With that unnerving experience behind me, I welcomed the news that the front had moved far enough forward for the 105mms to move to Tinian on 27 July, 1944.

I saw the DUKWs coming and walked out to wait for them. Corp. Harry Mefford hopped out of a DUKW and sauntered toward me with a wide smile on his face, "Hi, Sarge!"

"Hi, Mefford. How'd it go? Any of the men hurt?"

"Nah. You didn't miss a thing. It was a snap. The only excitement we had was when a DUKW backed over a small land mine. It blew out a tire but the DUKW wasn't damaged," he answered.

The other men yelled greetings. From their attitude, I didn't sense that they felt I had bailed out on them by staying behind. The friendly greetings made me feel better.

While away from the platoon, there wasn't anything for me to do except talk to the 105mm men. The liaison duty had apparently been only the captain's ploy to try to make me feel that I was doing my part in the invasion. But, the only liaison duty I had performed had been with the latrine!

After loading the 105s, the DUKWs went out through the channel at Charan Kanoa and the drivers swung the bows in the direction of Tinian. The company went ashore on the small beaches where the initial landings had been made.

The 105s were delivered to positions and then the company returned to a bivouac near the edge of a cane field, a short distance from the invasion beaches.

Corp. Orval "Smitty" Smith and I guessed that we would be in the bivouac for some time, so we picked up a heaping load of wooden ammunition boxes at a nearby artillery position. They were oblong in shape so we laid them flat for a floor and on their sides to make the walls of a hut. We left a few projecting to the inside to use as shelves. An opening in front served as a door and an opening on each side for windows pro-

The Quack Corps

vided cross-ventilation. We stretched a DUKW tarp over the top for a roof. Our foxhole was only a few feet away. Our Tinian mansion was christened my second night on the island, with the men clustered about for a housewarming.

Our deluxe living quarters measured about 8 x 10 feet. During rains, other men packed in to join us and enjoy its dry comfort.

Smitty and I were the envy of the others and some made plans to copy our mansion. Captain George didn't want his company's bivouac to become a shantytown and forbid building more. We assumed that we'd have to demolish ours, because it could cause resentment and hard feelings, but he didn't order it torn down. His failure to do so may have been because one of the officers had copied it with a miniature version.

Extra ammo boxes served as seats when more visitors showed than our two canvas cots could accommodate. An ammo box became our writing desk and our clothing hung on nails driven into the walls. I also propped my girl's picture on one of the shelves, even though she wasn't that popular with me right at the moment—later, I learned she had quit writing because she hadn't heard from me for two months.

I watched over my last lone bottle of sake with tender care and stored it on one of the projecting boxes. I hadn't sampled any from the other bottles that had been in the case and I was saving this one for a celebration. The Japs poisoned some bottles of liquor left behind on Tinian and a few Marines died after drinking the contents. Mine had been liberated before they began that practice, plus no one had suffered any ill effects by drinking from other bottles in the cases.

After an errand, I returned to the hut and noticed that someone had tapped the bottle's contents. Smitty informed me who had and I charged out of the hut to find him. My anger wasn't that I valued the sake so highly but it was because he had come into my quarters and taken something belonging to

Rest and Tinian

me. I cooled down some before finding him so after a good tongue-lashing, I threatened to wipe up the dirt of Tinian with him if he ever entered my quarters again without permission. He was an NCO in another platoon and could bird-dog liquor without it even being uncorked. Now that the sake had been uncorked, I took one swig and shared the rest with the 1st platoon'ers.

The sake incident had added a little variety to the Tinian stay but most of the days were routine, without the fireworks of Saipan. Describing the daily routine in a letter, I commented, "I spent the day working at Tinian Town. I didn't see a single house that hadn't been flattened by ship or shore bombardment."

On one of my forays, I saw a large aluminum pot laying in a field about 50 yards from the road. Gingerly, eyeballing for mines, I picked my way across the field for a look. I thought it might make a good container for washing clothes. The pot's metal was very thick and, except for a fairly large shrapnel hole, was in good condition. I used a hammer to mash the edges of the hole back together and, surprisingly, it didn't leak.

Instead of using it for a washtub, I decided it'd make a good pot for heating rations. After disinfecting the pot thoroughly, several varieties of C-rations were dumped in. The mixtures made some rather tasty meals. Possibly, the heat was more important than mixing varieties but, in any event, it was a change from cold "K" and C-rations. The large quantity was far too much for me so I invited other platoon members to join me for chow.

I didn't have to do my own chefing for long, because unlike Saipan, the company remained in the same bivouac during its entire stay on Tinian. As a consequence, we had a company mess hall a few days after I hit the island..

With the smaller size island, the 105s didn't have to move up much and they used less ammo. Most of our unloading runs

The Quack Corps

were to island dumps, which made for routine but long workdays.

With a regular schedule, I had time to write letters while the battle was still in progress. One of the first written on the ammo-box desk was to request an absentee war ballot for the upcoming presidential election. It would be my first time to vote for a president of the United States and I sure didn't want to miss the opportunity. Later, when the ballots were mailed in, the company officers wanted to check to make sure they were filled in properly. Lieutenant Blackburn didn't agree with my political philosophy. When he checked my ballot, he remarked, with a grin, "Sergeant, you're just wasting your vote." I felt irritated enough that he looked at my supposedly secret ballot, so his remark didn't serve to lessen my irritation.

The battle for Tinian wasn't lengthy and 2d DUKW suffered no casualties in the fighting.

After it was over, the 2d Marine Amphibian Truck Company was transferred, 6 August, 1944, to the 2d Marine Division. The 2d Division remained in the Marianas and the 4th Division was sent back to Maui.

The company's stay on Tinian wouldn't be long because it moved back to Saipan on 11 August. With the move, Smitty and I had to demolish our mansion; we had been proud of it and had enjoyed our temporary home.

Second DUKW's personnel had given a good account of themselves in the two invasions. Like all who know and do their jobs well, the officers and men were a confident group. None took it as an insult when other Marines quacked like ducks as the vehicles passed or called us "The Quack Corps," because they too had learned the capabilities of our hybrid vehicle.

For a five-day period, heavy weather caused Higgins boats to broach in the surf and LVTs to be unmanageable in the stormy sea. Less than 150 DUKWs provided the only means of supplying the Tinian invasion forces and proved, without qualification, the value of amphibian trucks in the Pacific island invasions.

The heavy weather spawned a lasting memory for Navy Commander Harold Stassen, a former governor of Minnesota and later a perennial contender in primaries for nomination as the Republican party's flag bearer in postwar presidential elections. A DUKW, of which Pvt. Harold Young was a crewmember, was being utilized by the commander as a taxi for getting ashore and returning to his ship. He not only learned the capabilities of the hybrid vehicle but also to pay heed to DUKW crew cautions.

On the commander's first return to his ship, he was offered the assistant driver's seat for a drier and safer ride through the surf but he declined and stood in the cargo space. The surf was huge and he was upended when the DUKW knifed through a towering and breaking wave. The paper-filled valise in his hand tore loose. Its catch came undone and papers scattered about in the cargo space and overboard. Sputtering and soaking wet he scrambled to recover as many documents as possible, then rose to his feet and enjoyed a laugh with the DUKW crew. Thereafter, he occupied the assistant driver's seat in Captain George's DUKW while being taxied back and forth.

Chapter 14
In the Marianas

Second DUKW moved into a tent camp on Kagman Peninsula upon its return to Saipan.

We had hardly settled in when Lieutenant Blackburn came to my tent. After the usual amenities, he informed me that the Marine Corps wanted to give out medals and asked who in the platoon we could recommend. I felt that an outstanding job was expected of every Marine without the expectation of or presentation of a medal just because a job was well done. I answered him this way, "Sir, every man did as he was ordered and went where he was sent. Whenever I requested volunteers for frontline or other equally dangerous runs, more responded than usually were needed. In my opinion, every one did an outstanding job. If one deserves a medal, then I feel they all do." A few medals were presented to men in the company but none receiving them were in first platoon.

We had little free time because the DUKWs needed thorough maintenance, scraping, painting, and repairs. We also had to train new men who had replaced those wounded or killed. Daily in-camp procedures and routines had to be established. We also were not off the hook in unloading ships because a mountain of supplies had to be stockpiled on the island. Saipan had limited dock facilities, though the addition of temporary piers helped improve the situation.

Here again, the versatility of the DUKW proved invaluable because ships anchored offshore and the hybrid vehicles ran from ship directly to inland dumps, leaving the decks clear for land vehicles to unload ships at the piers.

I had seen much of Saipan during the battle for the island, because the 1st platoon also made runs into 2d Marine Divi-

In the Marianas

sion territory. Later, I had occasion to make runs to Garapan and Tanapag but there were some areas I hadn't seen. So, with the battle over and duties lightening up, I made "justifiable" opportunities to take in the scenery.

The tale of a single Sherman tank crew knocking off several Jap tanks on a winding road from high country into a valley was common knowledge to DUKW men. So, with a DUKW crew, I took a side trip to check out the battle site. The Sherman had been positioned so it commanded an exit from a sharp curve. Several Jap tanks were traveling uphill on the road and as each one made the curve, the Sherman gunner picked them off, knocking each one off the steep road bank. He had a turkey shoot because the downhill side of the road was littered with destroyed enemy tanks. I could imagine the elation the Sherman crew must have felt when the last of the Jap tanks tumbled off the road.

I hadn't been in the central portion of the island north of Mt. Tapotchau but I heard of a large valley in that area. Again, I found a "justifiable" reason for a side trip to eyeball it. Later, the Army used the valley for vegetable gardens, enabling its personnel to enjoy freshly grown vegetables of assorted varieties.

After the island's capture, the engineers wasted no time in building new and improving existing roads. The improvements helped speed up stockpiling of war goods for future invasions and supplies for the troops occupying Saipan and Tinian. As 2d DUKW was relied on less and less for moving supplies ashore, our trips to the unloading areas lessened. As a result, each run was almost like seeing Saipan all over again because of the constant changes on the island.

The atmosphere was different, as if the occupying troops were pressing the combat units to "go take another island because now this one belongs to us".

After the company moved into the Kagman Peninsula camp and some semblance of routine was established, I had guessed that we would be there for an indefinite period of time. I unpacked some of my extra gear and began adding amenities to make tent living more pleasant.

As a prolific letter writer, one of my first items of business was to build a table to make writing easier. I also built a box for the men to throw their letters in so they wouldn't be scattered by the wind. The box hung on a clothesline stretched between two posts in back of my tent. They gave me a ribbing as they guessed whether it was a birdhouse, a clothespin holder, or whatever.

Lieutenant Blackburn censored most of their letters and I delivered them to him by a certain time each day. I didn't envy him that job.

Secrecy had been so tight prior to the Saipan invasion that we were not allowed to mail letters after leaving Maui, even when the flotilla had stopped at Eniwetok. As a result, we had a lot of catching up to do. In some cases, fences needed to be mended with those who didn't understand that men at war couldn't always let it be known that letters wouldn't come for an indefinite period of time.

On 6 July, mail had been delivered to the 1st platoon in the Saipan bivouac where the fighter plane had accidently fired on us. With mail arriving, I felt it probably would be only a short while until outgoing letters could be mailed.

I had returned to the bivouac on 8 July, just as dusk was sending shadows across the island, and learned that the mail clerk had passed the word that letters could be mailed. Starving, I wolfed my rations and then dug writing materials out of my pack. I sat on the dirt at the end of my foxhole, using a knee for a desk, and scribbled a short note to Dolores Alden who I had met in the San Diego aircraft plant. Most of its text was:

> *I haven't been able to write to you for almost two months due to circumstances beyond my control. I'm*

In the Marianas

not allowed to tell you why now but I will …. someday. I am well but very tired. With a little rest, I'll be okay.

I've received several of your letters the past couple of days. I want you to know how very much I appreciate them. It is almost too dark for me to see but I wanted to let you know that I'm all right. …

I received the letters referred to in my note, and then … nothing. The last letter in that group was dated June 7th. I had noted gaps between dates when they were received but hadn't been concerned; it wasn't unusual for letters to be received before others with earlier postmarks.

After a few days, I rechecked the dates they had been written and saw that the gaps between them had gradually become wider and wider. Other than concern that she hadn't been getting letters from me, she gave no hint that she was thinking of or planned to quit writing. The tone of her last letters hadn't changed and she had continued to relate, in minute detail, her daytime and evening activities.

I had begun a barrage of letters to convince her to wait for me after her first letter, received on 14 January, 1944, had reflected a change in the feelings she had expressed before I shipped out. My threat to quit writing, in February, had resulted in more frequent letters and a change to a more favorable tone toward me. But now, it appeared that I had fence mending to do.

As the line of X's marking the days of July off my calendar grew longer and longer, I assumed that she quit because I hadn't been writing. I convinced myself that she hadn't really been interested in me and that it gave her a conscience-salving excuse to quit.

My feelings of hurt and anger, combined with the knowledge that the platoon was going to Tinian without me, made me want to lash out at whomever and whatever was handy. I

The Quack Corps

sat in the driver's seat of the DUKW parked behind the 105s blasting Tinian and vented some of my feelings in a scathing letter to her.

In the bundle of mail I received on 26 July, only two days after mailing the angry letter, I spotted her beautiful handwriting on an envelope. I laid it aside because I didn't have the nerve to open it first ... I expected it to contain bad news. After reading my other letters, I picked up hers and held it for several minutes while raising the nerve to open it. Then, I told myself, "You may as well get it over with," and slit it open with my KaBar.

Her letter was short, and dated 5 July:

> *It has been a long, long time since I have heard from you. I believe you owe me a letter. In any case, I am writing to find out why you haven't written to me. I do hope and pray that you are all right. So many things can happen over there, and I may never know.*

My last letter before leaving Maui was dated 11 May. The last sentence of that letter was an expression that I had never used in a letter to her. I had been saving it for just such an occasion. It read: "I will write whenever I have the opportunity." I assumed she had reread the letter many times and should have caught the sentence's implications. Apparently, she had missed it. I hadn't dared write more than it contained.

My note of 8 July drew a prompt response so things began looking up. But, everything could be lost when she received my scathing letter. Before she received it, I had received her promise to wait. Then, unexpectedly, my angry letter brought her acceptance of my earlier marriage proposal. As a result, my overseas tour would be more bearable.

I made good use of my new writing table by penning almost daily letters to her. In one, I described the weather, thusly:

In the Marianas

The weather seems to be about like Hawaii, although probably a little more rain. I liked it on Tinian better, because we were more isolated and not so many servicemen around. I think these islands are beautiful. As long as I have to be overseas, I'd rather stay here.

The long water trips back and forth are so monotonous. Maybe, too, I'm anxious to see the development on these islands, now that we control them. But best of all, I don't have to be without letters from you.

High command relaxed censorship in mid-July. We still couldn't write about certain invasion incidents, such as the loss of men and DUKWs during the initial landing, nor about some of our daily activities. It was permissible to brag about our chow, including a new ration we had begun receiving. In my search for something I could write about, I decided to describe it to her, in this way:

We are getting a new ration that is called 10-in-1. It is surprisingly good. We will still eat K and C rations during the first few days of an invasion; they are more compact so don't take up so much space. Then as space becomes less dear, we will eat at least like king's aides. Each carton contains enough food for 10 men for three meals.

How do you like this for a menu on a Pacific island? Each carton contains: sliced bacon or ham'n eggs - roast beef or pork sausage - jam or jelly - preserved butter - crackers – napkins (no less!) - gum - cigarettes - canned cream - sugar -salt - cheese - fruit bars or caramels - matches - lemon powder or cocoa - cereal - can opener - water purification tablets and saltwater soap. The men use most of the napkins for toilet tissue.

The Quack Corps

While on the subject of rations, I decided to describe other items we had begun receiving at the same time, thusly:

> *I know you don't smoke, shave or use chewing tobacco, but you do brush your teeth, eat chocolate bars, chew gum and wash your face and hands. We also get a ration accessory box containing: twenty cartons of cigarettes - matches - razors - blades - tooth brushes and powder - Hershey tropical chocolate bars - pipe and chewing tobacco - gum and soap. As you can see, we don't and won't starve. We can also keep our teeth pearly white, smoke, chew and shave.*

Though I could write about things of that nature, I couldn't mention the Army Air Corps fighter airstrip located a short distance from our camp. I often walked across the small gulch separating the strip from our camp to engage in bull sessions with the pilots and ground crews. I could have written reams about the P-38 and P-51 fighters at the strip and my admiration for the sleekness of the P-51. A twin fuselage P-61 Black Widow nightfighter plane also used the strip; it was painted a dull black and looked deadly. I didn't envy its crew in their lonely night-time war with the Japs.

Second DUKW had hauled in most of the Air Corps' supplies when the units moved to the airstrip. One of the DUKW drivers, a corporal, made a habit of tapping the airmens' liquor supply. When his load contained liquor, he stashed a bottle in a gully by the side of the road paralleling Magicienne Bay. By the time he finished hauling, his stash amounted to 35 bottles of Schenley's Black Label whiskey. He donated enough to the 1st platoon men for a party and sold the balance for $100.00 per bottle.

Prior to becoming a Marine, he had been a professional card dealer in Kentucky. After the occasional paydays, he'd add to his bank balance by cleaning out many of the inexpert gamblers. Eventually, orders were issued that no more than $100.00 per month could be mailed out from the island. Though the reason given was to cut down on gambling, the enlisted men felt it was really to protect the officers' liquor from being appropriated and sold. Gambling in camp wouldn't have been allowed in peacetime but it was another regulation ignored in the forward war zone; it helped relieve free time boredom. Many of the nongamblers filled free time with cribbage and pinochle.

Personnel, ammunition, other armaments, and supplies packed Saipan. Explosives couldn't always be stored in the most logical areas. I didn't even want to write about the ammo dump located at the end of the fighter strip. The planes were barely airborne when passing over it.

One day, I stepped out of my tent and noticed smoke rising above the dump's location. I wondered who would be so foolish as to burn trash in that area. Moments later, a DUKW man raced through camp bellowing, "A P-38 crashed into the ammo dump!" DUKW personnel boiled out of their tents and headed for the hills laying to the west of camp.

Two men matched strides with me sprinting across the softball field to take cover behind a DUKW parked about 50 yards away. We cringed behind it while shrapnel and unexploded armaments scattered over the area. Good fortune rode again with 2d DUKW, because no men were injured or vehicles damaged.

There were other less explosive things to write about, as long as I used care in how I handled them. We had been in camp only a few days when the Army Island Administration refused to let 2d DUKW personnel attend its outdoor movie near our camp. A few of the men had taken boxes for use as seats and left them in the movie area. The no-movies edict was in effect for 15 days. It was a blow to morale because the men hadn't seen movies since leaving Maui. I informed Dolores

The Quack Corps

that she would be getting longer letters from me because I wouldn't get to spend any time at the movies.

The Island Administration's top brass seemed to delight in finding an excuse to lord-it-over the Marines on Saipan. I guessed they were getting revenge because Marine LtGen. H. M. "Howling Mad" Smith had relieved Army MajGen. Ralph Smith during the battle for Saipan. To me, it seemed childish for high-ranking officers to let interservice rivalries affect the morale of enlisted men. I wondered if they didn't realize that the Army, Navy and Marine Corps were fighting on the same side in the war.

I tried to ignore those irritations and not brood about them, because my moods were up and down like a yo-yo anyway. In a down mood, I didn't even attempt to write letters.

Censoring mail was boring for those required to do it. Censors had difficulty in keeping abreast of the frequent changes in what subjects were and were not forbidden. Though I had had little cutting done on my letters, Lieutenant Blackburn lowered the boom on one dated 19 August. He informed me next day that he had cut one-half page out of my letter. I didn't want to embarrass him by telling him that I had quoted from *Time Battle Baby*; one of the magazines published as a miniature of regular issues and sized to fit in the back pocket of dungaree pants.

On 20 August, the men of 2d DUKW received their first mail since the company's change from the 4th to the 2d Marine Division. With letters to answer, it was much easier to write letters of decent length. Fortunately, we now could write about past happenings if we avoided revealing casualties and damages to our ships and equipment.

So in a letter to Dolores, I wrote a little about the invasion:

> *I was surprised that I didn't have D-Day Eve jitters. We were close enough to see the flares and hear the booms when the big guns on the battleships and*

In the Marianas

cruisers fired. I watched for a couple of hours, then hit my sack for a good night's sleep.

The pre-landing bombardment was an awesome thing to watch ... the flashes of the big guns and then, in moments, the explosion that marked where the salvo hit on Saipan. And the huge column of smoke and flame boiling into the air when a fuel or ammunition dump was hit.

Although I knew death rode with some of them, it was beautiful to see tracer bullets filling the sky during an after-dark air raid on the fleet."

It wasn't unusual for me to jump back and forth between past, present and future in my letters and that one didn't differ in that respect. I quickly switched tenses:

Would you believe that there are a couple of fryer-size chickens running loose in camp? We've tried but haven't been able to catch them so we can enjoy a tasty meal of fried chicken. We also have several goats in camp. With no holes to crawl into, I wonder how they survived the pre-invasion bombardment and the battling on land that followed. The nannies look like they would appreciate being milked for their udders are gorged with milk. Some of the men have a snowy-white kid in front of my tent. Hold everything ... I'll be back in a minute.

After going out to pet and run my hands over the downy softness of the kid's hair, I returned to the letter:

It is only about five days old and is the cutest thing. When the Jap goats b-a-a, they sound exactly like the goats did back in Missouri.

The Quack Corps

We fought boredom by writing more letters, playing softball and cards, and engaging in lengthy bull sessions. We also battled hordes of mosquitoes. In August, most of the men suffered with dengue fever, with 50 so sick they had to be hospitalized at some period during the month. Though I used repellant lavishly and a flashlight to make certain none were inside my mosquito bar at night, I too caught it for what I felt was the second time; my symptoms made me believe that it had been dengue that prevented my making the initial Tinian landing. Even dengue was a worthy subject for a letter, as on 26 August:

> *I have dengue fever with a 102 temperature. Of course, the high fever could be the result of the letter I received from you today! Honey, don't worry about me because it will be only a memory by the time you get this letter.*

"I will be so happy to wear your ring. I will feel closer to you," was included in the letter I received on 12 September. She didn't realize the predicament her desire put me in because engagement rings couldn't be bought on Saipan, or to my knowledge anywhere in the forward war zone. I was going to move heaven and earth, if necessary, to get a ring for her but, at first, I couldn't think of any possible way to do it.

After stewing for several days, I thought of a solution ... Bill, my Marine brother, was now stationed in New Orleans. I'd ask him to select and buy one with a matching wedding ring. Though I didn't like having somebody else choose them, I didn't have any choice. He had excellent taste but, if I didn't like them, I'd buy another set upon my return to the States. I'd have him mail them to me and I'd send them on to her. I knew the rings could be lost while crossing the Pacific twice but I wanted to see them. I also felt she'd feel better if she didn't know just how I had managed to acquire them.

In the Marianas

I hoped to have them to her by Christmas, but it was mid-December before arrangements with Bill were completed. I decided to have him send the wedding ring along and I'd forward it to her for safekeeping.

I felt that 2d DUKW would probably remain in the Kagman Peninsula camp indefinitely so I had requested that Dolores send flower seeds so I could improve the area around my tent. I also was curious about how they'd do on Saipan. Some of my farm background surfaced and I knew growing flowers would help relieve boredom and occupy free time. Flowers would also give me another subject to write about. So I planted forget-me-not seeds on 14 September; they were popping through the soil on the 19th. Also on the 19th, I planted zinnia and larkspur seeds she had included later. If they grew well, my tent would be in an oasis of flowers.

To add to my flower garden, I planted watermelon and muskmelon seeds given to me by a next-door neighbor. Most of them came up. So maybe, in time, I'd enjoy fresh melon.

Gardening took a back seat to duties and I went to Charan Kanoa to pick up a new DUKW; a replacement for one of those sunk on D-Day. One of its tires was flat. While changing it, I saw movie star Betty Hutton and another woman swimming between the reef and the beach. Censorship had tightened up again so I couldn't mention Saipan or her name when I wanted to let Dolores know that I had seen her. So I handled it this way:

> *One day I was changing a flat tire by the ocean and I saw two women swimming; one was a blonde movie star and the other a stunning brunette. I've told you before that God put pretty women on this earth for men to admire, and that I never refuse to look at one. So my attention focused on the beautiful brunette. It took longer than necessary to change that tire.*

The Quack Corps

> *I saw the show a couple days later. The stage was in the boiling sun and perspiration cascaded off the blonde during her performance. I appreciated that she would put out so much energy in the heat, and I've enjoyed her zany actions in movies more since then. The brunette was a contortionist. A guitar player and a juggler were also in the show.*

The sexual stimulation caused by watching the scantily clad, voluptuous, contortionist seductively stretch and move her body added to the yearnings for the pleasures of Stateside. In the flesh, its effect was much greater than if it had been seen in the make-believe of a movie screen. I thought it was a mistake for girls to be sent to perform on the islands. I had to agree with a DUKW man's remark, as we walked back to camp, "There's sure going to be a lot of loads dumped in socks on Saipan tonight!"

Almost every subject was covered at some time or other in bull sessions, with girls and sex receiving the most attention. Most of the men expressed surprise that the lack of sex didn't cause them to feel horny an inordinate amount of time. Though none seemed to know whether saltpeter lessened sexual desire, it still didn't prevent some of the men accusing the cooks of dumping it in our chow. The more worldly realized that the reduction was more than likely the lack of exposure to the wiles of, or close contact with, and the smell and feel of girls. In any event, girls and sex did make for some lively, enlightening and long discussions.

Armistice Day, 11 November, 1944, showed on the calendar, giving another subject for letters, as in this one:

> *Today was always Armistice Day. No doubt there will be wild celebrations after this war too. I think we should have a day of solemnity and prayer that this time we will have a lasting peace. I don't think this is*

In the Marianas

the war to end all wars, because there will always be people struggling for power and ... more power!

Next day, the watermelons and zinnias began blooming. The zinnias' blossoms were yellow, pink, and white. I had earlier written Dolores that I'd press and dry the largest one so she could see, too, how big the blossoms were that *We* grew on Saipan. ... I still have it.

By now, most of those writing to me knew it would sometimes take regular mail two or three months to catch up. Fortunately, most sent everything airmail, keeping news of family and Stateside more current.

Even the flowers blooming and Christmas presents arriving didn't relieve the boredom of small island duty. So I welcomed the orders sending me, with Corp. Arthur Stover and his assistant driver, to Tinian to assist an LST that, after a breakdown, had been pushed ashore by wind and waves. An electric motor had to be taken to a tender for repair or replacement. The ship was so far up on the beach that its ramp was pushed into the air. She couldn't get underway until repairs were completed. We parked the DUKW on the beach and spent the nights aboard.

With the tank deck inaccessible, the motor had to be loaded into the DUKW alongside, which made for tricky work for the driver and the davit operator. If the timing of the rise and fall of the waves wasn't just right, Stover could be injured or the motor could go through the bottom of the DUKW. Both the driver and davit operator were experts so the maneuver was successful, as was the unloading of the DUKW when the motor was returned to the ship. The DUKW couldn't be tied to the ship so Stover had to jockey with the throttle to keep the vehicle in position. Stover was an expert behind the wheel and I had chosen him on several other occasions that involved tricky driving. It had been a welcome break for us.

The Quack Corps

Pier facilities had been added and others improved in the harbor area so demand for DUKW company services had lessened. As a result, our trips to other areas of Saipan became less frequent. Though it lightened our workload, it meant that we no longer could keep completely abreast of the changes being made in almost every section of the island.

Only so much time could be spent playing softball—my tent was adjacent to and faced the company's field—and writing letters or in bull sessions. To fill some of the free time, I walked to the top of a hill facing Magicienne Bay and spent hours watching the B-29s take off from Aslito Airfield (renamed Isely by the Navy but I always heard it referred to as Aslito). The heavily laden 29s became airborne at the end of Aslito and then dropped almost to the ocean's surface. A crewman informed me that they then flew for many miles in a gradual climb to altitude so the motors didn't overheat. At first, my heart was in my throat because I felt certain they were going to hit the water.

I earlier had written Dolores that I wanted to ride along during a bombing raid on Japan. I wanted to see Japan proper getting blasted and I thought I might be able to cajole the pilot and bombardier into letting me press the key to release the bombs; doing so would have given me a feeling that I had exacted direct personal revenge for Pearl Harbor. A B-29 pilot offered me a ride. When I requested permission from Captain George to make the trip, he refused to grant it, with the comment: "It's too dangerous and an unnecessary risk." Though disappointed at being refused permission, I could understand his reasoning because it *would* have been difficult for him to explain to higher command what one of his platoon sergeants had been doing in a B-29 lost in a raid on Japan. The plane crews were making the Japanese leaders realize the folly of the attack on Pearl Harbor, in a direct and dramatic way.

Jap planes quite often strafed the parked B-29s on Aslito. We could see smoke towering above the airfield after some of the raids. We didn't often see the planes as they arrived or departed because they usually didn't come by our camp. But during one of the raids, I saw three P-47s tailing a Zero by the point of Kagman Peninsula, at low altitude. They had the Zero boxed in, but apparently couldn't close enough to knock it down. When the north end of the Air Corps' fighter strip came into my line of sight, I noted a P-38 becoming airborne. Amazingly, it had left terra firma before the pilot got the second motor started. He approached the P-47s from aft, zoomed above them and dived on the Zero. A short burst from the P-38's guns sent it crashing in flames.

The P-38 made a tight turn, barrel rolled as it crossed the strip, made another very tight turn and sped in for a landing. The pilot taxied the plane to its parking spot, jumped out and began sauntering toward the ready tent, as if to say: "That'll teach you to interrupt my nap." He shot the Zero down so quickly, and acted so matter-of-fact about it, that I stood gaping with amazement.

Scuttlebutt floated that there had been a fourth P-47 that was shot down by a Navy tanker anchored in Magicienne Bay. I didn't know until later that Dolores had an uncle, a Navy lieutenant, aboard the tanker. Later, he denied that the ship shot down the P-47.

Censorship was relaxed and then the screws periodically tightened. I wondered whether it was done to try to confuse Japanese Intelligence or whether someone just wanted to issue orders. In any event, I couldn't let those I wrote know that 2d DUKW had moved back to Tinian in early December. I did let Dolores know in my letter of the 11th that I had been told that one of my muskmelons was ripe.

Tinian had limited dock facilities and heavy weather was forecast. The ships had to be unloaded before it hit. We worked 24-hour shifts for the first couple of days but then changed to shorter hours. The men hadn't worked very hard the past few months and welcomed the change of locale and routine.

I knew that information about Jap air raids was appearing in stateside news media but I didn't know how much. Just in case, I thought I should calm any undue concern Dolores might have about me, so on 16 December:

> *Censorship has been relaxed again and I can tell you that we have had several air raids. Falling flak worries me more than the enemy planes. Of course I hold my breath when they fly over our camp but I think it'd be an accident if they dropped any bombs on us. You should hear the men cheer when a Nip plane falls in flames—reminds me of a football game. The raids are why I've mentioned that I can't appreciate a full moon here.*

I avoided mentioning that the rear gunners sometimes gave a few parting shots to personnel areas.

In my letter of 17 December:

> *When we sit and talk it's called a bull session or shooting-the-bull. And a person who likes to talk a lot is called a sea lawyer. Although I may be a sea lawyer at times, there are times I like to be by myself so I can think not only about you but also other things.*
>
> *Yesterday, while by myself, a plane passed a short distance away. I began thinking about this modern world and nature. I thought not only about airplanes, television and electric appliances, but even about the alikeness of different animals' legs. Then my thoughts returned to television. I've never seen it but I've read many stories about that invention. Do you realize that in a few short years after this war is over we will*

In the Marianas

probably be able to sit in our living room and watch movies?

With the move to Tinian, our mail was delayed for about two weeks because stormy seas made it unsafe for the mail clerk to bring it over from Saipan. He managed to get it to us on 20 December. It was a real boost to morale for a large number of letters to arrive so close to Christmas.

Our mess hall on Tinian was well lit so most of the men gathered there to do their letter writing. I referred to it on 22 December:

> *You should see the crowd of men in this mess hall hurrying to complete their letter writing before the moon gets bright enough for the air raids to begin. Some of them are arguing the merits and demerits of the German V-3 weapon; it is a portent of the wars to come!*

The Thanksgiving and Christmas holidays were the loneliest days of the year for most of the men, particularly Christmas. In my case, I wondered whether and where my family had gathered, if they thought of me and were speculating about where I might be and what I was doing. They couldn't imagine how lonely I felt on those days.

I spent Christmas Day on Tinian, and in my letter written to Dolores that day:

> *This is the fourth consecutive year I've spent out of the United States. I was at sea on board the U.S.S. almost-didn't-sail in 1941; in 1942, I was on board the U.S.S. almost-never-sail at Nandi Bay in the Fiji Islands; in 1943, I was at sea on board the U.S.S. baby flattop; this year, I'm spending Christmas on the dirt of the U.S.S. military secret. I can't mention ship*

The Quack Corps

names when writing about dates and years because it could help our little friends break our code.

Our DUKWs were showing hard use and word was passed that the company was getting new vehicles. But, Army command decided that the Army would take the new DUKWs and the company would have to make do with the Army's castoffs. The decision added insult to injury for some of the Army personnel had been acting like they owned the islands. Saipan and Tinian had what appeared to be an over abundance of Army newly commissioned 2d lieutenants. Dressed in sparkling new khakis, they sped about in jeeps and recons giving the impression that now they were here the war would be quickly won. They appeared unaware of how lightly regarded they were by Marines and Army combat troops.

When Captain George heard that Army command intended to grab the new DUKWs, he jumped into a jeep and rushed out of camp with an angry set to his face. He returned a few hours later relaxed and cheerul. The Army's decision had been changed. I later learned what triggered it. After 2d DUKW had arrived on Oahu, Captain George had drawn the cash for the company payroll from V Amphibious Corps. He recounted it before paying the men and discovered that he had been given $100.00 too much; he rushed it back to V Corps. His honesty impressed a Colonel Anderson in V Corp so much that, thereafter, he made certain 2d DUKW got a square shake. The colonel knew which strings to pull to get the Army's decision changed. The men felt like they had Cadillacs because they could again inflate and deflate the tires just by moving a lever in the cab.

The New Year found 2d DUKW still on Tinian. But the company moved back to Saipan, and the Kagman Peninsula camp, on 5 January, 1945.

As the days of January moved past, my watermelons were nearing the ripening stage but they began disappearing. I won-

In the Marianas

dered whether some city slicker didn't know they should ripen before being eaten. It wasn't long until I discovered the thief's identity.

Late one afternoon, I glanced out of my tent and saw a billy goat, a few nannies and several kids heading my way. They headed for the melon patch and the billy lowered his head and began helping himself to a melon. I eased my KaBar from under the folded clothing at the head of my cot and threw it at him; it stuck in his flank. He jumped straight up in the air, then ran out of the patch with the others tailing. My knife dropped to the ground after a few hops. I had always considered goats to be rather stupid, but my knife attack had apparently been enough to keep them from raiding the patch again. Now I had another tale to relate in letters.

After the year 1945 dawned, its first month would be tension-filled for much of 2d DUKW because shortly after the carnage at Iwo Jima began, the company was ordered to standby because a move to Iwo was imminent. Packed and ready to move, we sweated out the wait. By a fluke of radio transmission, we could listen to the crews of Marine tanks as they fought the Japs. As the battle progressed, we got to feeling as if we knew the crew members of certain tanks personally. We sorrowed with their buddies on the scene whenever a crew was reported knocked out. Listening to the sounds of actual battle, it was as if we were already there and our days became tension-filled and nights sleepless. When the standby orders were cancelled a few days later, the superstitious men became even more certain that the humpback whales, at Maui, had been and still were 2d DUKW's guardian angels.

The personnel of 2d DUKW were unaware that the Marine Corps had formed other amphibian truck companies, until Iwo. Reports that many of the DUKWs used there had been lost, early on, in the surf made us wonder why a cadre of men from the battle experienced DUKW companies hadn't been sent back to impart knowledge gained to the personnel of the

The Quack Corps

newly forming companies. Of course, we realized the beaches of Iwo differed from those at Saipan and Tinian; nevertheless, the experience gained from additional months of battling surf by the men in 1st and 2d DUKW should have been utilized as other companies formed.

Scuttlebutt floated that the C.O. of 1st DUKW didn't rate very high with 2d Division high command. Reportedly, things got real sticky when a sentry shot the man relieving him with a shotgun. In any event, First DUKW moved to Guam, in February, and joined the 3rd Division there. The company didn't make Iwo Jima with the division and remained on Guam for the balance of the war.

Second DUKW had made *the* reputation, but possibly 2d Division high command just liked the fact that the Number 2 designation matched the division's number.

Also, notable in the month of February was the arrival of a small package on the 13th. With anticipation, I carefully removed the wrapping paper and opened the little box for my first look at the set of rings my brother had mailed on 13 December, 1944. I failed to remind him to ship them airmail and they had taken a trip across the Pacific in the hold of an extremely slow ship. Nevertheless, I felt grateful for his good taste.

Receiving an engagement ring by mail wasn't the most romantic way for a girl to become officially betrothed. I damned the Japs for making it impossible for me to slip it on her finger in person. Nevertheless, I felt pleased as I rewrapped and sent them out airmail on the 13th. She received them on 20 February; the 21st on Saipan because it is across the International Dateline. I was gratified by her pleasure when she wrote, "I'm so thrilled to receive them. I think they are just beautiful!"

The calendar flipped to March 1945 and we were amidst preparations for another invasion. Scuttlebutt floated that it would be the Japanese home islands. I also heard the name

In the Marianas

Okinawa mentioned. As I felt it was still a little premature for us to land on Japan, I thought it was the more logical one; even I could deduce by looking at a map that it gave American forces a good and close spot for the masses of men and materials it'd take to conquer the Japanese homeland.

In my letter of 22 March: "Keep writing please. ..." I hoped this time she'd catch that sentence's implications when my letters stopped coming.

After scaling the side to board the DUKW, I turned for one last look at my flower and melon patch. I had left my mark on Saipan because, in time, their seeds would drop again and again, renewing their life cycle over and over. I wondered whether they may be my last contribution to life on earth. After gazing at the patch for a few moments, I turned to the driver, and ordered, "Let's go!"

Chapter 15
Okinawa!

The heavily loaded DUKWs eased into the tank deck of *LST-725*. There was enough ammunition in the 16 vehicles and tank deck to blow the ship, crew and DUKW personnel to Kingdom Come!

Odd, how accustomed one could become to being near high explosives. It didn't do much good to worry because if they exploded, not many of us would be likely to survive.

The 4th platoon had been disbanded prior to 2d DUKW's return to Tinian in December, and the men and vehicles had been apportioned among the other platoons. With the addition of those men and others aboard from the maintenance and 2d platoons, two officers and 56 enlisted Marines were on the LST.

The flotilla consisted of nine LSTs, with a destroyer escort (DE) ahead of and behind. The escorts followed a zigzag course searching for enemy submarines. They also provided the main weapons for repelling enemy air attacks. It must have been extremely monotonous for them to travel at the slow speed necessary to avoid running away from the LSTs. The LSTs were not blessed with an over abundance of anti-aircraft weaponry and would be almost sitting ducks for determined enemy aircraft. I didn't feel very secure, even with the DEs as escorts.

Again, I spent many hours topside looking over the ship's bow and mulling over what might lay ahead. Tarawa, Saipan, Iwo Jima and Peleliu had been bloodbaths and we expected that this one could be the worst yet. I knew the Japanese would be feeling even more desperate, because we were getting very close to their homeland. They would pull out all the stops.

Okinawa!

The sea was rough for the first few days and some of the men were seasick. Because they had been on the water in bobbing DUKWs so much, I suspected it was probably caused by the skin-yellowing Atabrine we had been taking for several days; quinine was in short supply because of the war and Atabrine had supplanted it as a malaria preventative. Atabrine made me feel as if I was walking about two feet above the deck.

I spent some of my time reading the paperback edition of *Claudia,* a book noted for being risqué for the times. My attention had a tendency to wander, probably because of the Atabrine, and I had to reread parts at times. After reading for awhile, I felt like taking a snooze but when I laid the book down and closed my eyes, sleep wouldn't come; Atabrine also made me feel edgy and tense.

Then, Okinawa was disclosed as our destination; it is the main island in the Ryukyu chain, laying about 350 miles south of Kyushu, the most southern of Japan's main islands. It was pretty obvious that after Okinawa, Japan proper would be the next most logical target—victory was in sight, if I lived to see it.

The invasion, planned as a combined Army and Marine venture, would be under the overall command of an Army general. Marine and Army leadership differed in their thinking about how the islands should be conquered. Many of the Army high command felt that bombs and artillery could defeat the Japanese. The Marines had learned differently, because the Japs had to be dug out of the holes, tunnels and caves by close-in use of satchel charges, flame throwers, rifles, machine guns and grenades, and in some instances, with bayonets or knives. Marines felt that fewer men would be lost on each island with the use of Marine tactics. Fortunately, Okinawa would reveal that some of the Army commanders had learned that same lesson.

The Quack Corps

From my observations in the Marianas, I felt that the Marine way was the best, because the saturation pounding of Saipan and Tinian had left too many Japs alive. It had been proven that if we wanted their islands, we had to go in and take them. They had the rocks and solid ground to dig in; we had only the sandy beaches.

The word filtered through the chain of command that we could write one letter, to be left on the ship for mailing after we had landed. This time, we could tell that we were going into combat. The letter deadline was the day before the scheduled landing so we had four days to compose it.

It turned out to be the most difficult letter to write of any I've ever written. Usually, I avoided writing about things that would heighten Dolores' worry about me. With the opportunity to let her know why my letters would stop, I decided to take advantage of it. The iron would be in the fire long before she received it. She could have the option of thinking that I didn't have time or that mail wasn't allowed to leave Okinawa instead of wondering whether the worst had happened.

Probably, she wouldn't understand why I couldn't tell her how I truly felt about heading into combat again—I couldn't admit to my fears that my nerves might not absorb any more stress. Also, I couldn't tell her that I pretended toughness because it made my duties as a platoon sergeant easier. Too, I couldn't let her know about my worries that I might become crippled, upsetting my plans for a future together.

This could be the last letter she would ever receive from me and I wanted it to be cheerful. But, to write that type of letter under those circumstances was extremely difficult since I didn't feel the least bit cheerful. I'd try to write a memorable one she could treasure.

It was difficult to say goodbye without the letter reading as if that was what I was doing, and without becoming maudlin. I sat at the mess table and stared at the blank paper for several minutes, trying to ignore that others were also at the table.

Okinawa!

After writing for a while, I found it necessary to go topside and sit in the sun to control my emotions, and to renew my courage so I could keep a cheerful tone.

While gazing out over the ocean with unseeing eyes, I mentally examined each word and phrase. Each was tested to insure that the letter would express my feelings exactly like I wanted it to. I knew it could be weeks before I received any letters from her—letters I relied on to help me overcome discouragement and to give me the will to keep going.

I answered her questions and made references to comments contained in the letters I'd received just before sailing from Saipan. I wrote little about the forthcoming battle because I didn't want her to know how worried and concerned I was about it. Usually, I teased in my letters and so this one wouldn't differ in that respect. I ribbed about her enjoyment of going barefoot, and the 15 children I expected a wife of mine to bear and mother.

She didn't know how long it took for me to write the letter or of the many times I had torn a page, or pages, to shreds and started over because it didn't read right. Though I spent four days, 28, 29, 30 and 31 March, off and on, writing it, I still felt a nagging dissatisfaction. I wanted a *masterpiece* but felt it had failed to be one, though 12-pages were filled with my hard-to-read scrawl.

With the letter done, my attentions turned to the future. It wasn't long in coming for shortly after dawn on 1 April, 1945, the LST's PA system passed the word: "Unidentified planes are heading our way!"

I guessed that they were Jap and the pilots were looking for the biggest game. I knew there were hundreds of ships surrounding us, even though I couldn't see many of them.

"All Marines go to your quarters!" blared the PA system. I hurried to the 1st platoon's quarters, below decks in the ship's stern.

The Quack Corps

Moments after sacking out in my bunk, a mental picture flashed of a Jap plane's motor crashing through the thin steel of the ship's hull. I had been caught below decks once before and I wasn't going to let it happen again! I slipped topside and stood just aft of the superstructure. A 20mm mount was nearby with one man missing from its crew. I had learned how to use them on the battleships but, as I made a move to help man it, the crewman arrived breathlessly to his station.

Moments later, I saw four planes several thousand yards distant, flying just above the water and in a heading angling between the lead DE and the lead row of the LST flotilla; *LST-725* was the center ship of the three comprising the front row. The pilots had selected the LSTs of the flotilla to be their targets. They were trying to wipe us out before we even sighted land!

Were those four planes only the vanguard for others to follow? Did those pilots realize that destroying the LSTs in that particular flotilla would also destroy the AmTracs, tanks, DUKWs with howitzer-filled cargo spaces, and the men to operate them, and make it impossible for an entire division to make a successful landing? Did they realize that they were looking at the ships hauling the essential parts that made it all possible? If they decimated this flotilla, other means would have to be used to get the infantry units ashore, other means would also have to be found to keep them supplied with vital needs enabling them to continue fighting, and, they'd be fighting without artillery support until other guns could be acquired and brought in. Destroying this small group of LSTs would disrupt and possibly delay the Okinawa invasion.

Only seconds after I sighted the planes as they came over the horizon, flames erupted from the lead DE's 5-inch AA guns. In a matter of only seconds, the accurate fire by the guns brought down two of the enemy. The other two planes performed evasive maneuvers and as the range lengthened, the DE ceased firing. The 5-inch AA bursts hadn't deterred them

Okinawa!

from attacking and the planes continued bearing down on the front row of LSTs.

One plane disappeared behind the bulk of *LST-884*, to port of *-725*. Moments later, smoke and flame boiled up above *-884*. The plane had apparently deliberately crashed into the ship!

The remaining plane maneuvered to a course directly between *LST-884* and *-725*, and, skimming the wave tops, bore down on *-725*. I watched, almost with fascination, feeling helpless and mentally pulling for it to clip the top of a wave.

The 20mm and 40mm guns on *LST-725* began spewing projectiles and the noise rose in a crescendo. I silently implored *Get him! Get him!* The plane continued to bear down until, about 100 yards from the side of the ship, it suddenly veered to its right and crashed into the wake of the LST. A huge geyser of water, flame, smoke, and debris spouted skyward. Fractions of seconds later the noise of the explosion reached me. It became very quiet. I breathed a prayer of thanks.

LST-884 had stopped dead in the water and was burning. The DEs quickly came alongside to rescue men and fight fire.

The flotilla sailed away at its plodding pace. It looked as if they were deserting their sister ship, but there was nothing they could do. And the pillar of smoke would serve as a beacon for other Jap planes on the hunt for targets.

I watched from the ship's stern until the burning LST's silhouette gradually faded below the horizon. I wondered how much longer 2d DUKW could expect its luck to hold. Maybe the humpback whales *had been* our guardian angels.

As I thought about the close call, I wondered whether the pilot may have decided, at the last moment, that he couldn't be responsible for causing the deaths of men on that ship since I saw no flames, smoke, or other evidence to account for the sudden veering off during the approach to *LST-725*.

The Quack Corps

A huge column of black smoke hung in the air for several hours until it too disappeared below the horizon.

On 1 April, 1945, April Fool's Day, the 2d Marine Division feinted a landing at the southern end of Okinawa, then again on the 2nd. But the Japs didn't take the bait offered by the play acting. Then, the division withdrew and was held as floating reserve.

As the ships hauling the division cruised slowly and aimlessly in the East China Sea, the knowledge that Marines were fighting nearby and 2d DUKW wasn't lending a hand made me feel like the company wasn't doing its part.

The sea was calm, 13 April, and I was lolling topside watching a Jap plane flying just under the broken clouds, apparently taking photographs. Two Hellcat fighters headed toward it. The enemy plane ducked into a large cloud hanging off to starboard of *LST-725*. Occasionally, it dropped out of the cloud but quickly ducked back in when the fighters drew near. As the cat-and-mouse game continued, I began to feel grudging admiration for the Japanese pilot, as he continued to outguess the Hellcat pilots. Eventually, the plane ducked into the cloud and didn't come out. The Hellcats circled for a while then headed out of the area.

While I was watching the battle of wits overhead, the announcement of President Franklin Roosevelt's death came over the LST's PA system. I wondered what effect his death would have on the future conduct of the war. I also wondered what secret agreements he might have made with the Allies. He wasn't my favorite but earlier I had written Dolores that he was popular with many Marines.

Only a few hours after word of his death, the LSTs hauling 2d DUKW pulled out of the flotilla. Their bows pointed toward the hazy silhouette of Okinawa, peeking over the horizon. I guessed that something was up when Lieutenant Blackburn ordered me to muster the men on the fo'c'sle. After mustering, he announced that we were going to land on Okinawa

Okinawa!

and to take all our gear, including seabags. The 105s in the DUKWs would be unloaded and moved back aboard ship.

The LST headed straight to the island and ploughed through the light surf until her bow made contact with Okinawan soil. The huge bow doors opened, the ramp began its descent and continued until it, too, touched shore.

Nothing like variety for 2d DUKW because now it was making a landing just like any ordinary wheeled vehicle unit! Quite frankly, I much preferred it.

"Ye gads!" I blurted when I saw that the 1st platoon had been assigned a bivouac at the hub of a crossroads. Yontan Airfield was a short distance up the hill to the east; the beach, a few hundred yards to the west. It wasn't the most appealing place for a bivouac. I ordered the men to hold off digging foxholes until I checked with Lieutenant Blackburn to inquire whether we could get a change of bivouac.

I pointed out that it was a very likely place for the Japs to work over with bombs and strafing. I knew Jap planes were making raids almost every night. He agreed with me and hurried away to find Captain George. Apparently, the captain had been assigned a very specific area for his company to bivouac. He was unable to get it changed. We were stuck with the spot.

After the disappointing word, I ordered the men to make haste with their digging. I also warned them to roof their holes with sandbags. Luckily, we were able to find enough scrap lumber for roofs over them. Sandbags filled with dirt were piled on the lumber.

As anticipated, just after dark we heard planes coming in the distance, from the south. They appeared to be following the main road, which ran north and south about 25 feet from our nearest foxholes.

Just before reaching the crossroads, it sounded like the Japs dumped small bombs out of burlap sacks. As the planes completed their runs and climbed for altitude, the rear gunners sprayed the 1st platoon area. I could hear bullets hitting the

The Quack Corps

sandbags and splattering the ground. Fortunately, the hole tops were thick enough to prevent any men from being wounded or killed. Surprisingly, the DUKWs dispersed adjacent to the foxhole perimeter didn't receive any appreciable damage.

At dusk, the second night on the island, a DUKW crew and I were nearing the bivouac when we heard planes coming. The driver floorboarded the throttle and we reached the bivouac just as the first plane zoomed overhead. He set the emergency brake, the wheels locked, and we cleared the DUKW before it stopped moving.

I had to report to the command post, about 200 yards away, so I dove into a little ditch bordering the road to it. After each plane passed, I leaped to my feet and ran until I heard the next one coming then belly flopped into the ditch again. Jesse Owens would have had trouble matching strides with me on that run!

Finally, dirty and out of breath, I made it to the CP, which was located near the beach and between two little hills. I had to sit for several minutes regaining my breath, before reporting to Captain George. Admittedly, it felt much safer under the thick roof of the CP though it received no strafing.

Every bomb landed across the road from the 1st platoon's bivouac—we didn't lose a man or vehicle.

I wondered why the Japs concentrated on the other side of the road until I realized that the most logical place for men and vehicles would be in vegetation, for concealment, which the bombed area contained. They must have assumed the flat terrain in the barley field at the crossroads held only lower-priority materials.

The drivers had covered the DUKW windshields with the cab tarps and I doubt that the Jap pilots and gunners even realized the vehicles were parked there.

The day after the second strafing, the 1st platoon moved near a little knoll closer to the beach and doubled up in foxholes with other men in 2d DUKW. We hadn't moved far but

Okinawa!

it was just enough to end the sound of Jap bullets hitting the tops of our foxholes during subsequent air raids. I guessed it would have been only a matter of time until the Jap pilots decided to bomb our side of the main road, and I felt relieved by the move.

Though it ended the sound of Jap shells on our hole roofs, we encountered another problem. Inexperienced gunners, firing 20mms at the low-flying planes from the ships offshore, sprayed the bivouac. Several mornings, we found unexploded 20mm shells sticking out of sandbags. A 20mm penetrated the hull of a DUKW and lodged over a wheel well. The vehicle was out of service for several days before one of the men got up the nerve to fish it out. In time, the shelling stopped and scuttlebutt floated that the Navy had ordered that only warship gunners could fire at planes over land. For whatever reason, the air raids were a little less hard on our nerves.

A short time later, the company moved into the area of the two little hills. The 1st platoon bivouacked on the beach side of the larger one, adjacent to the road running between the two. I liked this spot much better because it lessened the likelihood of bombing and strafing. Also, we would have had a mud problem in the barley field, because it became a bog during heavy rains.

With the bivouac problems solved and a work routine established, we became anxious to receive and send out letters. But, it was 18 April before we knew what we should show for a return address.

Although carried on the rolls as an element of the Tenth Army, Second DUKW worked mostly in the area of and with the 6th Marine Division, which was on the extreme right of the front as the divisions advanced south.

Fortunately, Second DUKW's new address was simply: The 2d Marine Amphibian Truck Company, c/o Fleet Post Office, San Francisco, California. With that address, it would prevent long incoming-mail delays as the company switched divisions and islands. Apparently, the Fleet Post Office was informed immediately of company moves and our mail was redirected as it crossed the Pacific.

With the new return address on the envelope, my first letter to Dolores went out on 18 April. I reminded her to take note of it so her letters wouldn't be delayed. She received the letter on 26 April, to read:

> *You should see the burial tombs here. They are all over the place. I understand the Japs, or maybe the natives, place a body in a tomb for three years then burn what remains and dump the ashes in a jar and set it back in the tomb. Hearsay maybe, but they do have big jars in them and some have boxes that look like caskets.*
>
> *The natives run loose but don't bother anything. They salute or bow when meeting an American. It's funny as hell ... when I see one, I see at least a dozen, with the ratio of one man, six or eight women and the rest children. The women and kids carry the loads and the men are usually empty handed or carrying a stick.*
>
> *I miss you, Honey. Why don't you start digging your way over to me? If you come up under my foxhole, you'll have 6-feet less to dig! Come right away because I'm cold and need you to keep me warm on these chilly nights.*
>
> *I inflated five Navy lifebelts for use as an air mattress—it's like sleeping on a soft Stateside mattress so I'm fighting this war in style and comfort.*

I began constructing and acquiring various other items to make foxhole living more comfortable. A bright can made a reflector which helped the candle I'd acquired back on Saipan light my hole better. I also rigged a shower by using a barrel

Okinawa!

mounted on a wooden platform—showering in the solar warmed water was refreshing.

The candle was obtained in the manner Marines usually used to supplement meager supplies. A cargo ship off Saipan had dunnage (scrap lumber) and I had taken a DUKW and crew to pick it up for use in our Kagman Peninsula camp. The ship's captain requested that we haul a case ashore which had been left aboard by the Army engineer unit riding the ship to Saipan. After leaving the ship, I felt curious and wondered what engineers carried in boxes like that so I removed the packing slip from its envelope for a look. My eyes bugged when I noted that among the items in the case were four dozen, four-inch paintbrushes. Second DUKW hadn't been able to replenish its supply of paintbrushes, of any size, and I wondered why the engineers rated so many.

I made inquires upon reaching the beach but no one could tell me where the unit was located. So I thought, rather than run around the island with a heavily loaded DUKW, I'd take the case to camp and let the company office go through channels to locate the engineers. Lieutenant Blackburn was in camp and asked about the case. When I told my tale, he commented, "We sure could use those paint brushes."

"I know, Sir, but if the engineers check with the ship, they'll learn that a DUKW hauled it in and pretty soon they'll be here looking for it. If they spot the case, we'll have problems," I commented.

One of the men standing nearby piped up, "We can throw it into the trash pile and burn it." So the contents of the case became 1st platoon property, for a time.

Generously, I distributed three dozen of the paintbrushes to the other platoons and placed the other dozen under my cot. That night, I went to the nearby outdoor movie. After the movie, I returned to my tent and discovered that someone had appropriated the 1st platoon's share of the brushes. I didn't learn who had taken them until 40 years later!

The Quack Corps

In addition to the improved lighting and the shower, I strung a duplicate field telephone wire to the radio in the CP. It wasn't loud enough until I cut off part of a cardboard megaphone and put it over the receiver to make a loudspeaker. My phone could ring with the wire attached but I had to disconnect it to converse. With piped-in music in the foxhole the leisure hours passed more pleasantly.

The amenities helped to maintain our reputation as scavengers supreme. A maintenance platoon sergeant acquired 110 pounds of steaks from a cargo ship. What a feast! My letter of 25 April was filled with raves about it.

My duties or scavenging didn't give me much time for writing but I managed a letter every two or three days. Sometimes, the air raid siren howled and I'd have to quit in mid-sentence and wait until the next day to finish it.

Darwin "Nick" Nicholson, now a sergeant, shared the hole with me. We were compatible foxhole buddies. He snored but it didn't create any unusual problems since the frontlines were some distance away. We could see the flashes and hear the explosions when shells hit Jap territory. Nick liked to putter. After moving a bivouac, it usually wasn't long until he could be spotted taking off with a couple of wrenches peeking out of a dungaree pocket. I occasionally related his activities to Dolores, as in this letter:

> *Nick has been scavenging again. He found a Jap hand pump, used to transfer liquids from barrels, and he has been working on it most of the day. He has two barrels setting by our foxhole and has been pumping water back and forth from one to the other. He just told me, "I think I've got it fixed. Now we don't have to pass water by hand into our shower barrel but can pump it in."*
>
> *That squeaky pump has been driving me crazy while I've been writing to you. I don't want to be*

Okinawa!

driven crazy ... except over you!

Second DUKW's reputation for scavenging must have preceded it from Saipan. One afternoon, Lieutenant Blackburn came to my foxhole and inquired, "Sergeant, do we have any mortars in camp?"

Surprised by the question, I wondered if he had lost his marbles. After staring quizzically at him for a moment, I answered, "Lieutenant, that is a strange question. Why do you ask, Sir?"

"Men are here from Army ordnance and they say they are missing some mortars. Someone told them that our company has them."

"Sir, I know the men make it a practice of lugging stuff to camp but I haven't seen or heard of any mortars."

"I haven't heard rumors of any in camp either," he replied.

"Sir, are you sure the doggies aren't trying to pull a fast one? What use do they think this company has for mortars? Whoever told them that must be off his rocker."

"I told them, 'I think you've been misinformed but I'll check with the men,'" he replied.

"Sir, if I hear or see anything I'll let you know."

"All right, Sergeant. You do that." He turned and headed back to the CP. Second DUKW may have hauled the mortars but dropped them at the wrong location.

With Yontan Airfield only about a mile from our bivouac, we sometimes had much more to worry about than missing mortars. Japanese planes strafed the field frequently. One afternoon, I watched two planes as they made a run down its length. The machine gunners stationed around its perimeter hit both of them. Flame and smoke streamed behind the planes and they banked in my direction. One crashed just before reaching the bivouac and the other soared over it and hit a short distance off shore. The gunners used their weapons with

The Quack Corps

deadly accuracy because I saw many enemy planes shot down by them.

Censorship was more relaxed so I could write about seeing the planes shot down and other incidents, including more of my own activities. In my letter of 2 May:

> *I watched a Hellcat coming in, escorted by a Corsair, with half of its tail assembly dragging behind. I didn't see any smoke when it landed so apparently the pilot made a safe landing. Our planes are so much sturdier than the Nip planes.*

Then I switched the subject, and continued:

> *I'm going to try finding some of the red lacquer this place is noted for. It is touted as being very beautiful but thin and easy to break.*
>
> *I made a run several miles inland last night. I saw the first bridge and river that I've seen in a long time. I'd like to take a fly rod and see what could be caught in the river. I became very sleepy about 3:30 A.M., because it took most of the night to complete the errand* [I avoided military time designation in letters to civilians].
>
> *I usually work a 12-hour shift, followed by the other two senior platoon sergeants working 12 hours each. It means that I work all night every third night. The company usually works 24 hours each day until it finishes unloading a ship. Of course, we have to shut down when the air raid sirens howl, then it's back to work.*
>
> *I didn't do much dreaming during the other invasions but I've been making up for it lately. A few nights back, I dreamt of being on an ice floe (must have kicked my blanket off and got cold) and the Japs*

were firing artillery at me. I was scurrying for cover but every time I tried to run, I'd slip and fall. Finally, I began crawling over the ice. Why is it that in a person's dreams, no matter how hard one tries, one can never run?

I daydream about you. But the dreams I have about you at night seem to end up with us fighting about something, which reminds me ... you mentioned in your last letter that you got very angry when the foreman wanted to switch your work hours. I'm wondering if you are the kind of hellion that throws dishes? Well, are you? Maybe I'd better bring my flak jacket back with me!

Second DUKW's personnel used Army Air Corps flak jackets during the Okinawa invasion. This may have been their first use by a Marine ground force unit or even the first use by an American ground unit.

I watched the planes, enemy and friendly, approaching and leaving Yontan. Also, I watched enemy attacks on the ships offshore. Occasionally, enemy aircraft appeared to fit into a free-of-fire zone in the air. Not so, I noticed, when American planes were fired on by mistake because it seemed that someone always became a deadeye then. It must have been a terrible feeling for American pilots, when apparently among friends, to be fired on and sometimes shot down. I first saw American planes shot down by mistake at Saipan when four TBFs headed toward the ships carrying the landing forces and were shot down. I also saw it happen at Okinawa when pilots made the mistake of flying toward or over ships at low altitude; I believe they had orders not to do it.

The CP for directing the DUKW drivers where to take loads and for keeping tallies was located on a small beach north of our bivouac. A bulldozer pushed up dirt on three sides, with the front of the CP left open. One evening, during

The Quack Corps

an air raid on Yontan, Lieutenant Blackburn and I were standing in the CP talking. Suddenly, bullets c-r-a-a-a-c-k-ed between us. We belly flopped on the dirt. Later, we learned that a machine gunner clearing his gun had let it get away from him.

Another evening, I was directing traffic at the beach CP and noticed a fire at sea. Since we didn't unload ammunition ships after dark, the DUKWs should have been in by then and I began to worry. In time, I heard one coming and waited at the water's edge. I stopped the driver, and asked, "Why are you so late getting in? You know you are supposed to be in by dark. Do you know what caused the fire?"

He answered my last question first, "Yes. A Jap plane crashed into the stern of the ship we were unloading. We've been rescuing the ship's crew."

"How come the ammo ship didn't blow?"

"One of the crew said that the captain ordered the sea cocks opened. It went down before the fire reached its cargo."

"Are all of the men okay?"

"Yes. They're coming in just as soon as they get the rest of the crew aboard another ship," he answered.

We didn't unload ammo ships at night because they anchored so far offshore that the drivers couldn't find their way in. Also, the ships didn't like to show lights and we couldn't use a beacon light on the beach, for obvious reasons. The ammo ships were required to anchor well away from other ships.

At dusk another day at the beach CP, I heard a jeep coming from inland with its motor whining at high RPM. When it neared, I saw that it was being driven in reverse. The driver, Corporal Guy Burton, jammed on the brakes and the tires kicked up a cloud of dust and gravel. "The Japs are coming!" he yelled.

We hadn't had any reports of the Japanese infiltrating the area. It was considered secured, so I questioned him, "Are you

Okinawa!

sure they're not natives?"

"They're not natives! They're Japs!" he adamantly insisted. Suddenly, he jammed the jeep in gear and took off with the tires spewing dust and gravel. He headed down the rough road, parallel to the shoreline, toward camp at high speed.

The CP was isolated and no units were bivouacked within several hundred yards. Three men were at the CP with me. "Grab your carbines and take cover in the CP!" I ordered.

"We don't have them with us," one of the men answered.

I blew my stack! "What the hell do you mean, you don't have them with you? Don't you men know this island is far from being secured?"

"We left them in camp," the same man replied.

"You sure as hell better grab some rocks then! If they're Japs, I sure can't hold them off long with my .45," I fumed.

The men had become careless and complacent because we were running from a ship just offshore to a close-by dump. Also, the dust was thick on the roads which necessitated frequent cleaning of weapons.

After I had paced back and forth in front of the CP for a few minutes, a DUKW roared to shore. The driver hopped out to replenish his canteen water. I scaled the side of the vehicle and quickly backed it behind the CP mound. Then, I manned the .50-caliber machine gun, it fortunately had on its ring mount.

After waiting for a few minutes, I heard chatter in a language I couldn't understand. The group wasn't making any effort to be quiet. I wondered ... *could they be Japs masquerading as natives?*

Most of the light had faded by the time the group came within hailing distance, so I challenged, "Halt! Who goes there?" The voices quieted but no answer came to my challenge. I cocked the .50. The cocking noise brought a prompt "Ho!" in English. "Advance to be recognized!" I commanded.

The Quack Corps

The group came closer and I halted them again. "Give the password!" I commanded.

The English-speaking individual gave the correct password, then continued, "Sergeant, this is Lieutenant Blackburn. These natives were turned over to me and I've brought them here until the MPs can come get them."

He lined the group, about 15 natives, up alongside the road. One of the men stepped out of line to in front of the lieutenant. Dropping to his knees and clasping his hands in a prayerful position, he looked into Lieutenant Blackburn's face and pleaded with him. He apparently concluded that the lieutenant lined them up for me to mow them down with the machine gun. It looked like the native was pleading for their lives.

Though he didn't speak the language, Lieutenant Blackburn made him understand that we wouldn't harm them. So the group sat down in the dirt to wait, their faces beaming with broad smiles. Later, I learned they were caught by nightfall before they got back to their village.

Lieutenant Blackburn was a little put out at me. So I said, "Sir, you should have answered my first challenge."

"Yes, I know I should have. It sure scared little peach seeds out of me when I heard you cock the .50," he replied, with a wry grin.

A few days later, I had a scare of my own. I had to have a wisdom tooth pulled! It turned out to be a memorable visit to a dentist. While in the chair, a plane flew over that didn't sound American so the dentist, his assistant and I rushed out of the tent. We were in time to watch a kamikaze dive into amidships, on the boat deck of the battleship *New Mexico*. We didn't see or hear a single shot fired at the plane. Though none of us saw it, a bomb dropped by a second plane also hit her. *New Mexico* had 54 killed and 119 wounded by the attack. A Marine told me later that only 12 Marines in her detachment escaped death or injury. I wondered whether any of them had been aboard during my time on *New Mex*.

Okinawa!

At night, I often sat by a radio jeep belonging to an adjacent unit and listened to the nightfighter pilots while they devastated flights of Jap planes attempting to get to the island or our ships. The pilots had my admiration; what a tremendous job they did!

From the beginning, the Nips sent planes over at high altitude, at night, to drop a few bombs and harass American forces. We referred to them as Washing Machine Charlies because of their rough sounding motors. Though they kept us awake, they didn't do much damage. I felt the Charlies were also sent over to help Jap ground forces' morale so they knew they had friends in the sky. None of our guns ashore had been able to hit them so the pilots disdained even trying to evade the searchlight beams.

The Army brought in a few 90mm AA guns which were reportedly radar controlled. I watched as vehicles towed them by our bivouac. Washing Machine Charley was in for a surprise. *Sure enough, the first night he made an appearance after the 90's came in, the crew didn't eat breakfast in Japan the next morning.* I saw the flashes when the AA guns opened up and, moments later, the plane's motors stopped. Fractions-of-seconds later, a bright flash lit the night as the plane exploded in a massive ball of flame. Cheers reverberated up and down the island! The Jap pilots soon avoided the areas where the 90's were positioned.

While snooping around Yontan Airfield one day, I noticed a Marine Corsair with the motor cowling pushed in. The propeller and adjacent areas didn't show any evidence that an AA shell burst had caused it. While I was eyeballing it the Corsair's pilot walked up. We talked and I asked, "Sir, I'm curious about how your plane got damaged that way?"

He didn't seem to be a smart ass so I had no reason to doubt when he answered, with a grin, "I tangled with a Zero and he got on my tail. I shoved the stick forward and went

The Quack Corps

down in a power dive. He stayed with me but while trying to follow me out, the Zero lost its wings."

I knew it'd take tremendous speed to push the cowling in, and asked, "Sir. How fast were you going?"

"Damned if I know. I glanced at the needle just before pulling out and it was way past the pin."

Our bull session was lengthy. When I left, I wished him good luck and, my parting words were, "Knock as many of those bastards down as you can."

"Thanks. I'll do my best," he replied.

I didn't write about the Corsair or the Zero losing its wings because I thought the pilot might have devised a new way for downing Zeros. But, I did write that I had been to the graves of the men lost by Admiral Perry during his visit to Okinawa in 1854. I also wrote that a white schoolteacher and other Caucasians were buried in the same plot.

Sometimes, Dolores wrote about things that reminded me of my duty. She described two new dresses she had purchased; one was yellow. Commenting about the dresses:

> *I'll bet you look nice in yellow. Speaking of yellow, it reminds me that it's time to hold Atabrine call. I'll be back later. ...*

After making sure all of the men had taken their Atabrine tablets, I dismissed them and returned to the letter:

> *I'm as yellow as a dried peach seed because of taking Atabrine. Everyone looks like they have yellow jaundice.*

The fear of catching malaria I felt should be reminder enough but some of the men had to be nursemaided into taking the Atabrine tablets. I suspected there were a few in the company who felt malaria was preferable to battle.

Okinawa!

With the tensions of over three years of war and my platoon responsibilities, I was feeling much older than my 23 years, as reflected in my letter of 15 May:

> *Although I'm young in years, I feel and think like an old man. When I get back and all of the pent up emotions and tensions have an outlet, I'll be as frisky as a new born colt.*

And a change of subjects:

> *You should have been here to share noon chow with me today. Here is my menu: fried bacon, mixed C-rations consisting of chicken and vegetables, frankfurters and beans, and corned beef hash. I topped off the meal with peas and ham 'n eggs (dehydrated). In addition to all of that, I had apple jelly, crackers, and grapefruit juice. The men wonder where I put all of that food and consider me to be a true "chow hound."*
>
> *A woman's touch would come in handy here. Want a job? I can understand why, in medieval times, husbands took their wives to war with them.*

During work-hour lulls, I mentally cataloged things to write about. When time came to put them on paper, the Japs sometimes interrupted my plans, as they did on 25 May. They didn't bomb or strafe the bivouac, they found another way to disrupt the routine.

When I returned to camp a dusk, Nick was standing in front of our hole holding a .30-caliber air-cooled machine gun, appropriated earlier off a destroyed tracked vehicle. We hadn't acquired a tripod yet so he had the barrel slung from a piece of wire. When I asked why he was armed that way, he replied, "Didn't you see that plane come by camp?"

"No. What happened?"

"We were shooting the bull and a Jap plane suddenly roared by from the ocean side. It was so low that its belly almost scraped the little hill. We were so startled that we didn't even take a shot at it. But I'm ready now. If another comes by, I'll get 'em."

"How come it was so low?"

""I don't know but it headed for Yontan," he answered.

A few minutes later, my field telephone rang. It was Captain George with orders for me to report to the CP. I reported in and was told, "Sergeant, the Japs have landed men on Yontan. We've been ordered to send reinforcements. You will go as senior NCO."

"Which officer will be in command, Sir?"

"I will," he replied.

Based on my observations, when the men had tried to run a compass course I laid out while the company was on Oahu, I knew that, within reason, the fewest men taken along the better things would be. So, after some discussion the captain decided to take only two 10-man squads because control would be difficult in the darkness. The men chosen had infantry experience and those who best retained their wits under fire. They gathered their gear and mustered near the DUKW park, because, to speed things up, we'd ride part way. Fortunately, word came cancelling the order before we left. Airfield personnel had things under control and we wouldn't be needed. I breathed a sigh of relief because 2d DUKW had never placed any priority on field training in infantry tactics.

The Japs intended to satchel charge or grenade the planes but most were killed before they reached them. I learned that, of the few who managed to do damage, some had hacked at the planes with knives.

With that excitement out of the way, our routine returned to normal. We operated as the DUKW's inventor may have envisioned: ship to inland dumps. We made some frontline deliveries with the usual cringing in holes, behind rocks or a dirt

Okinawa!

Photo by PlSgt. Tom Black—March 1945
Packed top deck of LST heading for Okinawa invasion.

Photo by PlSgt. Tom Black—June 1945. Okinawa
PlSgt. Arthur Wells—tanning Atabrine-yellowed body dressed in prewar-issue skivvy shorts.

The Quack Corps

Photo courtesy Robert Freer—June 1945
2d Amphibian Truck Company DUKWs hauling Japanese prisoners of war, Okinawa. No. 94—1st platoon.

bank when mortars or artillery opened up. Our exposure to direct enemy fire was much less frequent than it had been on Saipan. The men were bored with ship unloading.

Though I recognized the DUKWs' importance in quickly getting supplies to the island, in a way I felt almost left out of the battle. I knew the efforts of the 46 men in my platoon resulted in many more killed Japs than if they were firing rifles and machine guns on the frontlines. The armaments and supplies they delivered made it possible for thousands to fire guns and kill Japs. Even with that awareness, I still felt the Marine Corps was wasting my varied weaponry and other training, as was the case with several others in 2d DUKW.

But, there wasn't the mind-deadening mental and physical fatigue like on Saipan and my letters to Dolores reflected it. My moods didn't bounce up and down like a yo-yo as they had before. Only once since landing on 13 April had I begun a letter and quit because of a bad mood. Perhaps, a good part of that was because she had made the commitment to be my wife.

Okinawa!

At times, Dolores showed impatience at the seemingly long wait before my return. She had high hopes that war's end in Europe meant I'd come home sooner. I knew that wasn't likely to happen. The Marines had too much experience in amphibious landings and I didn't feel they would send in a new team to replace them. Too, high-ranking Marine officers, as a matter of Corps pride, would agitate to make certain that the Corps wasn't left out. The Marines had been in the forefront of the relentless march across the Pacific and they expected to be in on the kill. So I wrote in late May:

> *I know it takes lots of patience during times like these. Sometimes, I've had the feeling that maybe it's not good to plan for the future—you know ... make merry today for tomorrow I may die. But I've never been able to resist making plans.*
>
> *Even though the war is won in Europe, it probably won't have any bearing on when I'll return because there are few Marines in Europe. Discharging men from the Marine Corps in large numbers cannot be done. But the additional Army personnel shipped to the Pacific will help make our job of finishing the Japs easier and quicker. You must remember too that, percentage wise and man for man, the Marines have had the most experience at fighting the Japs on land. We'll be in the middle of it until it's finished. On the whole and regardless of how much we may "beat our gums," I don't think Marines would want it any other way. We just need a vacation from it now and then.*

My morale, on the whole, was good because her letters arrived regularly. But, I welcomed what appeared to be good news at the tail end of May, 2d DUKW was going to leave Okinawa. Admittedly, bivouacking so close to Yontan Airfield

The Quack Corps

too often made it like 4th of July fireworks; sooner or later one of the Jap planes would end up in our laps.

My guess was that the company would rejoin the 2d Division. I knew it was still on Saipan but I suspected it was about ready to make a landing someplace though I hadn't heard any scuttlebutt to support my suspicions. With the tough fighting on Okinawa and the casualties being taken, I thought it odd that the 2d Division hadn't been committed to the battle.

We removed the tarps from over the foxholes and cleaned up the bivouac. Our gear was loaded into the DUKWs. This time, the drivers drove the lightly loaded vehicles to the beach and up the ramps into the tank decks of the LSTs. The ramps raised, the huge prow doors closed, and the ships backed slowly away from shore.

Chapter 16
A Second Invasion of Okinawa

LST-1029 turned and headed away from Okinawa. I looked at the landmass and silently prayed for my buddies-in-arms, soldiers, sailors, and Marines, who remained and were still fighting to make it ours. I also gave thanks that I had survived another invasion.

The 2d Marine Amphibian Truck Company, I felt, must be leading a charmed life. Again good fortune had smiled on 2d DUKW because not one man or vehicle had been left on the island as a result of enemy action. So little loss in three invasions was almost a miracle. The law of averages would catch up with the company sooner or later I feared.

Instead of heading for Saipan, as the company's personnel expected, the LSTs sailed to and anchored at an island near Okinawa. We wondered what high command had in store for us. Scuttlebutt floated that the ships needed shelter to ride out a typhoon forecast for the Okinawa area. In open sea, the ships could be lost in stormy seas and us with them. After about three days, the LSTs got underway.

Captain George later informed me that the brass *had* planned a different job for us ... we were to land on and capture one of the small islands near Okinawa. Radar and AA guns were to be installed to detect and shoot down Jap planes heading for Okinawa. But, someone decided that the planes would just fly a different route and bypass the island once they knew the equipment was on it. Captain George didn't specify whether other units had been scheduled to help us, but he did say that DUKW personnel casualties had been expected. The only weapons aboard the vehicles were our carbines, BARs, Thompson submachine guns, .45-caliber pistols, grenades,

The Quack Corps

and the .50-caliber machine guns mounted on several DUKWs. I wondered if high command thought that the men and thin-skinned hybrid trucks were somehow indestructible.

Shortly after leaving the anchorage, Lieutenant Blackburn ordered the men mustered. Then, he announced that the heavy rains had made Okinawa a quagmire and we were to return to the island for further duty.

Oh! Oh! I thought, maybe I was too hasty with my thanks. I decided that someone was keeping close tabs on 2d DUKW. The men who called the tune recognized the DUKWs' versatility. They needed us and we heeded their call.

On 4 June, 1945, the LSTs nosed up to the same shore from which they had departed such a short time before. Second DUKW returned to the camp between the two hills to occupy the same foxholes. Thank goodness, we didn't have to expend energy digging new ones. The conveniences we had constructed, such as the barrel shower, were still intact.

The muddy conditions meant that, once again, 2d DUKW would become jacks-of-all-trades.

The three drive wheels on each side of the DUKW ran in the same track, enabling the vehicle to travel over muddier terrain than the 6 x 6 truck could. But, we found it quicker to go by water to near our final destination and then head to shore to complete the delivery.

After dropping a load, each DUKW swung by the aid stations near the front and transported the casualties to offshore LSTs. Those ships delivered the wounded to rear-area hospitals or hospital ships. With the DUKWs ability to climb the ramps and enter the tank decks of LSTs, it reduced the time involved to move casualties aboard ships. It was an ingenious way to quickly get the wounded to better care facilities.

Heading toward Naha by sea one day I saw a spotter plane heading north flying parallel to the shore. Its fuselage covering, from forward of the pilot's seat to the tail, was missing. I could see the pilot in his seat and the fuselage framework but

A Second Invasion of Okinawa

the second seat was empty. I guessed that Jap AA fire tore holes in the fabric and the wind had peeled it off. The little "grasshopper" planes were used for scouting and to spot for and report the accuracy of artillery fire.

In fact, I saw what I assumed was the same plane on two different days. I guessed that the pilot didn't mind flying his open-air craft. He apparently was doing the observing too since in both cases an observer was not aboard.

The fighting front advanced farther south which resulted in long and time-consuming drives for us to make delivery of supplies. So, after a couple of days in the two-hills bivouac, we moved to one located a short distance to the north of Naha.

The drivers made many runs into the northern outskirts of the destruction-filled city. Snipers often crept close to the road leading into the outskirts. Seldom did a DUKW travel on the road without its crew hearing the zing of a sniper's bullet … shades of Saipan! Two men were hit and some of the DUKWs sported bullet holes. When the road was drier and packed, the vehicles barreled along at about 40 miles per hour; the snipers didn't often have the opportunity for a second shot.

A hill, about 200 feet high was between our bivouac and the front. It shielded us from artillery fire. We dug foxholes on the lower part and parked the DUKWs in the flat valley. Only good fortune prevented a sniper problem inside the bivouac because three Japs had holed up inside our night defense perimeter. A 1st platoon man stumbled onto them while nosing around on the hill. After they were discovered, the Japs scrambled up the hill.

Unarmed, the 1st platoon'er ran down the hill bellowing for the rest of us and the men rushed to their holes for weapons. I remembered their pursuit of the Japs in the Saipan canyon had been like a bunch of wild banshees and I blew my whistle. I didn't want an undisciplined pursuit because someone might be accidently shot. Though a squad was organized, I doubted that the Japs would quit running until they had

The Quack Corps

cleared the area. They didn't get very far before they ran into another Marine unit and all three were killed.

Even though the Japs dug their hole under a bush and carried the dirt away, I thought it odd they had gone undetected so long. I guessed they knew their war was lost and were holing up until an opportune time to surrender. Their weapons consisted of one saber so they had been in no position to do any sniping. Their hole was well stocked with 10-in-1 rations. I guessed they had been eating, in part, from our supply, though they had several packs of Lucky Strike and Camel cigarettes whereas our rations contained Raleighs.

I felt it was bad enough for censors to read my letters but even worse that Japs were close enough to read over my shoulder. Even with this much help I took care not to forget to mark dates off my calendar. To help keep them correct, I called each letter to Dolores a "Foxhole Gazette" and gave it an edition number. But, I hadn't begun the practice until my first letter from Okinawa, on 18 April.

Dolores was aware of my involvement in the Okinawa invasion and she inquired about my activities. I wrote about some of them but without all of the details, especially the hairy incidents. Later, those letters enabled me to tie an incident to an exact date—though in some instances, I didn't need any reminders. Except for the date, I didn't need the other information in "Foxhole Gazette," Edition 26, to recall vividly the details of a delivery made on 7 June, 1945.

I returned to the bivouac after making a supply delivery. A group of nine DUKWs was loaded and ready to head out. Lieutenant Blackburn approached and I hopped off the DUKW to be greeted with, "Sergeant, I want you to take those DUKWs and make delivery to a tank unit operating near Naha. They are almost out of gas and will have to be pulled off the line unless you get it to them. You'll have to go into Naha Harbor to get to the unit."

A Second Invasion of Okinawa

"Aye, aye, Sir. How will I know exactly where it's located?"

"The tankers sent a field radioman to show you the way. He'll also maintain contact with them."

The cargo space of one of the DUKWs was heaped with rations and other supplies, an 8-man volunteer work detail was also aboard, and the other eight were loaded with 55-gallon barrels of gas. As I recall, a cargo space held 17 barrels.

I made a quick stop by my hole. Then, as I headed for the lead DUKW, the lieutenant called me aside, "I'm told there's a Jap machine gun on the south side of the harbor that hasn't been knocked out. You be very careful" ... a remark characteristic of him.

"I will, Sir. Do you know what caliber and exactly where it's located?"

"They didn't tell me its size. It's in a pillbox or cement blockhouse at the south side of the entrance. They're going to try to knock it out before you get there."

"Lieutenant, I sure as hell hope they're successful!"

"They're dozing a road down the harbor bank so you can get out of the water. If they're not ready when you get to Naha, pull to shore north of town and wait until it's done."

"Aye, aye, Sir." As I headed back to the DUKW, I thought this might turn out to be a hairy run. I scaled the side of the DUKW, gave the crank-up and follow-me signals, then headed the convoy west through the small hills between the bivouac and the sea, because we'd make most of the trip by water.

We reached the northern outskirts of Naha. The tankers didn't have the road ready so we headed to shore and dispersed the vehicles on the beach.

I saw puffs of smoke and heard gunfire of all sizes from the front lines on the hills surrounding the inner reaches of the small harbor.

The Quack Corps

The platoon was organized into four sections with four DUKWs each, with a sergeant as section leader. I walked toward one of the vehicles to talk to a section leader and a shell, that I judged to be about 37mm size, zipped past and hit the water just off the edge of the beach. Instinctively, I began to run one way but changed my mind and headed the other direction. After a couple of steps, I realized there wasn't anything on the beach to hide behind, so I decided I may as well walk. I really didn't need to talk to that section leader after all, I decided, and returned to the lead DUKW.

Corporal Harold Reynolds was one of the eight who volunteered to go along to help speed up unloading. He not only was the star softball pitcher for the 1st platoon but he was one of the first to step forward when volunteers were requested for frontline runs and other dangerous missions. As I neared the DUKW, he was lolling on the rations and looking at me with, what Missourians called, an "opossum-eating" grin on his face. The others aboard joined him in laughter and razzed me about my antics when the shell passed. They welcomed almost any reason for a way to relieve tension. I could only respond with a sheepish grin.

The tankers radioed that we could come ahead, the road was almost finished. So I reboarded the lead DUKW, ordered the driver, "Head out!" and gave the follow-me sign to the other drivers.

We had to go by sea for about one mile to reach the mouth of the harbor. So, the driver headed the DUKW into the water near the mouth of a small canal that ran inland into Naha.

Shortly after we became waterborne, I noticed a rock jetty projecting seaward on the north side of the harbor entrance. It's purpose was to help calm harbor waters during stormy weather.

Oroku Peninsula bordered the harbor on the south. The shoreline extended out beyond the mouth of the harbor and then gradually curved south.

A Second Invasion of Okinawa

Before reaching the harbor entrance, I had the field radioman contact the tank unit to check whether the machine gun had been knocked out; its command post didn't know.

The mouth of Naha Harbor was narrow and it looked about 300 yards wide. We would be setting ducks for the machine gunner if he was still there.

When we were about 100 yards from the seaward end of the jetty, a Marine AmTrac headed into the harbor's mouth. As it neared the harbor end of the jetty, a huge geyser of water spouted into the air a few yards in front of it. The driver spun it around and, with trac-cleats hurling water high into the air, sped out of the entrance to duck behind the jetty for protection.

Oh boy! I thought, not only do we have the machine gun to worry about but the biggies too! I ordered the driver to veer to sea about 500 yards so we'd have maneuvering room if the Japs shelled us.

After we reached a point directly seaward of the entrance, I radioed Sergeants Darwin Nicholson and Harry Mefford, section leaders, to keep the DUKWs moving in a large circle. I wanted to see if the Japs fired more shells at the AmTrac, or shelled us to discourage harbor entry. They did neither.

Scared, and with the high probability of losing the men and DUKWs in the harbor, I hesitated several minutes before getting up the nerve to enter. I decided it'd be better to take one DUKW in first to test the Japs' reaction. So I radioed the section leaders: "I'm going to take one DUKW in to see what the Japs have to say about it. I'm transferring to another DUKW and leaving the work detail with you. I'm taking the radioman with me." We transferred to another DUKW, loaded with barrels of gas, and, with a .50-caliber mounted on its gun ring.

"Keep the DUKWs moving until I give the word to come in. In case they have to take a swim, remind the men to be sure their shoes are untied and that their flak jackets and cartridge belts are undone. When you come in, keep your eyes peeled for mines and any movement on the harbor banks. If the Japs

231

The Quack Corps

get us, take the DUKWs back to north of Naha and one of you return to camp to see what the lieutenant wants to do," I radioed.

I reminded the assistant driver to keep the .50 trained on the cement structure at the south side of the harbor's mouth. Then, I ordered the driver, "Let's give it a try!" He goosed the motor and turned the DUKW toward the entrance.

With the prospect of swimming through burning gas on the calm water and the anticipation of shelling, I felt extremely tense. The Japs could undoubtedly read it on my face through their powerful spotting binoculars and telescopes. Only the AmTrac was near if we ran into trouble. It stayed behind the jetty with its crew sticking their heads above the vehicle to watch us enter. I hoped they were praying for us.

The volume of fire had picked up on the front. I could only guess that it was to divert the enemy's attention so they'd lay off us because not a single shot was fired as the DUKW progressed through the harbor mouth, and the machine gun didn't open up. I assumed it had been knocked out and the tank CP hadn't gotten the word, or its crew had scrammed, or the Japs decided not to duel with the .50-caliber trained their way from that different looking boat. Also, the AmTrac crew might have taken care of the gun.

I worried about bypassed Japs and those who may have infiltrated back in on Oroku Peninsula after the Marines had advanced up it. The demolished buildings also provided good cover for snipers. And we were in range of their famous "knee" mortars.

I stood resting my arms on the tarp rail in back of the cab with my eyes scanning the water ahead, the hill paralleling the south bank, and the demolished buildings of Naha on the north bank.

We were about halfway through the harbor when the tankers radioed: "Hold up! We're not quite ready for you."

A Second Invasion of Okinawa

"Hold it here!" I yelled at the driver, and fumed: What a hell-of-a-place to sit and wait!

I glanced toward the harbor entrance. *Oh damn!* I swore when I saw the other DUKWs coming single file through the harbor entrance. Nicholson and Mefford had decided to come in after they saw us make it okay. Our handheld walkie-talkies were short range and unreliable. Later, I learned they decided my radio had malfunctioned when they couldn't raise me.

A heavy firefight was in progress on the front. I could see splashes as shells hit the water nearby and hear various calibers passing by or overhead. I judged that most were over-fire or ricochets from the front.

A demolished building was on the harbor's north side, with cement steps lining the bank to low tide mark. So I ordered the driver, "Head over and anchor the front wheels on those steps. We'll take cover behind that cement wall until they're ready for us." The wall was about all that was still standing of what had been a passenger terminal; the harbor appeared to be too small for other than inter-island ships. The other drivers dispersed their vehicles along the steps, using front wheels to anchor, with the crews and work detail joining us behind the wall.

Sergeant Nicholson and a couple of men scouted the area and discovered that we were on a small island, about 50 yards from the mainland on the Naha side.

Upon re-entering the terminal, I stood and looked out over the DUKWs through a large shell hole in the wall. Machine gun bursts periodically splashed water near their sterns. I began to worry they'd be destroyed and we'd be marooned on the island. I guessed it'd be some time before anyone took the risk of coming after us even if they knew we were there. I also didn't know how secure the area immediately inland from us was, in case I had to lead the men back to camp by land—we'd have to swim 50 yards or so to the mainland because I hadn't

The Quack Corps

spotted any bridges. Then came the welcome message: "We're ready for you now."

I reboarded the DUKW hauling the work detail. After proceeding a short distance, I noticed a ferry cable stretched across the harbor and in the middle hanging very near the water. I anticipated that it was heavy and wondered what the best and quickest way to get the DUKWs under it would be. There was room to get under at the south bank but with the heavy vegetation along it, I didn't want to risk that Japs might throw grenades into the DUKWs. I didn't feel it was smart to have each DUKW sitting still while its crew tried to work it under the cable so I radioed: "Nick, go check the weight of the cable in the center. If you and the crew can hold it up, the others can get under it quickly."

Fortunately, the cable was much lighter than I had anticipated—Nick stood on the bow alone and held the cable as the ration DUKW passed under it. He gave me a baleful look, his mouth opening and closing. I couldn't hear what he said, but I had no doubts that he was cursing. Maybe, it was just as well I couldn't hear him. He kept his position until all of the DUKWs had made it under the cable. Later, he informed me that a Jap machine gunner had persistently tried to hit the DUKW. As, at the terminal, I guessed that the range was too far for the gunners to see exactly where their rounds hit.

As we moved farther into the harbor—I estimated it to be about a mile and a-quarter in length—I saw the tank unit's CP on the south bank and about one-quarter mile from the inner end of the harbor.

"We're going to unload the rations first so this detail can get out of here as soon as possible. Disperse the DUKWs along the bank. I'll look things over and let you know the layout," I radioed the section leaders.

The steep road up the dirt bank was about 50 feet in length. With its 6-cylinder motor roaring and water cascading off its hull and undercarriage, the DUKW's six drive-wheel

A Second Invasion of Okinawa

tires ripped and clawed the dirt until reaching the top—the road would become slicker and slicker as each succeeding DUKW came up.

A small CP tent sat at the edge of the bank to port. An 81mm mortar position, about 75 feet to our front, fired round after round as fast as the crew could drop them down its tube. Parked nearby was the dozer-equipped tank. The small flat area was protected from direct small arms fire by a hill projecting toward the harbor, laying in a northerly direction.

"There's room up here for only two DUKWs. Tell your drivers that as soon as a DUKW returns to the water, I want another headed up that bank. When empty, I want them to get the hell out of here and head for camp!" I radioed the section leaders.

With the battling at the front so close, the work detail unloaded the rations with more zest than any detail I'd ever had—they needed no prodding! They unloaded the gas with an A-frame.

After the last DUKW was empty, I paid my respects to the tank unit's commanding officer. He thanked me for getting the supplies in and asked me to thank the men.

"Good luck, Sir. Give 'em hell!" I said, and scaled the side of the DUKW.

We worked our way back under the ferry cable. The driver didn't need reminding to floorboard the throttle and get to open sea. As the harbor entrance faded behind the DUKW, I breathed a sigh of relief.

After my nerves had settled a little, I laughed to myself at the look on the tank unit's C.O.'s face when I had jumped off the ration DUKW. I had looked ready to take on the Japs single-handed! As the DUKW had approached the bank road, I had gathered all of my gear because I wouldn't ride that one back to camp. My gas mask, carbine, and radio were slung from my shoulders, binoculars hung from my neck, and I wore

The Quack Corps

a flak jacket, helmet, ammo clip belt, .45 pistol and Navy life belt.

Though I could have guessed that, at his first sight of me, the tank unit C.O. thought I was fresh from stateside and scared that a Jap was in every bush, his demeanor had changed by the time the last DUKW was ready to leave. He seemed impressed by the quick and efficient way the 2d DUKWers had gotten the supplies to the flat area and unloaded.

After returning to camp, I checked to make sure all of the men had safely returned. Then, I made my report to the lieutenant.

The DUKWs from 2d DUKW were probably the first American craft to enter Naha Harbor from the sea and proceed to its inner reaches entirely by water; the Marines had landed on Oroku Peninsula, outside the harbor, and fought their way inland.

The 27th edition of my "Foxhole Gazette," dated 11 June, reveals that I took another 9-DUKW load to the tanks. Delivery was made on a beach near the outer point of the peninsula. The Japs shelled us while we proceeded through the general area where the DUKWs circled on the 7th, but they inflicted no damage.

On almost every subsequent run to Oroku Peninsula or farther south, company DUKWs were shelled while waterborne, usually by a single gun or mortar. Fortunately, they appeared to travel faster in the water than actual speed. My gunnery experience on the *Pennsylvania* and Palmyra Island taught me how difficult it was to visually spot and hit a moving waterborne target. I also considered that by now most of their more-expert gunners may be casualties and the replacements just hadn't acquired the knack. Even though the Japs didn't pick off any of the DUKWs, each run felt like a new invasion.

On 12 June, scuttlebutt floated that the Japs were going to surrender. If so, it would be a complete turnabout so I doubted

A Second Invasion of Okinawa

it was true, but they *were* doing some things differently on this island. I hadn't heard of any large-scale banzai attacks and they didn't appear to be infiltrating as much to the rear areas. Surely by now they had learned that those tactics wasted irreplaceable manpower. I respected their tenacity as fighters but I thought the banzais stupid. Their use of artillery on Okinawa impressed me as being better than I'd seen in the Marianas, except for the inability to hit DUKWs.

The engineers began to span Naha Harbor with a Bailey Bridge. The Japs waited until it was partway across, then shelled it and knocked it out. The engineers tried again; the Japs knocked it out. After several repeats, the engineers' persistence and determination to span the harbor won the day. It probably was to the engineers' benefit that the enemy had been pushed farther south on the island.

Two DUKWs and two AmTracs combined forces to take supplies to a unit south of Naha. En route, a rope wound around a DUKW's propeller shaft and caused the shear pin to snap. Corporal Dwight Rector and PFC Joseph Takats of the maintenance platoon were along in case mechanical repairs became necessary. Rector dived under to remove the rope while Takats replaced the shear pin. The DUKW caught up with the other vehicles on the coral reef just in time to be caught in a barrage of mortar fire. The drivers headed their vehicles for protection behind a seawall paralleling the shore. They waited while a tank took care of the mortar. Then, they watched an Army unit push through a small village with the Japanese retreating headlong before them. With the Japs cleared out, the soldiers filed by the DUKWs and AmTracs to fill their ration, water, and ammunition needs.

In another instance, DUKW men had to make a choice between remaining in the open or taking cover from mortar fire in a ditch running knee-deep with raw sewage ... the ditch won!

The Quack Corps

When possible, AmTracs accompanied DUKWs on runs south of Naha to provide additional firepower. On one of the runs a DUKW broke down. An AmTrac crew stood by while the DUKW men attempted to repair their vehicle. Darkness fell before repairs were completed so the DUKW crew spent the night under the AmTrac. After an uneventful night, they completed the repairs and the vehicles returned north.

Conventional land vehicles were being used more often to supply the units south of Naha, thanks to the Bailey Bridge. Working hours slacked off and enabled the men to write more letters, perform DUKW maintenance, and relax.

During the latter stages of the invasion, most days I was on the go from daylight until dark. I had used up my candle supply so my letter writing had to be done in daylight. As a consequence, my letters to Dolores became sporadic.

My first one had been sent on its way to her on June 8th, only four days after our second invasion of Okinawa. I related tidbits of my activities, things I saw and company tales. With the less-strict censorship it wasn't hard to fill up to eight pages with prattle. The censor probably hoped I'd be jilted or lose my fountain pen. A part of what I wrote on the 8th was:

> *No mail for over a week but I suppose you've noticed the lapse of time between my last letter and the date of this one. Sorry, I can't tell you why.*
>
> *The first sergeant acquired a monkey. It's a cute little devil. They act so much like a human it's comical. This one sees herself in a mirror and tries to smell the monkey staring back at her. She also tries to put her arms around it.*
>
> *Did I tell you that my hair is getting long enough to comb? Thought I'd be prepared, just in case. I don't know whether my uniforms still fit. If they don't and I should return unexpectedly, I at least can marry you with my hair combed.*

A Second Invasion of Okinawa

Do you have that white satin squared away yet? If not, I'll even let you marry me in slacks. Of course, I won't object if you just wrap yourself in a sheet.

A guy has a Jap truck stuck on the muddy road near camp. They don't have many equipped with front-wheel drive and their vehicles are helpless in the mud. I'd be a good Joe and pull him out with a DUKW but it'd be a waste of time and gas, because he wouldn't get far before he got stuck again. I believe it's taken him at least two hours to come the last mile.

Our mail usually arrived from the States in 10 to 12 days. At times, it was delayed and came in bunches. At one mail call, one of the men received 67 letters—I was far behind with only 30.

In my letter of 15 June, I described a native's vegetable garden in the valley near our DUKW park. After describing the sweet potatoes, sugarcane, radishes and cabbages, I added:

I raided a native's patch three days ago. Although I knew that I shouldn't, I just couldn't resist eating a head of raw cabbage. No side effects showed up or maybe I should say, "After effects." I felt it worthwhile because I hadn't eaten raw cabbage since leaving Missouri.

On 18 June, Dolores included a stick of Wrigley's chewing gum in her letter. She thought I wasn't getting gum. I repaid her with stick of Beechnut out of my rations. Chewing gum was on the restricted mail-back list. Lieutenant Blackburn let it go through because of the small quantity. The stick of gum is still in the envelope and it does feel a little stale. I chewed the stick of Wrigley's because it had been months since I'd enjoyed the flavor.

The Quack Corps

On 18 June:

The secured portion of the island is lit up like a big city at night. Big guns on a hill near camp are bombarding Jap territory. Our camp shakes and we can hear the shells passing overhead as they head out. We can see the sky light up when they hit. I'm sure glad they're going out instead of coming in. What a war this has turned out to be.

I've shoveled dirt as a boy on the farm, and I've wallowed in dirt a good part of the time since then. I've done so much shoveling this past year and a-half that I never want to touch another shovel. We'll just throw the seeds on the ground, scratch the dirt with a rake, and those seeds the birds don't eat will grow to be our flowers and vegetables.

She never asked me to send anything but I picked up on our previous long-distance conversations by referring to gum in my letter of the 19th:

In addition to chewing gum, here are just a few of the items we are forbidden to send to the States: fountain pens, Eversharp® pencils and razors, in fact, anything that is in short supply or rationed Stateside.

I made a dunnage run to the east coast today and returned with enough lumber to build company mess tables. Now, we'll eat like human beings again. Of course, when we sit on the dirt to eat, it's like a picnic. Yes? No!! It is much prettier on that side of the island.

Have you heard of the offer "Rosie" [Tokyo Rose] *made to the first 500 Marines to enter Tokyo?* [She reportedly had offered to take care of them sexually]. *If you haven't, I'll just let you use your imagi-*

A Second Invasion of Okinawa

> *nation for now and tell you some day. I suppose she thinks we're flattered. She'll rue the day the first Marine enters Tokyo! We laugh at her accounts of the war action. She's had the Japs sinking our fleet so many times that I don't know where we obtained all the ships I see here. She does broadcast better American music than we hear on our own island stations.*
>
> *None of the men have been bothered by illness on Okinawa. We were warned about so many things before making the landing. I think most of the men worried more about snakes and illnesses than they did the Japs. At our bivouac, during the early part of the invasion, a Marine killed a big snake a short distance up the hill from my foxhole. But that is the only one I've heard about.*

With the work pace at almost a standstill, I spent even more time writing letters. I watched for and thought back to my earlier days on Okinawa for subjects. On the 23rd, I took up the subject of our company cavalry:

> *After we landed on Okinawa, one of the men brought a small pony to camp; it was even smaller than many Shetlands. I've told you about Smitty's* [Orval Smith] *height and I laughed while watching him ride the pony. Not only did "super" horse have trouble carrying his weight, Smitty had to hold his long legs up to keep his feet from dragging the ground.*
>
> *The sleek horses I wrote you about are still tethered in camp* [Fat and well cared for, we guessed they had belonged to high ranking Jap officers]. *I rode one of them the other day and, as I did on the farm, bareback. I didn't ride very long because as you probably know, one does get a little sore riding without a*

The Quack Corps

> *saddle. Many of the men are "city slickers" and have never rode a horse ... I do find things to laugh about.*
>   *The men aren't doing their usual free time horsing around. They are showing the wear and tear of being in combat and subjected to air raids and long work hours during most of the past year. There are probably exceptions, but most appear to have lost about 10 pounds. They have lines in their faces that were not caused by age. They're tired and need rest and recreation. Others have had it even tougher but these men have had it tough too. They haven't had a **real** liberty since Maui.*

The hills surrounding the valley blocked the ocean breezes and sometimes the heat and humidity were stifling. So to be more comfortable, I stripped to skivvy shorts, fore-and-aft cap, and boondocker shoes. To expose more of my Atabrine-yellowed body to the sun, I rolled the shorts into bikini style. Though cameras were against regulations, Platoon Sergeant Thomas Black used his to snap my picture for posterity.

On 22 June, 1945, Okinawa time, the island was declared secured. Again good fortune had ridden with the 2d Amphibian Truck Company. Almost unbelievable that 2d DUKW suffered only two casualties: PFC Douglas S. Leathe and Corp. Macon R. Wills were wounded by sniper fire. Now that it was ours, I knew the next invasion would undoubtedly be the Japanese home islands. I had seen enough during the war to know that tens of thousands of my buddies-in-arms would die and hundreds of thousands would be wounded. The Japs would be even more fanatical when fighting on home soil *if* they could find a way to do it. I already felt sorry for the children and women, because the hail of steel and firestorms already devastating Japan were not choosy in selecting victims. If we had to invade, the soil would shudder and heave like a constant

A Second Invasion of Okinawa

earthquake under the uncountable tons of explosives pulverizing it.

With excess free time to fill, the men spent many hours in bull sessions. They knew the value of DUKWs in invasions. They knew they'd be there whenever and wherever the next landing might be and they felt awed that 2d DUKW had been so fortunate. It was hard to believe they had survived three invasions while riding six feet above ground with no protective armor, in attention-drawing DUKWs, while making many runs to and near the fighting fronts. The superstitious men still felt the humpback whales at Maui continued to be their guardian angels.

They suffered nerve-wrenching fear from enemy shelling while the DUKWs were waterborne. Even if not blown to "Kingdom Come" by a cargo space load of gas or high explosives, they could have been wounded and drowned because they wouldn't have been able to make their way ashore. There also had been danger while loading alongside ships because a cargo net could snap and dump its load on them. Two men in another DUKW company were killed that way at Saipan. Furthermore, the grapevine had spread the word about a 6th DUKW company driver killed and his assistant suffering a broken back in the same type of accident at Okinawa.

The men were aware that the Marine Corps was scraping the bottom of the barrel for manpower to replace casualties. They had hauled too many fuzzy-cheeked, inadequately trained young Marines off the front on Okinawa and they knew their chances of getting out of the combat zone were almost nil, unless they, too, were seriously wounded. They also felt 2d DUKW's good fortune must be the lull before the storm, because there had been too many close calls.

Then, the word came: "Prepare to break camp. We're leaving Okinawa." I assumed we'd head for Saipan and the 2d Division.

The Quack Corps

The tents were broken down and folded. They joined the rest of our gear in the DUKWs and the 1st platoon's 16 DUKWs entered the tank deck of *LST-649*.

The LST got underway and I watched the landmass of Okinawa fade over the horizon. I resumed my usual at-sea routine of sitting or standing topside in talk with other men or thinking of Dolores and home.

Chapter 17
War's End!

On 9 July, the company landed on Saipan and rejoined the 2d Division.

The company's rear echelon had our Kagman Peninsula camp ready and we moved into the tents we had previously occupied. The personnel in the Fleet Post Office in San Francisco had been on the ball, too, so our mail was waiting for us, as was our share of Coca Cola® and beer rations issued during our absence.

Saipan was about 1,000 miles closer to the United States than Okinawa but the States were still far away and seemed to be in another world.

Second DUKW personnel thought it strange that the company could move over a thousand miles farther away from Japan, and those issuing censorship regulations decided it should be kept a secret. Of course, we realized that open speculation about the anticipated landing on the home islands shouldn't be allowed. We also knew that movements of certain elements in a division could tip off its probable activities and the timing. None of us were so naive that we thought the Japs didn't already know the 2d Division was on Saipan. At this stage of the war, we knew they were in no condition to do much about American troop movements except to make a landing more costly if they knew when and where it was to be made.

A change in censorship regulations was reflected in my first letter to Dolores on the 9th:

> *Censorship has been tightened again and I can't tell you where I am. I can't write about my activities or say anything about this place. It's going to be diffi-*

The Quack Corps

> cult to write long letters so reconcile yourself to them being shorter.
>
> I felt wealthy for awhile today. Payday, yes really, and after only five months. I went to the post office to get money orders for the men in my platoon. I don't recall that I've ever had $1,750.00 in my pocket before, but I'm sure that I haven't. I never gave any thought to the possibility of being robbed.
>
> Since the war began and every Tom, Dick and Harry have been inducted, thievery has ballooned. I use the same precautions I would as a civilian to protect my personal gear. A month or so ago, I returned to my foxhole [Okinawa] and found that the padlock on my seabag had been broken but nothing was missing.

Our letters kept each other abreast of the songs we liked, which song topped the Hit Parade, magazine articles, books and radio shows. We never knew whether the Hit Parade she listened to while writing to me was the same one I tuned in [Saipan Armed Forces station] while writing to her. So I teased that we not only had a long-distance romance but also a delayed-action one.

In my letter of 17 July:

> General Vandegrift lost popularity with me today. He said, "No Marines will be discharged while the war is still going on." He was also quoted as saying, "As long as the war is going on, the Marines will be fighting." I don't mind if they will give me a little Stateside duty. It would refresh and give me a taste of what I'm fighting for. If I could get back for a short time, I wouldn't yell about coming back over for the duration ... Oh well, not too loud anyway. As it is now, I sometimes don't give a damn whether the sun comes up in the morning or not.

War's End!

I was mentally and physically fatigued and, at times, found it difficult to avoid discouragement and self-pity. Our duties were light and the let down had hit me after the tension of the Okinawa invasion. My morale was at rock bottom; even Dolores' frequent letters didn't perk me up anymore.

During our previous stay on Saipan, the Red Cross had a booth a few hundred yards from our camp. Because the attendant charged me for a cup of coffee and a doughnut, I patronized it only once. Charging for them made the other men and me extremely angry. We thought the Red Cross was pulling a fast one on the American people by having stateside fund-raising drives *for the boys* and then charging *the boys* for the goodies.

In another incident, a DUKW crew that included PFC Dewey Reed, hungry and fatigued by extremely long hours, swung by a Red Cross booth to check whether they could get hot coffee and a snack. When told by the attendant, "We don't feed Marines!" the driver used his DUKW for a battering ram and demolished the booth. Apparently, the attendant felt it better not to make a complaint because his remark triggered the driver's action.

On Okinawa, I was desperate for stationery and a razor and filled my needs *free* at a Red Cross booth. I guessed that it had been at no charge because the fighting was still in progress. Much later, I learned that an agreement had been made with the British that American servicemen wouldn't be given goodies free by the Red Cross because the British servicemen didn't get freebies.

On 21 July, the Red Cross donated 1,000 doughnuts to 2d DUKW. At the time, and based on previous policies, I assumed they were bought by someone in the 2d Division as a "welcome back to the division." Apparently, the agreement with the British had expired or was being ignored because of war's end in Europe.

The Quack Corps

With my four sisters, five brothers, numerous aunts and uncles, and friends too, I sometimes had problems keeping my out-going letters straight. The only slip ever called to my attention was a letter written to a sister but addressed to Dolores. When she saw that the letter wasn't for her, she hastily folded it, included a note, and sent it on its way. As I wasn't one to bypass opportunities for using a slip to good advantage, I covered my tracks by writing:

> That should convince you that I'm not lying when I tell you, "You are always on my mind." At least, it wasn't to another girlfriend! One of the men writing to two girls did get the letters mixed. Luckily for him the censor noticed it and put them in the correct envelopes.

I didn't realize how right I'd be when writing on 27 July, but rumors of Japanese peace feelers through neutral sources triggered these comments:

> Maybe I'm being overly optimistic but I've a feeling this war will be over shortly ... say this year. Everyone is keeping ears tuned to the radio for news. We're not going to coast along waiting for it because that is exactly what the Japs want and we're not out here to please them.

With Okinawa now ours and the U.S. Fleet running wild in Japanese home waters, we wondered why censorship remained so tight. It meant devoting letter space to subjects that would usually have drawn slight or no mention. So to give the letter of the 27th reasonable length, I used much space describing my watch problems. It had quit running and the Marine watchmaker had broken the crystal while trying to remove the back so he informed me that it was full of rust. With the watch already kaput, I used a hammer and punch to get the back off. It wasn't full of rust but as I wrote:

> *The thing-a-mi-jig that engages the gadget that rotates around the gidget, or in plain language, the winding stem gears are stripped.*

Watches couldn't be mailed to the States, even for repair. I judged that the watchmaker didn't care whether mine or any other watch got repaired. Rather than wait for him, I bought a new watch on a ship. I needed one for use in performing my duties. The Marine Corps was supposed to issue one to me but never did.

Though anxious to get stateside, I realized the job had to be finished, as revealed in this letter:

> *I believe the Jap warlords know the game is up and have for a long time, but they're holding out for easy peace terms. As anxious as I am for this to be over, and to come home, I don't want anything but an unconditional surrender. If we don't finish it completely this time, our sons may have to do it in a few years. I wouldn't want to raise sons knowing they had to finish the job we failed to complete.*

With rumors that the Japs were going to surrender frequently beamed over the airwaves, it was difficult to give full attention to duties. When an errand took me away from camp, I rushed to do it and hurry back to be within earshot of a radio. Talk and other noises in camp were subdued because no one wanted to miss the announcement ... if it came.

My sleep was not disturbed in the wee hours of the morning on 6 August, 1945, when the Enola Gay's motors roared and she became airborne at Tinian that fateful day ... a day

The Quack Corps

which would not only change history but, also, the future of the world.

I didn't see her leave Tinian but I may have watched her return from a distance as she glided gracefully to a landing after she had dropped the first atomic bomb.

When the bomb's nature had been divulged, I felt extremely hopeful that I had been involved in my last invasion. More A-bombs would be used if necessary, I felt, and Japan would have no choice but to surrender. I thought the number who probably had died in that holocaust were only a pittance to the number that would die if we physically had to conquer the Japanese home islands. To the other men and me, *it was a trade-off ... their lives for ours ... we preferred to keep ours!*

In my letter of 8 August, 1945:

> *How about the Atomic Bomb? It* is *the most frightening thing in warfare today. It's hard to even attempt forecasting the future with it in existence. It's a cinch the Japs won't last long now. I feel they'll surrender in the near future. What scares me is if it should ever fall into the wrong hands.*

The rumors became persistent that the war might end at any moment. Camp activity almost came to a standstill. The men seemed to withdraw within themselves and little talk was heard in the tent area. Was the war finally going to end? they questioned themselves. Am I really going to survive?

And then ... JAPAN SURRENDERS! ... boomed out of the radio speaker. The word spread about the island like wildfire.

It was almost unbelievable that the war had come to an end. War had become a way of life for me. The blood that had flowed from the wounded at Pearl Harbor had been only a rivulet for a river that grew to become a torrential flood before that final word came.

War's End!

PEACE AT LAST! My letter to Dolores began with those three joyful words, on 15 August. I continued:

> *No one cheered because we have been subjected too many times to apparently good news, then discovered that it was a false alarm. I think that everyone reacted as I did ... they just breathed a prayer of thanksgiving and relief. It just doesn't seem true. Tears flowed from my eyes as I listened to the newscasts. How happy the World must be! It shouldn't be long now until we'll be together and this time, it will be for always.*
>
> *I can't relax entirely because I don't know whether I'll be heading for Japan or the United States. I don't know if My war is yet over.*
>
> *Surrender came quicker than I expected. Maybe it is the main reason I can't digest the fact of peace. Honey, what a day this would have been for me if I could have been with you to celebrate it. It has taken so long. Those who expected it to end in a matter of a few months after Pearl Harbor were so wrong. I am on needles-and-pins wondering whether the Japanese fighting men will accept the surrender. We may have to fight our way ashore to occupy the place. Hopefully, it means that I will see you earlier than expected.*

But I couldn't relax until I knew that Japan was accepting occupation peacefully.

I felt that I'd be among the first men returning to the United States—I hadn't re-enlisted or extended my enlistment when my four-year hitch expired in mid-1944. I served at the Convenience of the Government [COG]. During that year and a-half, I had jokingly told company officers, "You shouldn't count on me because I'm a nothing ... neither an official Marine nor a civilian."

The Quack Corps

"Sergeant, things are tough all over," they retorted.

After 2d DUKW had returned from Okinawa, the staff NCOs of the company and the 2d Motor Transport units nearby scrounged enough materials to build a staff NCO club adjacent to our tent area. To celebrate its opening on 19 August, we invited the officers of our units as guests. But there was a catch ... each had to bring a bottle of liquor as the price of admission.

With peace now a fact, I felt the time had come to really celebrate so I got rip-roaring drunk. Eventually, I realized it was time to head for my tent and cot. The tent guy ropes along the path kept getting in my way! I thought that odd because it was a *straight* path during daylight hours. In time, I reached my destination.

With frequent trips for a drink of water, that must have almost drained the 36-gallon listerbag by morning, I decided an officer must have distilled his own liquor though we had specified that their admission bottle contain a *good* alcoholic beverage.

The staff club gave us some of the benefits of stateside duty but we wouldn't get to use it long—Second DUKW was to be a part of the occupation forces and orders were passed to sharpen up the men with close-order drill and improve their military bearing. The vast majority of Marines in the Marine Corps entered after war began. Most hadn't been involved with much close-order drill since leaving boot camp. After boot camp my duty prewar in the 6th Regiment and seagoing had provided close-order drill opportunities for me but most of the company sergeants hadn't had much, if any, practice drilling units. After a short brush up, I let them drill the platoon while I instructed and supervised.

Second DUKW had in excess of 15 percent pre-war Marines which would much benefit helping the transition to the peacetime Marine Corps by the other men.

War's End!

Transfer out of 2d DUKW by request hadn't been permitted. It would have been devastating to morale if the men had felt there was no chance for advancement in rate. So the company was authorized an excessive number of NCOs, resulting in it having seven platoon sergeants by war's end; apparently, it was never authorized to have a gunnery sergeant.

I explained to the men the differences between the wartime Marine Corps and what they could expect in peacetime. I reminded them that a higher priority would be placed on spit-and-polish and close-order drill. I also covered military protocol, courtesy, and Navy and Marine Corps regulations. Also, I advised them that punishment for offences would be more severe and certain offences, such as thievery, would get them kicked out of the Corps. With a smile, I pointed out that gambling in camp would no longer be permitted.

I felt that I wouldn't be with the platoon much longer but I wanted the men to show their pride in being Americans, and Marines, with their military bearing and conduct in Japan.

I bragged about them in a letter to Dolores, thusly:

> *I've never served with a better group of men. Not one refused to obey a combat order, even though he knew obeying it could result in his death. I've had serious problems with only two of them; one I decked when we were on Tinian the second time, for getting too handy with his mouth and calling me insulting names. I could have lost my stripes for hitting him, but keeping my self-respect was more important to me.*
>
> *The other man mouthed off, just before peace was declared, because I reprimanded him for criticizing an officer to me with other men present. He didn't call me insulting names so I handled that incident in a different manner.*
>
> *I've been with these men for almost two years. Except for those two incidents, the problems with them*

The Quack Corps

were minor. I'm proud of the men in this platoon!

Being called a son-of-a-bitch were fighting words to most of the men, particularly those off farms or from small towns, because they took it to mean just what it said. An officer or NCO who used an excess of vulgar language while commanding men lacked the intelligence and ability to express themselves in any other way I felt. Maybe it fed their ego and they felt it made them sound tougher. Cursing a subordinate was forbidden by Navy and Marine Corps Regulations. I had learned that voice inflection and a right look in the eye had a greater effect in generating prompt obedience to commands.

The platoon leader of 2d DUKW's 3rd platoon frequently addressed his men in ranks as sons-of-bitches. I hadn't been in ranks with him in command but I seethed when hearing him address them that way. Possibly, most of them didn't know it wasn't permitted or were afraid to call his hand, so I became determined to stop it. His platoon sergeant worked close enough with the officer that it'd be less embarrassing to those concerned if I handled it through him instead of the commanding officer, and I reminded him of the officer's habit. Apparently, the platoon sergeant didn't talk to him, or if so, the officer didn't pay heed. I was primed and cocked when he mustered the entire company for close-order drill and ordered, "Attention!" His very next words were, "All right, you sons-of-bitches!"

Without a moment's hesitation, I stepped forward out of ranks, saluted, and addressed him, "Sir! I don't feel that I'm a son-of-a-bitch and I don't think these other men in ranks feel that they're one either!"

Startled, he stared at me for a few moments, then stammered, "Sergeant, resume your place in ranks." He proceeded with the drill.

War's End!

Only minutes after the drill ended, Captain George sent for me. I had been put on report for insubordination but it backfired on the officer because the grapevine spread the word about how Captain George had reamed him out for addressing subordinates that way. He also reportedly advised the officer to learn to conduct himself like a Marine officer was supposed to.

I knew he would be laying for me but he'd have a hell of a time catching me off base, because I knew the ways of the peacetime and regulation Marine Corps better than he.

On 1 September, I listened while a radio announcer read the peace terms Japan would sign. Although they had surrendered, V–J Day wouldn't be declared until the surrender documents were signed and the war was officially over. I prayed that the Japs wouldn't have second thoughts.

While waiting out the official surrender, I continued to write almost daily. Portions of my letter, dated 2 September, 1945:

> *The staff NCO's celebrated V-J Day this afternoon. I didn't drink a drop but spent my time talking. I also heard the surrender ceremony at 11:30 A.M., and the President's speech.*
>
> *When President Truman spoke of that day of infamy* [the attack on Pearl Harbor], *it brought back vivid memories. Details of that day will always stick in my mind ... even my thoughts and detailed actions. I really felt low after the attack was over. I felt that the people back home had let us down. It's not a very good feeling when a person realizes that, but for a lot of shortsighted people, he and his buddies could have had the proper guns to fight back with. If we had had just one of our battleships properly armed with AA guns, what a different story it could have been. The Japs would have done damage, yes, but we wouldn't*

have had to watch as many of our ships burn and sink. I cursed with the best of them that day.

I would have liked to have been on the Missouri today. While the ceremony was going on, I was thinking of you. The right and privilege of coming back to you has made what little I've done and the months spent overseas worthwhile. I'm just a very small cog in a great machine and you are my stake ... you understand what I mean. Take that in terms of millions and it gives you an idea of what we were fighting to preserve ... add it all together and it spells America!

When they made arrangements for the surrender ceremony, I hoped the brass would realize that those of us present during the first act at Pearl Harbor wanted to be there for the final act of the war. I hoped they'd try to make it possible for those nearby to be in Tokyo Bay for the surrender ceremony. Most of the high-ranking officers and officials appeared to be jockeying for a visible position in history and weren't too concerned about the feelings of others. For me to be present and see the humiliation of the Japanese high-ranking officers and officials in surrender would have been the most satisfying act of the war for me.

But, I wasn't there and my attention turned to other things, most importantly, my return to the States and Dolores. The company office notified me that I was in the first priority category for return to the U.S. I wasn't feeling very cheerful because my return hinged on the availability of a suitable replacement. I was on edge for fear that my orders wouldn't come before 2d DUKW sailed for occupation duty. Though I pointed out to 1stSgt. Harold Pohlad and Lieutenant Blackburn that Billy Kerslake was now a platoon sergeant, it didn't appear to hurry my orders.

With the Japanese peacefully accepting occupation, I felt that my job was finished so now I didn't have any desire to go

War's End!

to Japan. Also, occupation duty could mean many more months of overseas duty.

I wasn't superstitious but I was grasping at any straw. I hoped that Dolores' letter of 4 September was an omen:

> *Any news as to when you will be coming home? I walked across the lawn and happened to look down and, Honey, all that I could see was a four-leaf clover; let's hope it means good luck!*

While I fumed and fretted about the delay in orders, the days seemed to fly by, drawing closer to the day 2d DUKW would board ship for Japan. And, on 9 September, I nearly exploded with frustration when I had to board *LST-785*, in preparation for sailing to Japan for occupation duty.

God, please let my orders come before this ship sails, I entreated in silent prayer. I was ready to go home!

Chapter 18
Going Home!

While *LST-785* waited at Saipan for orders to sail, I spent most of the daylight hours topside, watching each small craft headed toward the ship. They either passed by or stopped for reasons other than to deliver my orders.

As usual, I spent some of my time writing to Dolores, getting things off my chest and making comments about current events, as in this letter:

> *There will be many happy people in the States when the war prisoners return. Men given up for lost will show up and relatives of others will have their hopes dashed because their loved ones will never come back.*
>
> *I wonder how the Japs can expect any sympathy after the way they have treated prisoners. Now that they're beaten they're so anxious to be friends—I call it "two-faced."*

The factories and plants that made war goods had laid off workers by the hundreds of thousands since the German surrender. Dolores had been one of the very last women terminated at the aircraft plant where she worked. She wrote about filing for unemployment insurance. In my answer to the letter, I responded:

> *Gee whiz! Do you mean that you actually draw $20.00 per week for not working? How do you go about getting that? See how much I've missed out on the news? That's a good deal and it'll keep you going*

Going Home!

until I return. Do you realize that's as much as I made per month before enlisting in the Marines.

As in most of my letters, I quickly switched gears:

> *I was thinking yesterday that those of us God saw fit to let return, and in one piece, have so much to be thankful for. We shouldn't even mind the delay in returning, but I still sweat it out.*
>
> *I received the August 27th issue of Time today. Golly, this world is in a political mess! It surprised me that the world wasn't ready for peace. Now that it's here, let's hope it isn't messed up.*
>
> *I've made a rough estimate of how much it'll take to completely outfit myself in civilian clothing. I'd guess about $200.00, but I'm probably over-estimating. I'm basing it on two good suits, a couple pairs of dress shoes, plus all the other articles I'll need. I'm starting from scratch because I've outgrown everything and, too, the few things I may have at home still usable may be outdated. It will cut a hole in our nest egg, but we'll still have enough to live on for awhile.*
>
> *You're my future and whatever I do will be to make you happy. Now that the war is over, we can make plans without that hanging over our heads. We have nothing to worry about except just us.*
>
> *I'd like to fly back but I suppose that is wishing for too much. I don't think many officers will even go to the States by plane. Wouldn't that be something ... leave here and three or four days later be in the States? I'd ride a DUKW back if that was the only available means to get back to you. I'm anxious for*

censorship to end. I'm sure the lieutenant will be glad because he won't have to bother reading my "books."

Censorship ended on 10 September, except for on a spot basis, and the lieutenant was off the hook.

Censorship regulations required the letter writer to print first name, middle initial and surname at the bottom of the last page. After almost four years of writing letters that had to pass censorship, I found that I still adhered to regulations. In my letter of 10 September, I printed my first name and the initial before I realized it was no longer necessary, so I crossed them out.

I continued using the edition numbers I had begun on Okinawa but I dropped the "Foxhole Gazette" from them. Edition number 86 contained, in part:

I'm not flag waving but I love our country. It hurt when the draft law was enacted. I couldn't understand why a man would have to be forced to fight for his country. Just the thought of it being over run, the women raped, the children mistreated, and all of the other things that would have been daily routine if the Japs had been successful, should have been enough to make any man want to be in it. I'm not belittling the physically unfit. I know many of them tried to volunteer. And I'm not belittling the men who were not allowed to enlist because of essential jobs. Most of them made a greater contribution to the war effort than they could have in uniform. We young bucks realize we'd have been very impotent without the supplies to do it with.

As each day dawned, I wondered if it would be the one when I'd feel the engines throb and begin to move the LST out

Going Home!

of the harbor. I even hoped for an engine malfunction so the ship couldn't sail.

On 11 September, I leaned over the rail and watched as a small craft pulled alongside. I saw a small packet among the items coming aboard and wondered if it contained my orders, and those for 27 others in the company. The small craft delivered the answer to my prayers. It also delivered the last letters I would receive overseas but I didn't know it at the time.

I read and re-read the orders directing me to return to the United States, and the Great Lakes Naval Training Center, to be processed for discharge from the United States Marine Corps. What a joyful day it turned out to be.

> *I'm packed and ready to start the journey back tomorrow or maybe I should say, "I transfer out of this company," but it could be a few days before I leave here. Isn't it wonderful? I was supposed to leave today but was delayed; that's why I'm on needles-and-pins until I actually get underway,*

I began my letter of 11 September.

> *In a way, I hate to leave this company. I have some very good friends here, but I wouldn't pass up the chance to come back for anybody.*

I spent the next few hours making the rounds to bid goodbye to all the men in the platoon. After a short visit with each of them, I paid a visit to Lieutenant Blackburn's quarters for one last talk. He was not only my superior officer but had become a friend. And, he had become a pretty good officer just as I had anticipated in the company's early days.

I wondered whether I would see anyone from the company again. We had been through much together and it created a strong bond but some of it would disappear once we left the

The Quack Corps

Marine Corps and began civilian pursuits. I hadn't broken the bond with some of them yet because they'd begin the trip back with me. My foxhole buddy during our entire stay on Okinawa, Sgt. Darwin "Nick" Nicholson, was one.

We boarded a small ship at Saipan on the 12th but didn't sail until the morning of the 13th. On that date, Dolores wrote in a letter I received later:

> *I'm still keeping my fingers crossed that I will receive a letter soon saying, "Don't write anymore because I'm on my way home."*

By coincidence, in my letter also dated 13 September I was this:

> *I exult with every vibration made by the turning of the ship's screws. I'm enroute to Guam to catch transportation back to the U.S. I don't have any idea when I might leave Guam, or, when I'll show up in the States. It will take almost a month for most of the ships to make the trip. I might be lucky and board a warship—if I do, it'll be quicker. Will you pinch me so that I'll know returning isn't just a dream?*

In the balance of the letter I speculated about how I would get across country and informed her that I'd call at the first opportunity after reaching the States. I also asked her to keep her fingers crossed that my orders would be changed so I'd be discharged in San Diego.

At the transient center on Guam, I tent-mated with Nick and two men I didn't know. He left many days before I did because the center sent out men based on their home states. It was the first time I knew the *W* for Wisconsin and the *T* in Texas fit into the alphabet before the *M* of Missouri! Apparently, they used that system because a state, or a combination

Going Home!

of two or more, matched the exact number of men a ship could handle. Usually the ships made other ports-of-calls and already had men aboard when they stopped at Guam.

It was an emotional time for both of us when Nick's time to leave came. We had faced fear and death side-by-side innumerable times. We had borrowed from the other, stamps, ink, stationery and envelopes, and sometimes even the pen to write the letters. Also, we had spent uncountable hours scouting and in one-on-one bull sessions. Neither of us could say much before he picked up his gear to leave. We knew the probability of seeing each other again was remote since he didn't plan to stay in his Wisconsin hometown and I planned to live in California. As we shook hands upon parting, we couldn't meet each other's eyes ... war had taught us to hide emotions and feelings but this moment ripped away that shield.

My last contact with the men of 2d DUKW was cut by Nick's departure because I hadn't seen other 2d DUKW'ers in camp; apparently, they had already left for home.

The transient center served the worst mess hall food of any I had eaten as a Marine. The meals were, at the most, lukewarm and the cooks didn't seem to care whether the food was even warmed. So I stocked up on Vienna sausage and salt crackers at the PX and rarely responded to chow call.

Guam was out of the way for ships returning to the U.S. from Japan or Okinawa, so I guessed that my wait could be long. Few men were leaving the center. It made me feel like the men in camp were considered G.I. surplus that no longer rated any priority.

Writing letters helped relieve some of the frustration but, sometimes, I waited until my mood improved so they wouldn't be filled with gripes about the tedious wait and poor camp conditions. Even with those irritations, I felt elated that I was on the first leg of the trip home. With no duties or other things to occupy time, I spent most of the awake hours sacked out on my cot thinking.

The Quack Corps

Though most of my thoughts were of my girl waiting and stateside, some were of the war years. I realized I had participated in a war that had seen the transition from the old to the new in weapons, ships, planes and methods. In that transition, I had seen the advent of the semi-automatic rifle for each infantryman; the use of armored vests by ground force personnel; the beginning of the jet age with the Germans' use of jet fighters; modern rocketry in battle and the saturation bombing by masses of airplanes. And, of course, the dawning of the use of A-bombs in warfare.

Also, I had witnessed the change from slow, inadequately AA-gun-armed massive capital ships that had been designed for battle against other ships on a liquid battlefield, to gigantics so fast they had to reduce speed while turning in evasive maneuvers so inboard AA guns could depress enough to fire on attacking planes. Ships whose design had incorporated enough AA guns to throw up a curtain of steel that few planes penetrated while attacking them in a new method of war ... airplanes pitted against surface ships.

While watching small helicopters flying near our Kagman Peninsula camp on Saipan after our return from Okinawa, I didn't envision their eventual use in war or that I was looking at the craft that ended the need for DUKWs.

During the bull sessions following the dropping of the A-bombs, most of the men appeared to react to them much as I did ... just another weapon of war, but, what an awesome one! Most felt we owed our lives to the A-bombs because they undoubtedly hastened the end of the war and insured that we wouldn't have to invade Japan. Most agreed that instant vaporization was preferable to being shredded by shrapnel, or burned to the crispness of overdone toast by the flash of conventional explosives or napalm, or to spend one's life fighting for breath after breathing poison gas. Even with the reported destruction and the A-bomb residual effects most feared poison gas equally as much.

Going Home!

My thoughts didn't dwell for long on the changes in war I'd seen or my feelings about the A-bombs for, without volition, they quickly switched back to stateside.

Lieutenant Blackburn's censoring of my letters cramped my style while I courted Dolores by mail. Though the conditions of war meant that some things, from a practical standpoint, couldn't be done in the most optimum way, I felt the military should have used special units whose only job was to censor mail. An immediate superior censoring letters put a subordinate in an almost untenable position. In my case, I felt that it was almost as if Dolores wrote to the lieutenant too. He could deduce what she had written by the comments, answers to questions, and so forth in my letters. It also placed him in an embarrassing position because he was privy to the innermost thoughts of those under his command. There were many things I didn't write about because I didn't want to divulge my innermost thinking about some things to anyone except the individual to whom I was writing.

I had felt determined that nothing was going to delay my return to the States, as reflected in this letter:

> *When I got ready to leave the LST at Saipan, I put on my pack, threw my seabag on my shoulder and slung my carbine over the other one. Half-way up the ladder from below decks, the ship rolled and I stuck out my arm to keep from falling. It jammed my shoulder and threw my neck out of joint. They have been sore as a boil since but I'm not going to report to sickbay because I'm not taking any chances on this trip. If need be, I'll crawl up the gangway.*

Bored with the waiting, I decided to see some of Guam. I hitched a ride to Agana, Guam's largest city. While nosing in the area, I spotted *Pennsylvania* in Apra Harbor with quarterdeck almost awash. I felt nostalgic about the old ship and attempted to board her for one last visit. A sailor at the pier informed me that only crew was allowed aboard.

Later, I learned that she had been torpedoed at 2045, 12 August, 1945, in Buckner Bay, Okinawa. An undetected Jap plane had dropped a torpedo that hit her in the stern and killed 20 men. Those 20 and the 24 killed at Pearl Harbor were the only men she lost to enemy action during the war though she earned eight battle stars. Damaged the first day of the war, she also may have been the last U.S. major warship damaged by the Japs.

Then, much later, I learned that after surviving two A-bomb tests at Bikini in 1946 and still too radioactive to crew, the gallant old *Pennsylvania* was towed to sea off Kwajalein and scuttled on 10 February, 1948.

Depressed by seeing my old ship damaged, I returned to camp and the routine of laying on my cot thinking and having one-sided mental conversations with my future bride.

My thoughts about stateside, and the girl waiting there, were interrupted at times with curiosity about the whereabouts of 2d DUKW. I wondered whether it had sailed from Saipan and, if so, when it had reached Japan; too, where it had landed and was stationed. Also, I wondered whether the men had to be constantly alert to avoid injury or death at the hands of die-hard Japs.

As I spent another boring day 23 September, I didn't know that 2d DUKW was landing at Nagasaki with some of the men stretching their legs on the beach before proceeding through the devastated city to the Isahay Naval Barracks for billeting.

Later, I learned that the company was absorbed into the 2d Motor Transport Battalion, 2d Marine Division, on 6 December, 1945, and ceased to exist as a company; most of the men returned to the U.S. shortly thereafter.

With the superstitious men who had considered the humpback whales as 2d DUKW's guardian angels now gone, some

Going Home!

of the good fortune that had ridden with the company ran out for the men who replaced original personnel.

After landing, some of 2d DUKW's men helped disarm Japanese, while others ferried men and supplies along the coast and between islands. In some areas, they contended with huge whirlpools that could suck small craft to a watery grave. The original personnel's expert handling and knowledge of the capabilities of the DUKWs enabled them to avoid getting sucked under. Later, replacement personnel were towing a disabled DUKW with another when both vehicles and several men were lost in a whirlpool.

I was oblivious to the company's activities when I wrote on 25 September:

> There are only a few Marines here waiting to come back. One ship could carry us all, with room to spare. I keep hoping that elements of the Third Fleet will stop by to pick us up. I'm so tired and weary of being over here. One consolation though ... I didn't go the other way! See, there's a bright side to everything.

Several days had passed since the camp office had called men out by states. The gap between ships widened. Most of the original men had already left. I worried that the camp would fill with lower-discharge-point men and I might be overlooked or forgotten so I made another check by the office to make certain my name was still on the list.

I was feeling hopeless by now, and trudged slowly to the office when the PA system passed the word for all men awaiting stateside transportation to fall out. Each time before, I had slowly walked back to my tent, dejected, with my head drooping and eyes on the ground. On 2 October, I responded without enthusiasm. The names were being read by the time I arrived. But as usual I gave closer attention when the names, called alphabetically this time, neared the *W*'s. Then almost unbelievably, "Platoon Sergeant Arthur W. Wells!"

"Yo!" I bellowed exuberantly. The trip back to the tent was with spring in my walk, shoulders squared, head erect and a smile on my face.

The truck wouldn't show until later in the day so I secured my gear, sat down and, joyfully, wrote my last and 306th letter to Dolores. She outdid me because I received 343 from her. Number 306 was written with the fountain pen I had purchased on *Pennsylvania* [I still have the pen], it included:

> *I'm lucky this is my last letter because I'm using the last of my stationery and very last stamp. I have only a few cents in my pocket* [I had previously made out allotment forms for $90.00 of my monthly pay to be sent to my oldest sister, Evelyn, for deposit in my savings account]. *If I have to call you long distance after reaching the States, it'll have to be collect.*
>
> *Honey, pray that it is a fast ship.*

Those three weeks on Guam were the longest three weeks I've ever spent. The wait was not interrupted by the arrival of a single letter addressed to me. Those already en route to my DUKW company address went to Japan and the company mail clerk returned them to senders. When Dolores decided to take the chance I'd get them and wrote to the transient center address, every one of them arrived after I had left.

I didn't want any more delays so I was already at the designated place, waiting, to board the truck the moment it arrived. Fortunately, *U.S.S. Crockett*'s captain was also anxious and ordered her underway the instant the last passenger set foot on deck. Darkness was approaching so I felt thankful he didn't wait until morning to sail. My prayers that she would be a fast ship were not answered and the days stretched endlessly.

Going Home!

Except for the short hop on *U.S.S. Henry Clay* from Oahu to Maui, when 2d DUKW joined the 4th Marine Division, I had never sailed on a troop transport. The chow lines were long and for food little better than that in the transient center on Guam. Mess kits had to be washed in a barrel of greasy water. ... I ate only to survive.

The bunks were tiered five or six high with mine midway up. With ventilation almost nonexistent, I spent little time in the odor-filled compartment.

After fighting so fanatically on the islands away from home, it was hard for me to believe that the Japanese had completely turned around and accepted occupation peacefully. I knew there must be some still willing and ready to die for their Emperor. I wasn't unmindful that a submarine may have been caught far from home when Japan surrendered and her crew had decided to pretend they hadn't received the word, or if so, made the decision to send American ships to the bottom until their sub no longer had armaments with which to fight. With that possibility, and to escape the odor-filled compartment, I sacked out on the steel deck topside. Just as I had on the battleships when it was too hot to sleep in the Marine compartments, I used one woolen blanket for a mattress and another draped over a rope for rain protection.

It seemed almost unbelievable that I was finally on the last leg of my trip to the States. During those long days I thought again of the things I had seen and done, and the battles; I wondered if I'd refight them in my dreams. I also thought of the loneliness and aloneness I felt during the lengthy war and the many months, at times, without the sight of, the smell of, or the feel of a woman. Soon, I'd be able to bask in Dolores' warmth, softness and nearness. The scent of her perfume would again please my senses.

Then, I exulted at the announcement: "The ship is heading for San Diego!" I felt so excited about her destination that I walked miles on the deck to calm myself. My actions re-

The Quack Corps

minded me of an old mule I had worked on the Missouri farm that just couldn't wait to get back to the barn at noon or day's end, impossible to rein in.

I spent hours each day and night leaning against the rail mentally urging the screws to turn faster. Many of the other men also stood or sat alone. The bull sessions and card games usually so prevalent at sea were almost non-existent.

Marines joining a new group usually made new buddies quickly. But this shipload of men acted edgy, introverted and disinterested in conversing with men they didn't already know. Maybe they also felt almost revulsion at the sight of another strange face or another uniform. I was the only 2d DUKW man aboard. Surprisingly I met only one man, PlSgt. Del Dassow of prewar 6th Regiment days, who had served with me in any of my previous units—surprising, because this ship was filled with long-timers who had been Marines since before or shortly after war began.

As daylight broke 31 October, 1945, I joined others at the ship's rail. My eyes strained to see beyond the horizon. Each man at the rail was engrossed with his own thoughts and emotions and little talking could be heard. Conversation was difficult in the emotionally charged atmosphere. Just as I did, when the U.S. coastline faded over the stern of a ship, many probably had had the premonition they wouldn't come back. Just as mine did, their eyes misted when the hazy outline of Point Loma hove into sight on the horizon.

The *U.S.S. Crockett* sailed slowly through the harbor to her berth and I remained by the rail with my eyes feasting on San Diego's familiar features.

Even after the ship secured to the pier, the men aboard acted unbelieving and as if in shock; I didn't hear a single cheer. I wondered if I'd awaken to find that coming home was … just a dream.

Though only a few of us had been in the Pacific at war's outbreak, it was truly a shipload of veterans of war because

Going Home!

each had fought in multiple battles.

It seemed to take forever for the long line of men to file off the ship. My eyes scanned the faces of the civilians waiting on the dock—some probably had met every arriving ship with the hope and prayer that their Marine was aboard. The numbers waiting were small. I felt disappointed. Even a welcome by a brass band would have made me feel more like we had returned as victors. I had enjoyed a more enthusiastic welcome when returning to San Francisco in defeat after the Pearl Harbor attack. Except for those with men returning from or remaining overseas, the populace's attention had already turned to peacetime pursuits.

The women on the dock with organizations offered fresh milk, ice cream and cookies. A year and a-half had passed since I last tasted fresh milk but I hadn't forgotten its taste. Fearful of overdoing, I drank a small quantity of milk, ate a small container of ice cream and a few cookies. Some of the men gorged themselves and then suffered the consequences.

After the gedunks, I tossed my gear into the back of a truck for my last ride in a military vehicle. The Separation Center on the Marine Corps Base at San Diego would be my home until discharge, because my orders had been changed.

Chapter 19
A Warrior Returns!

After assignment to quarters in a small hut, near where I had lived in a tent during boot camp days, I lay on my bunk and waited for the posting of my discharge processing schedule.

As my thoughts roved, I wondered how much, if any, Dolores had changed in appearance. The five snapshots I displayed in my tent, in which she looked so different in each that the men accused me of having five girls on the string, and a large studio photo kept her overall features in mind. But, I realized some details had become hazy. I had written about it in my next-to-last letter from Guam:

> *Strange as it may seem, I hardly remember just what you look like. For that matter, the details of my relatives' features are a little dim. Of course, I'll know you at first glimpse but in two years recollections do get hazy. All of your mannerisms I remember. But, the sound of your voice and the lines of your face and figure are a little dim when it comes to recalling them in exact detail. ...*

I phoned and made arrangements for her to meet me at the base reception center that evening. She was surprised but pleased that my orders had been changed and I'd be discharged on the West Coast.

We arranged to meet at seven so I didn't return to quarters but roamed around the base at a brisk pace to stifle my excitement. After about an hour, I went to the reception center in case she arrived early. It had multiple entrances and I paced back and forth on the base side of the building. As the minutes slowly ticked off, anticipation built and I broke out in a nervous sweat.

I watched every slender, brown-haired woman approaching the center until she got close enough that I could see she wasn't Dolores.

Occasionally, I stepped inside the reception center to make sure I hadn't missed her. My eyes flicked over the room full of people, then I returned outside and resumed pacing.

Shortly before seven, I glanced through the glass in the door and saw her step through the entrance on the opposite side of the building. She hesitated while her eyes scanned the faces of the occupants seated around the room. I stood for several seconds looking through the glass ... savoring my first look at her. My eyes rested for a moment on her brown hair that I remembered so well, then another moment on her dark brown eyes, her full lips with their half-smile of expectancy, and her slender body. She looked exactly as I had so often pictured her! I hadn't really forgotten anything! I pushed the door open and stepped into the room. She saw me, smiled, and began walking to meet me. I hurried to meet her ...

As civilian curfew time of 2200 hours neared, I escorted her to the main gate. Then, I dawdled during my return to quarters.

Waiting for sleep, I realized that the dreadful aloneness I felt out in the Pacific was now a thing of the past. Out there, I was surrounded by thousands of Marines but still felt as if I was completely alone. *I will never forget that dreadful feeling of aloneness.*

I was constantly aware that, if I died, I would be known to those burying me only by the name and serial number imprinted in the dogtags laying against my chest. To them, I would be just another dead Marine to be covered with sand. Though I had had that awareness, I didn't brood about dying.

The Quack Corps

I just didn't want to be buried in the sand of some God forsaken island.

If only one had to die, I preferred it be the other man. He had felt the same way toward me though either of us would have risked our life to save the other without taking time to consider the consequences.

The day after my death those who knew me would have said: "It's too bad Wells got his yesterday." I heard that comment about other Marines so many times. Not a tear would have been shed over my grave, because there wasn't any tears left for buddies and comrades-in-arms.

While still courting sleep, I re-evaluated the thinking I'd done en route to the United States about what I had learned in the Marine Corps that could be utilized in civilian life. I knew the knowledge of how to kill or maim with a variety of weapons, including bare hands, wouldn't be of any benefit. But learning to lead men, size up situations and make quick judgments and decisions, the ability to mix with people in all stratas of society, deal tactfully with touchy situations, control my temper and conceal my emotions and feelings when it seemed best to do so, and self-confidence, could all be of extreme benefit in whatever postwar career I chose.

The next morning, I waited impatiently for the discharge process to begin. First on the list was a physical examination to make certain that I was fit to return to civilian life. I refused to heed the doctor's suggestion that I be a Marine a little longer and have my enlarged tonsils removed.

During the interview following the physical, Captain William Murphy offered a gunnery sergeant rate if I'd re-up. I reminded him that the Marine Corps had had plenty of time to give me gunny's stripes; I'd take my discharge.

The Marine Corps feared a serious shortage of experienced senior NCOs because so many were taking discharges; I talked to some with as much as 12 years of service. Apparently, the Corps was offering selected men the next higher rate if they'd ship over. But most of the senior NCOs were bitter because they had spent so much time overseas that it had made them feel like forgotten men. They realized that it was their duty to fight the Japs but they didn't like the feeling of being considered expendables. They knew they had been, and would have continued to be, sent into the maws of Japanese guns with no hope of being relieved from combat unless seriously wounded or killed. Also, the strain of battle had fatigued them mentally and physically. Later, I learned that many of them, after a rest and a taste of civilian life, returned to the Marine Corps and served until retirement, with some adding two more wars under their belts.

I signed papers and waited impatiently for the day's activities to end so I could shower, dress, and hurry to the main gate to meet Dolores. During the brisk walk to it, I felt a little self-conscious wearing Marine greens because dungarees had been my uniform of the day for the past two years.

Without a pass, I usually wouldn't be allowed through the main gate. I approached the corporal manning it, "Corporal, I'm expecting my fiancée in a few minutes. Is it okay if I wait at the curb for her?"

"Go ahead, Sergeant," he consented.

As Dolores and I passed through to enter the base, he commented, "Sergeant, I don't blame you for wanting to wait at the curb for *her.*"

"Corporal, I've been waiting two years for *this one,*" I replied proudly, with a pleased smile. "Thanks for letting me wait at the curb."

As we strolled toward the bleachers on the east side of the parade ground, Dolores offered, "Harriet [her sister] insists on bringing me to get you tomorrow."

"Honey, I don't know what time I'll get my discharge. I can ride the bus and save you a long wait."

"But she insists! Anyway, it'd be rather hard to carry your suitcase on the bus."

The Quack Corps

"I don't have a suitcase," I chided, with a laugh. "I have a sea bag just like the sailors, except mine is khaki [I still had my 1940 issue sea bag] and theirs are white. If Harriet insists, I won't argue."

Again, our stroll to the main gate lasted until the last minute. And, for the last time, I watched the car's taillights fade from view.

On 2 November, 1945, Captain Murphy passed my discharge papers to me, smiled, offered his hand, "Good luck in civilian life, Mr. Wells."

Grasping his hand, I returned his smile, "Thank you, Captain. After being addressed as Sergeant or Wells for so long, I'll have to get used to being called Mister." I was no longer a Marine and suppressed the usual reaction of saluting and addressing him as, Sir.

Hoisting the sea bag to my shoulder, I began the walk to the main gate. Partway there, I sat it on the asphalt of the parade ground and my eyes roved over the base—at my old barracks during 6th Regiment days, the boot camp area where I had learned to march in step to an NCO's cadence, the Sea School barracks where I had learned how to be a seagoing Marine, and the parade ground where I had marched so many miles with a Marine's fierce pride. In a way, I felt sad. I had spent 20 percent of my life as a Marine and undoubtedly would, at times, miss parts of that life and the comradeship of fellow Marines. But now, I was ready to walk away from it to face the challenge of civilian life.

On 11 November, the wedding band I slipped on Dolores' finger was the same one that had caused my worries as it traveled the 8000-miles from New Orleans to Saipan and then the 6000-miles back to her. And standing by my side as best man was one of my first Marine Corps buddies, former PlSgt. Del Dassow.

Postscript
Grey? Bald? Paunchy?

The Navy corpsman attached to 2d DUKW, Rex Rollins, was a native of Chico, California. He became a good friend and, in our bull sessions, sold me on the idea of settling there. As a result, Dolores and I planted roots in Chico.

After 29 years as the owner of a successful sporting goods and general merchandise store in Chico, I transferred my activities upon its sale in 1978 to the care of a small almond orchard near Chico that Dolores and I had purchased in 1974.

Then as December 1980 approached, I realized that some of the details of the Japanese attack on Pearl Harbor were beginning to dim in memory. I also realized that each person becomes a part of history with some actions, deeds, and thoughts becoming part of written history but others are lost forever. Those realizations prodded me to make the decision that I should write about my experiences during that surprise attack.

After that story was written, I further realized that I had participated in other historical events. My sons, grandchildren, and future descendants wouldn't know the details of my involvement unless I compiled a written record. In doing so, it precipitated an almost unbelievable chain of events.

While picturing the faces that matched names as I wrote about the events of those years, the desire to know what happened to some of those men became overpowering ... were they still alive? If so, where did they live? How has life treated them? I decided to try to find the answers. As I nosed through mementos of my service in the Marine Corps for verification of information, I discovered a copy of the First Platoon's Embarkation Roster for the Saipan invasion; it included next-of-kin names and addresses, as of early May 1944.

The Quack Corps

When my orders had come aboard the LST at Saipan, I was so excited about returning to the States that I failed to make arrangements to make later contact with my buddies. And, with a new wife, state, city, and job, rating highest priority in my thoughts for a few months, the company disbanded and the men spread with the winds. By the time I made the attempt, my letters were returned so I made no further attempts at that time.

As the result of a conversation with a Marine recruiter in the 1950s, I made contact with the former platoon sergeant of 2d DUKW's second platoon, Master Gunnery Sergeant Thomas Black, at Camp Pendleton, California. He also had wondered what had happened to the men of 2d DUKW.

A few years after returning to civilian life, I tried to contact Darwin "Nick" Nicholson in Glen Flora, Wisconsin. He had moved away, as had Donald "Dutch" Shults from Bend, Oregon.

I knew finding the DUKW men would be difficult because so many years had passed. To add to the difficulty, the Privacy Act of 1974 forbids government agencies divulging certain information about individuals. Maybe I could at least locate a relative of the seven men comprising my priority list which, in addition to Nick and Dutch, included Sergeants Harry Mefford and Orval "Smitty"Smith, Corporals George "Jerry" Tolar and Harold "Hal" Reynolds, and First Lieutenant James Blackburn. In early 1982, I began the search for them.

Starting with Nick, I began by checking phone information in the Badger State of Wisconsin, but that source was unsuccessful. Glen Flora is a small town so I guessed that the postmaster might know some of his family or maybe even know his whereabouts. I wrote him a letter of explanation. The postmaster turned out to be a postmistress. She knew that Nick's sister lived in a nearby city and passed the information on to me. I phoned the sister and learned that Nick had died in 1977.

Gray? Bald? Paunchy?

My search then switched to Malvern, Arkansas, and Orval Smith. It was unsuccessful though the postmaster did all possible to help, which included conversing with a woman in her 80s who remembered the family but could give no information about their whereabouts.

Undaunted by the failure to find Smitty, I tried next for Harry Mefford. There wasn't any Mefford surnames in his former hometown of Decker, Montana, but I remembered that he frequently spoke of Sheridan, Wyoming, a few miles from Decker. The telephone information operator provided a phone number and dialing it hit the target in Sheridan.

Now that I had located Harry, I decided to try next for our mutual buddy, George "Jerry" Tolar. Harry had received a phone call from him a few months prior to my call but had recently moved and was unable to find Tolar's address or phone number—he didn't remember from what city Jerry had made his call. Jerry wasn't on my platoon roster but I remembered that he hailed from the Peach State—a search in my photo albums verified that it was Atlanta. Several phone calls to Tolar surnames there proved fruitless. I hoped that Harry would eventually find the information.

Continuing my quest, I probed next for James Blackburn, in Glenmora, Louisiana. The phone operator furnished two numbers for Blackburn surnames. My first call put me in touch with his sister-in-law. I dialed the number she provided and reached his office in Lafayette, Louisiana. His return call about an hour later completed the connection.

In April 1982, Dolores and I visited relatives in Texas City, Texas, and my former platoon leader, with his wife, Eleanor, came to see us. We met at a supermarket during a pouring rain. Dressed in a raincoat and hat, I walked toward his car. He opened the door and stepped out with hand outstretched, "Well I'll be damned ... you haven't changed one damned bit!"

The Quack Corps

"Oh yes I have!" and fingered graying sideburns. And, more details of the events of the memorable two years in 2d DUKW came flooding back during a six-hour luncheon visit.

My impression had been that Captain James L. George, 2d DUKW's commanding officer, called Montana home. But Jim, as I now call my former platoon leader, informed me that he believed it was Iowa, Dubuque in particular.

About two weeks after I returned home, I decided to try to reach my former commanding officer, who I considered as one of my two best. Again, phone information provided a number and dialing it put me in contact with him.

"Jim," who I also now call my former C.O., believed that the company's first sergeant, Harold "Chug" Pohlad, lived in the Minneapolis area. Ma Bell's facilities were again put to good use and I contacted Chug.

During our conversation, I really hit the bull's-eye when he asked, "Do you know that Orval Smith lives in this area?" And, by a stroke of good fortune, my search that had begun in Malvern, Arkansas, switched to the Minneapolis area and contact with Smitty.

Making contact with Smitty led me to another man ... I had decided that finding Hal Reynolds in the Los Angeles area would be like trying to find the proverbial needle in a haystack, so I hadn't even tried. But Smitty told me, "I believe Hal lives in Whittier [California]."

Phone information couldn't give me a number for Hal in Whittier, but did furnish two numbers for the same name ... one in Covina and the other in Pico Rivera. Playing a hunch, I dialed the latter number first and contacted him. He furnished leads to four men.

My good fortune continued, because shortly after mid-day on 19 October, 1982, the telephone rang. Dolores answered and a man asked to speak to me. She called and I took the receiver, "Hello."

Gray? Bald? Paunchy?

"Hi, Ol' buddy! This is George Tolar!" Former Corp. Richard King was one of the men on Hal Reynolds' list and I had contacted him in the Dallas, Texas, area. He had phoned Jerry about me. I had made two phone calls to the Atlanta area just the day before trying to get a lead on Jerry ... the hunt ended in Carlsbad, California!

Contacting Jerry left only Donald Shults to be located out of the seven on my priority list. He didn't have a phone listing in Cornelius, Oregon, and I wrote to him at the address sent by Hal Reynolds. My letter wasn't returned nor did I hear from Dutch. Assuming that it had either been lost or mis-delivered, I mailed a special delivery letter about one month later. I assumed the worst when I noticed that another man had signed the receipt—that man didn't have a Cornelius phone listing either. I could only hope that he'd let me know about Dutch.

October 31st, I answered the phone and a man questioned, "Art Wells?"

"Yes."

"This is Dutch Shults." And telephone company stock must have gained considerable additional value by the time our conversation ended.

My letter had been forwarded to Gleneden Beach, Oregon, where Dutch was building a golf course—the golf pro there had signed for it.

Other men added their enthusiastic efforts since the beginning of my search, and by November 1982, twenty-one of 2d DUKW's officers and men had been accounted for. By May 1983, the number had risen to 95, with 75 still living. Of the 75 living, thirty-five men representing 21 states attended a first reunion in Denver, Colorado.

The search for 2d DUKWers continued and 131 had been accounted for by the end of 1983, with 108 still alive. The company's second reunion at Dallas, in 1985, drew 50 men of a possible 114. By the end of 1986, 154 men had been accounted for, with 118 living.

The Quack Corps

In addition to phone information and letters forwarded by postmasters, men were located by contacting high school principals and alumni associations of high schools, colleges and universities, and from information furnished by located men or contained in WWII address books or written on captured Jap battle flags. In a few instances, contacting city police chiefs and county sheriffs brought results.

As I began talking with each man, his conversation was reserved for the first few moments. I sensed his shock at hearing a voice from the distant past and as mental wheels spun while he tried to place Art Wells. But, with a "Do you remember? ..." and the relating of an amusing incident, time rolled back and once again he was a talkative, young and proud United States Marine of 40 years before!

INDEX

A
A Quack Marine 79
A Second Invasion of Okinawa 225
A Warrior Returns! 272
Alden, Dolores 2

B
Bacon, Sergeant Edgar 107
Bandy, Wayne 43
Barnett, Robert, Corp. *48*
Barron, Thomas N., Corp. 9, 30, 31
Bass, Sgt. Estes 75
Batey, Odis, Pvt. 160
Biddle, Colonel, Marine knife expert 130
Black, Thomas, Sgt. 85
Blackburn, 2dLt. James B. 79
Board, Woodrow W., Pvt. 30
Bowman, Vernon, Corporal 138
Bozek, Walter J., Pvt. 30
Brown, Major Wilburt S. "Slew Foot" 49
Burton, Guy, Corporal 214
Bush, Curtis, Warrant Officer 85

C
"C" Battery, 1st Defense Battalion 63
"C" Company, 1st Battalion, 6th Marine Regiment, Second Marine Brigade 63,
"C" Company, Marine Barracks, Navy Yard, Pearl Harbor 61
Carr, William H. W., Corp. 124
Chapman, Phillip, PFC 116
Cochrane, Red, World Welterweight Boxing Champion 66
Cooke, Jr., C. M., Captain 32
Cooper, Corporal Billy 46
Crawford, Claude C., Jr., Corp. 30
Crawford, James 96
Cushman, Jr., Captain Robert E. 49

D
Dale, Tommie J., PFC 30
Dassow, Del, PlSgt. 270
Dewey, Edward F., Sgt. 85
Dillon, George J. Jr., PFC 30
Donham, Stanley, Corp. 131
Draben, Warren C., Pvt. 30

E
Enola Gay 249
Eue, Gordon A., PFC 30

The Quack Corps

F

Fiji Islands (Fiji) 54, 56, 55, 56, 59, 193
Fire Storm in West Loch! 100
First Defense Battalion, Palmyra Island 6, 67
Fluegel, Jr., Paul H., Corp. 126
Ford Island 9, 12, 13, 14, 26, 42, 62
Francis, Hollis B., PFC 30
Furlough and Camp Elliott 70

G

George. James L., Captain 95
Going Home! 258
Gordon, Roger A., Pvt. 30
Postscript 277
Guam 49, 166, 196, 262, 263, 265, 268, 269, 272

H

Harris, William B. "Bucky", Gunnery Sergeant 49
Croix de Guerre 49
Hawaiian Islands (Hawaii) 6, 62, 83, 102, 181
   Maui 95, 96, 98, 100, 159, 178, 180, 183, 195
   Oahu 88, 194
Hines, James, Sgt. 85
Hitting Hawaiian Surf 89
Holcomb, T., The Major General Commandant 28
Holman, Nelson R., PFC 17, 30

I

In the Marianas 176

J

Tokyo 110, 241
   Tokyo Bay 256
Jensen, William, Corp. 161
Jones, Ervin B., Pvt. 30

K

Kalain, Eugene, Sgt. 154
Kimmel, Admiral Husband E. 12, 48
King, T. S., Captain 48
Knox, Frank, Secretary of the Navy 26
Kuehl, Russell K., Pvt. 30

L

Lassitor, Patrick H., Warrant Officer 85
Laughlin, Raymond "J", Private First Class 24

M

Mabey, Kember D., Pvt. 30
Mangnall, Richard 85
Marine Barracks, Navy Yard, Pearl Harbor 6

Index

Marshall Islands 109
   Eniwetok 109, 178
   Kwajalein 266
   Namur 109
McAdams, William 85
McClelland, Robert, Gunnery Sergeant 85
McFall, John H., Pvt 30
Mefford, Harry, Corp. 86, 130, 154, 171
Moffit Field 72
Moving forward on Saipan 140
Murphy, William, Captain 274

N

Nations, Morris E., Corp. 30
Naval Court of Inquiry 107
New Hebrides 58, 94
Nicholson, Darwin "Nick", Corp. 141
North Island 83
   North Island Naval Air Station 74

O

Okinawa! 198
Okinawa 6, 197, 199, 200, 202, *204*, 205, 212, 213, 218, 221, 225, 226, 228, 237, 238, 241, 243, 245, 247, 248, 260, 263
   Naha 226, 227, 228, 229, 230, 231, 232, 233, 236, 237, 238
   Oroku Peninsula 230, 232, 236
   wounded 242
   Yontan Airfield (Yontan) 205, 211, 217, 224, 213, 214, 220
Osipoff, W. S., 2dLt. 74

P

Palmyra Island 61
Parsons, Wilbur, PFC 161
Patrick, Robert 85
Pearl Harbor 9, 20, 22, 33, 35, 36, 44, 53, 59, 60, 62, 68, *85*, 100, 107, 108, 109, 190, 250, 251, 255, 256, 266, 271
   10-10 Dock *12*, *20*, 32, 44, 62
   Battleship Row 12, 15, 20, 43
   Hospital Point 25, 42
   Number-1 Drydock 12
Pearl Harbor Bombed! 9
Phillips, E. H., Lt. Col. 67
Pohlad, Harold, 1stSgt. 85
Pye, William, Vice-Admiral 5, 48, 51

R

Raleigh, George 85
Reams, Lester, PFC *93*
Rector, Dwight, Corporal 237
Reed, Dewey, PFC 247

285

The Quack Corps

Reeves, Harold, PlSgt. 63
Rest and Tinian 163
Return to Pearl Harbor 42
Reynolds, Harold, Corporal 230
Riddell, Robert S., Captain 49
Rodland, Bert W., Pvt. 30
Rogers, Leyton M. 2dLt. 12
Rogers, William W., Colonel 109
Rollins, Rex 277
Roosevelt, Franklin, President 204

S

Saipan! 113
Saipan 6, 110, 112, 113, 132, 140, 143, 147, 157, 158, 159, 161, 162, 163, 164, 165, 166, 168, 169, 173, 176, 177, 178, 183, 184, 185, 186, 187, 190, 193, 194, 196, 198, 200, 201, 209, 211, 213, 225, 243, 245, 247, 262, 278
   Agingan Point 161, 169
   Army Air Corps 148
      B-29 190
      P-38 182, 183, 191
      P-47 191
      P-51 182
      P-61 Black Widow 182
   Aslito Airfield 133, 141, 154
   Blue Beach(es) 113, 114
   Charan Kanoa 113, 115, 119, 129, 133, 137, 165, 171, 187
   Chalan Kanoa 113
   Kagman Peninsula 176, 177, 187, 191, 194, 245
   Killed in Action 159
   Smith, H. M. "Howling Mad", LtGen. 184
   Smith, Ralph, MajGen. 184
   Tanapag 177
   Wounded in Action 159
   Yellow Beaches 123
Samoa 59
San Diego 5, 6, 72, 75, 80, 82, 108, 126, 168, 178, 269
San Diego Marine Base 83, 84
San Francisco 5, 33, 34, 35, 36, 41, 44, 48, 68, 72, 245, 271
San Francisco Bay 33, 37, 38, 41
   Golden Gate (Bridge) 37, 40, 70
   Hunter's Point Naval Shipyard 33
Schaikoski, Marvin P., Captain 66
Sea School 5, 45, 159, 276
Sellers, Victor, Second Lieutenant 85
Shults, Donald J., Corp. 114
Smallwood, Lee D., Corp. 118
Smith, Orval C., Corporal 94
Smith, William, 1stSgt. 27
Solomon Islands 56, 58

Index

South Pacific 6, 53, 54, 62
Stassen, Harold, Commander 175
Stewart, Floyd "D", PFC 30
Stover, Arthur, PFC 119
Stringfellow, Platoon Sergeant 45

T

Takats, Joseph, PFC 237
Tarawa 123, 198
Taylor, R. L., Sgt. 15
The City by the Bay 32
The Quack Corps 109
Time Battle Baby 184
Tinian 6, 134, 140, 147, 148, 161, 162, 166, 167, 168, 169, 171, 172, 173, 177, 179, 180, 189, 191, 193, 194, 196, 200, 250
    Tinian Town 173
Tinker, Bud, Sgt. 11
Tobin, Patrick P., PFC 30
Tolar, George, Private First Class 81
Treasure Island 35
Truman, President 255

U

U.S. Navy Hospital 22
U.S.S New Mexico 51
U.S.S.
   Arizona 43
   California 13
   Cassin 10, 19
   Colorado 38, 39, 40
   Corrigedor 82, 83, 85
   Crockett 268, 270
   Crosby 40
   Downes 10, 19, 29
   Enterprise 21, 26
   Helena 12, 14, 20
   Henry Clay 95, 269
   Indianapolis 157, 158
   Lexington 26
   Maryland 25, 38
   Neosho 13
   Nevada 15, 43
   New Mexico 5, 6, 48, 50, 51, 53, 61, 216
   Oklahoma 13, 25, 44
   Oglala 12, 14
   Pennsylvania 5, 9, 10, 11, 12, 14, 19, 20,© 23, 28, 29, 30, 32, 33, 34, 35, 36, 37, 38, 39, 40, 41, 42, 43, 44, 48, 50, 51, 52, 62, 90, 108, 158, 236, 265, 266, 268
      killed 12/7/41 30
      wounded 12/7/41 30

The Quack Corps

    Sabine 62
    Saratoga 25
    South Dakota 58
    Tennessee 38, 59
    West Virginia 13, 43, 44
U.S.S. LST
    -1029 225
    -121 98, 106
    -205 100
    -23 98, 106
    -340 98, 106
    -353 107
    -354 98, 106, 107, 108, 109, 124, 127
    -649 244
    -725 198, 202, 204
    -785 258
Unterkoefler, Warrant Officer George 85
USAIT Comet 62
    Arrow 68

V

V Amphibious Corps 194
    Anderson, Colonel 194
V–J Day 255
Vincent, Jesse C. Jr., Corp. 30

W

Wade, George H. Jr., PFC 30
War's End! 245
Weatherly, Marvin, Corporal 34
Wells, Arthur W., PFC 30
West Loch 100, 101
    Hanaloa Point 106
    Intrepid Point 106
    LST explosions 101
    Tare 3 106, 108
    Tare 5 106
    Tare 8 102, 105, 106, 107
    Tare 9 106, 107
    West Loch Naval Ammunition Depot 100
White, Raymond H., Captain 65
Wills, Macon R., Corp. 242
Winker, Fredrick 85

Y

Young, Harold, Pvt. 175

Z

Zero 9, 138, 154, 191, 218